Structure as Architecture

Structure as Architecture presents a comprehensive analysis of the indispensable role of structure in architecture. An exploration, as well as a celebration, of structure, the book draws on a series of design studies and case study examples to illustrate how structure can be employed to realize a wide range of concepts in contemporary architecture. By examining design principles that relate to both architecture and structural engineering, Andrew Charleson provides new insights into the relationship between both the technical and aesthetic aspects of architecture.

Now in its second edition, the text has been extensively revised and updated throughout. Features include:

- a brand new chapter on hidden structure, adding to the material on exposed structures
- two new chapters on using structure to realize common architectural concepts through a combination of precedents and creative design
- over fifty new case studies from across the globe
- easy-to-understand diagrams and a highly visual design to aid understanding and accessibility

More than two hundred case studies of contemporary buildings from countries such as the UK, the US, France, Germany, Spain, Hong Kong, Australia and Japan illustrate how a thorough integration of structure adds layers of richness and enhances the realization of architectural design concepts.

Andrew Charleson has visited, photographed and analysed almost all of the case-study buildings included in this book. He is an Associate Professor at the School of Architecture, Victoria University of Wellington, New Zealand. Bringing over forty years' structural engineering experience to the topic, he has also written *Seismic Design for Architects: Outwitting the Quake* and published many papers relating both to the subject of this book and to his other main areas of research interest – earthquake engineering and architecture.

'*Structure as Architecture* cuts to the heart of the architectural and engineering relationship. This book explores how form and function blend, where structural and architectural concepts interweave and support each other for a technically and aesthetically enhanced work. Andrew Charleson demonstrates his holistic approach to architecture and engineering through stunning case studies where designers seamlessly and elegantly blend structural engineering with the architect's design intent. As a structural engineer and architect, I truly believe this book is a must-read.'

Holger S. Schulze Ehring, Structural Designer, New York City

Structure as Architecture

A source book for architects and structural engineers

Second edition

Andrew Charleson

Routledge
Taylor & Francis Group

LONDON AND NEW YORK

First edition published 2006

by Elsevier

Second edition published 2015

by Routledge

2 Park Square, Milton Park, Abingdon, Oxon, OX14 4RN

and by Routledge

711 Third Avenue, New York, NY 10017

Routledge is an imprint of the Taylor & Francis Group, an informa business

1007234634

British Library Cataloguing-in-Publication Data

A catalogue record for this book is available from the British Library

Library of Congress Cataloging-in-Publication Data

Charleson, Andrew.

Structure as architecture : a source book for architects and structural engineers / Andrew Charleson. – 2nd edition.

pages cm

Includes bibliographical references and index.

1. Structural design. 2. Architectural design. 3. Architecture–Aesthetics. I. Title.

TA658.C454 2014

720–dc23   2014000980

ISBN13: 978-0-415-64459-4 (pbk)

ISBN13: 978-1-315-756657-7 (ebk)

Typeset in Univers by
Servis Filmsetting Ltd, Stockport, Cheshire

Printed by Bell & Bain Ltd, Glasgow

Contents

Figures

Preface

The second edition of this book is based largely on the first, with a number of significant enhancements. Three new chapters have been introduced, of which two consider the topic of structure in architecture from a new perspective. The first edition concentrated upon an *analysis* of architectural structure. It analysed and illustrated the many architectural roles structure plays in both physical and conceptual ways. Its starting point was structure as manifest in existing architecture. Now, the additional two chapters focus on the same topic, but from the perspective of *design*. They begin from the basis of architects' design concepts and architectural qualities and show how structure positively reinforces the most common contemporary design concepts and facilitates desired spatial and other qualities.

This new emphasis on design, rather than analysis, brings a welcome balance to the book. The process of developing this material involved an interesting journey to identify and summarize current architectural concepts and qualities, and then illustrate them from existing works of architecture. One of the most rewarding aspects of this design-orientated emphasis was the design study undertaken by one of my postgraduate classes. Students designed spatial structure to convey a wide range of design concepts. The most relevant outcomes are presented in Chapter 11.

As well as the introduction of this design-related content, the third new chapter shifts the focus upon *exposed* structure to structure that is *hidden*. This exploration not only acknowledges pragmatic aspects of structural hiddenness, but also aims to stimulate greater creativity in the concealment of structure.

This new edition has also provided an opportunity to update case-studies, and broaden their geographical catchment. Thirty per cent of the case-studies are new additions, many from countries previously unrepresented, most notably Japan.

In spite of all of these and other improvements, the central theme of the book remains unchanged: where structure contributes architecturally, other than in its primary load-bearing role, it contributes other layers of aesthetic and functional richness to designs. It reinforces architectural design concepts and intended architectural qualities, thereby increasing the interest in and enjoyment of buildings, raising the spirits of their occupants.

Andrew Charleson
February 2014

Acknowledgements

The support of Victoria University of Wellington, which provided a period of research and study leave during which most of this second edition was researched and written, is gratefully acknowledged. During the time spent in Tokyo, Professor Masato Araya's support was much appreciated.

Thanks to Catherine Mooney, who updated the previous diagrams and drew all the new diagrams for this edition, and once again to Paul Hillier, who scanned and modified hundreds of images. Eric Camplin provided much-valued computer support.

I thank the following 2012 fourth-year architectural students, whose ARCI421 design assignment coursework has provided the inspiration and been modified for the design studies presented in Chapter 11: Emily Batchelor, Hamish Beattie, Alexandra Sawicka-Ritchie, Thomas Seear-Budd, Annabel Fraser, Amber Marie Gray, Henry Velvin, Jae Warrander, Bronwyn Phillipps, Qing Liao, Jorle Wiesen and Monique Mackenzie.

Many individuals have provided images and given permission for their use. They are acknowledged in the figure captions. Unless otherwise noted, photographs are by the author.

Finally, thanks again to my wife Annette for her support and encouragement throughout this project.

one

Introduction

Structure is columnar, planar, or a combination of these which a designer can intentionally use to reinforce or realize ideas. In this context, columns, walls and beams can be thought of in terms of concepts of frequency, pattern, simplicity, regularity, randomness and complexity. As such, structure can be used to define space, create units, articulate circulation, suggest movement, or develop composition and modulations. In this way, it becomes inextricably linked to the very elements which create architecture, its quality and excitement.[1]

The potential for structure to enrich architecture

Clark and Pause's statement above begins by describing the architectural qualities of structure and then suggests how structure might enrich architecture. But is such a positive attitude to structure realistic? What was the last building *you* experienced where structure either created the architecture or contributed a sense of excitement to it? Where do we find examples of structure playing such active architectural roles as defining space and modulating surfaces? And, how else might structure contribute architecturally? These questions set the agenda of this book, informing its focus and scope, and initiating an exploration of architecturally enriching structure.

Some readers may consider Clark and Pause's attitude towards structure as a fully integrated architectural element rather unrealistic. So often our day-to-day experience of structure can be described as unmemorable. In much of our built environment structure is either concealed or nondescript. Opaque façade panels or mirror-glass panes hide structure located on a building's perimeter. Inside a building, suspended ceilings conceal beams, and vertical structural elements like columns, cross-bracing and structural walls are either enveloped within partition walls or else visually indistinguishable from them. Even if structure *is* exposed, often its repetitive and predictable configuration in plan and elevation, as well as its unrefined member and connection detailing, can rarely be described as 'creating architecture, its quality and excitement'.

Fortunately, in addition to these ubiquitous and bland structural encounters, sufficient precedents of positive structural contributions to architecture exist. They point towards bolder and more exciting possibilities and have convinced critical observers, like Clark and Pause and others, of the potential for structure to engage with architecture more actively and creatively. Peter Collins, the architectural theorist, shares similarly constructive convictions regarding structure's architectural roles. In concluding a discussion on eighteenth- and nineteenth-century Rationalism, he suggests:

> However much the emphasis on structural expression may have been exaggerated in the past by a craving for ostentation, or reduced by the competing emphases on spatial effects, sculptural effects and new planning requirements, it is still potentially one of the most vigorous ideals of the modern age, and it would not be an exaggeration to say that it is the notion which offers the most fruitful prospects for the future development of modern architectural thought.[2]

Like the authors quoted above, I will also be looking beyond the physical necessity of structure towards its functional and aesthetic possibilities. Just because structure is essential for built architecture, providing it with necessary stability, strength and stiffness, it does not have to be architecturally mute – unless of course its designers make that choice. This book provides many examples of structures 'speaking' and even 'shouting' in their architectural contexts. In these cases their designers, usually both architects and structural engineers, have made structural decisions that do not detract from but rather strengthen their architectural ideas and requirements. Structure no longer remains silent; it is a voice to be heard.

Where structure is given a voice, as illustrated in the following chapters, it contributes architectural meaning and richness, sometimes becoming the most significant of all architectural elements in a building. Endless opportunities exist for structure to enhance architecture and thereby enrich our architectural experiences. As designers we can allow structure to speak and to be heard; or, to change the metaphor, we can design structure so that its viewers not only see and experience it, but, due to its well-considered architectural qualities, are enticed into 'reading' it.

Experiencing structure: reading and listening

Architects analyse structure by experiencing and reading it. In their succinct summary, Clarke and Pause suggest the ways structure might be read or analysed architecturally. In some architectural reviews of buildings, particularly where structure is exposed, structural readings are made. Although reviewers usually make little more than a passing comment, analysing structure in this way remains valid. The following two examples illustrate architecturally focused structural readings.

Fontein offers a reading of the interior structure of her School of Architecture building. She concentrates upon a single column, differentiated from others by virtue of its circular cross-section and increased height. She asserts that this column 'plays a pivotal role in the building' by marking and sheltering the intersection of two internal streets. It also connects that street junction to the school's main collective space whose activities it both supports and obstructs. Ultimately it 'establishes structure as a primary ordering device in the architecture of the School . . . and has the palpable effect of anchoring the life of the School'.[3]

LaVine tends towards less personified readings as he discerns significant architectural roles played by structure in his four house case-studies.[4] He notes how a ridge beam can symbolize the social centre of a house, and how a superstructure orders space by virtue of its regularity and hierarchy. In other examples, columns 'signify human activities of special significance' or 'portray a mechanical idealism'. He reads walls as separating occupants from the outside world, and frames as ordering interior space. As he reads structure, each structural element is laden with meaning and makes an important architectural contribution.

For many, the reading of architecture is as natural as breathing. For example, Stan Allen comments on the Tama Art Library, designed by Toyo Ito, that

> it is impossible not to read the arches as a sign, a reference to a recognizable form in the repertory of classical architecture. They *are* that, but they are many other things, too . . . Ito produces work that is richer and more nuanced precisely for its capacity to hold these multiple readings in a delicate equilibrium.[5]

All architectural readings incorporate a degree of subjectivity. To a certain extent, each reading is personal. It reflects the reader's background and architectural knowledge. The quality of their experience of a building is another factor which depends on the duration of the visit and the depth of reflection during and after it.

The views of two or more readers are unlikely to be identical. Each person brings their own perspective. For example, an architect and structural engineer will read a structure quite differently. Each approaches it with his or her professional interest and concerns to the forefront. Whereas an architect might focus on how structure impacts the surrounding space, an engineer will most likely perceive structure as facilitating a load-path.

The discussion above considers structure as a passive architectural element – like a book waiting to be read. However, could it be that structure plays a more active role and actually speaks to us? So as well as reading structure must we also listen to it? According to Alain de Botton, we should.[6] To ease us into this possibly surprising idea, in his chapter 'Talking buildings' he reminds us how sculpture generates in us a thoughtful and responsive attitude towards objects. 'The great abstract sculptures', he says, 'have succeeded in speaking to us, in their particular dissociated language, of the important themes of our lives'.[7] The argument continues that if objects in a gallery can speak, and even pencil squiggles on paper can convey emotions, such as peacefulness and confusion, how much more can buildings communicate? Buildings are therefore pregnant with expressive potential, as are their elements, including structure, and de Botton acknowledges this by suggesting that 'we can be moved by a column that meets a roof with grace'.[8]

So, my architectural analyses of structure inevitably reflect who I am, how I read and listen to structure, and this is affected by my structural engineering background, my experience of teaching in a school of architecture, and my intense interest in how structure can enrich architecture.

Before commencing to read building structures and explore their architectural contributions, the next section clarifies the meaning of the book's central focus – exposed structure.

Structure and its degree of exposure

At this stage it is necessary to come to a common understanding of what constitutes structure, and to comment on aspects of its exposure. For the purpose of sensibly limiting the scope of the book, structure is taken to mean any structural element that bears load other than that arising from its self-weight or self-induced loads, like those from wind or snow.

This definition therefore excludes consideration of purely decorative elements without wanting to deny any significant architectural roles they might play. Imitative structure and authentic structural members that are not load-bearing, even though they might clearly express their materiality and display standard structural dimensions, lie outside the scope of this book. Examples of the latter category include exposed frameworks whose sole purpose is to contribute to a building's composition, perhaps visually linking together disparate forms.

Although this discussion omits structure whose rationale is *solely* aesthetic, structural elements and details with minimal structural effectiveness *are* included. Structural details like the attached shafts on Gothic piers fall into this category. Even

though their architectural contribution may be seen as more aesthetic than structural, by increasing the cross-sectional area and depth of a pier, the details slightly increase its compression strength and overall stability.

Having established a working definition of structure, an explanation for the focus upon *exposed* structure is warranted and quite simple. Where structure is not exposed but concealed, perhaps hidden within wall cavities, screened by suspended ceilings or undifferentiated from partition walling, it possesses very limited opportunities to enrich architecture. In these situations, where the architecture must rely on other devices and elements for its qualities, any skeletal, wall-like or expressive structural qualities remain latent – structure cannot be read.

Architects take an unlimited number of approaches towards structural exposure. In its fully exposed state, the raw materiality of structure is visible, be it masonry, concrete, steel or natural timber. Even if coatings or claddings partially or fully veil structural members and their materiality, structural form can still play significant and expressive architectural roles. Steel structural members may be wrapped with corrosion and fire protection coatings and even cladding panels, but their structural forms can still enliven façades and interior spaces. Hence, in this book, *exposed* structure includes any visible structural forms, irrespective of whether their materiality is concealed.

This apparent preoccupation with exposed structure does not mean it is a requirement of exemplary architecture. Exposed structure has rightly been deemed inappropriate on many past occasions given the design ideals current at those times. Cowan gives examples of periods in architectural history, such as the Renaissance and the Baroque, when exposed structure would have detracted from the forms and embellished surfaces that designers were attempting to achieve.[9] Absence of exposed structure in contemporary buildings may also be completely defensible. For example, exterior exposed structure might compromise architectural forms exhibiting sculptural qualities and curved surfaces, and interior exposed structure would impact negatively upon an architectural goal of achieving spaces defined by pure planar surfaces.

Decisions regarding the extent to which structure should be exposed in an architectural design, if at all, are best made after revisiting the design concept and asking whether exposed structure will enhance its realization. Then, irrespective of the answer, design ideas will be communicated with greater clarity. Structural exposure should therefore be limited to buildings where structure integrates with and clearly strengthens the expression of architectural ideas.

Book outline

The following chapter analyses the structures of two contrasting buildings to set the scene for more focused and detailed explorations of many other buildings in the remainder of the book. Both buildings exemplify structure contributing architecturally in the context of specific architectural programmes. Exposed structure plays significant architectural roles on the exterior of the first building, while in the second, structure creates special interior spaces. Due to the inevitably limited range of architectural contributions illustrated by the two case-studies, the following chapters explore and illustrate exposed structure enriching specific areas of architecture in more detail.

Beginning with Chapter 3, chapter sequencing up to and including Chapter 9 reflects a typical progression of experiences when visiting a building. First, imagine approaching a building from a distance. When only architectural massing may be discerned, the diversity of relationship between architectural and structural form is explored. Then, in Chapter 4, drawing closer to the building, one observes structural elements enlivening façades in various ways, including forming surface patterns and textures, providing visual clues of entry, connecting exterior and interior architecture, and playing diverse expressive roles.

Having entered the building, the next three chapters consider relationships between the structure and interior architecture. Chapter 5 examines how structure enhances and, in some cases, defines building function. Structure maximizes planning flexibility, subdivides space to facilitate separate functions, and articulates circulation paths. Chapter 6 focuses on interior structure as an architectural element in its own right. It addresses the question of how structure enlivens and articulates interior spaces and surfaces. Examples

illustrate structure providing a wide range of surface and spatial qualities. Some interior structures read as responding to aspects such as a building's geometry or function, or, alternatively, expressing external factors like soil pressures or other site-specific characteristics.

Exploration of interior structure narrows in scope in Chapter 7 with an examination of structural detailing. After noting the importance of detailing being driven by a design concept, examples of expressive and responsive details are provided. They comprise two categories of details, one of which gains its inspiration from within the building, and the other from without. Some structural members are so elegantly detailed as to be considered objects of aesthetic delight, considerably increasing one's enjoyment and interest in architecture. A plethora of structural detailing languages with diverse architectural qualities strengthens designers' abilities to realize overarching architectural design concepts.

Chapter 8 investigates the relationship between structure and light, both natural and artificial. It illustrates structure's dual roles, as both a source and modifier of light, and introduces a number of different strategies designers use to maximize the ingress of light into buildings. Chapter 9 reflects on the symbolic and representational roles structure plays. Structure references naturally occurring objects like trees and processes such as erosion, as well as human artefacts, notions and experiences as diverse as oppression and humour.

Having completed explorations of exposed structure, Chapter 10 enters the world of hidden structure and contemplates its contribution to architecture, even though it is concealed. Then, in the following two chapters, the focus shifts from analysis of structure to design. Rather than analysing the roles of structure beyond load-bearing, the intent of Chapters 11 and 12 is to show how structure can reinforce architectural concepts, and realize specific architectural qualities.

The final chapter offers a brief distillation of the main themes that have emerged throughout the book – namely the transformative power of structure, the diversity with which it enriches architecture, and implications for the architectural and structural engineering professions.

Notes

1. R. H. Clark and M. Pause, *Precedents in architecture*, Hoboken, NJ: Van Nostrand Reinhold, 1985, p. 3.
2. P. Collins, *Changing ideals in modern architecture 1750–1950*, 2nd edn, Montreal: McGill-Queen's University Press, 1998, p. 217.
3. L. Fontein, 'Reading structure through the frame', *Perspecta* 31, 2000, 50–9.
4. L. LaVine, *Mechanics and meaning in architecture*, Minneapolis: University of Minnesota Press, 2001.
5. S. Allen, 'Toyo Ito's patient search', in J. Turnbull (ed.), *Toyo Ito – forces of nature*, New York: Princeton Architectural Press, 2012, p. 24.
6. A. de Botton, *The architecture of happiness*, London: Hamish Hamilton/Penguin, 2006.
7. Ibid., p. 81.
8. Ibid., p. 98.
9. H. Cowan, 'A note on structural honesty', *Architecture Australia* 1, 1980, 28–32.

two

Two building studies

This chapter presents structural analyses of two very different buildings. Between them, they exemplify structure enriching most aspects and areas of architecture. These analyses introduce the many ways structure contributes to architecture and prepares the way for a more detailed investigation and categorization of the architectural potential of structure in subsequent chapters.

The following two case-studies illustrate the considered use of exposed structure in very different architectural contexts. First, the National Stadium, Beijing, displays an exuberant and chaotic exterior structure, but it is more muted when experienced from the interior. Exterior and interior expression reverses in the second building, the Baumschulenweg Crematorium. Within its formal minimalist exterior envelope, impressive exposed interior structure in the form of 'randomly placed' columns transforms the main space, leading to alternative architectural readings.

National Stadium, Beijing

Built for the Beijing XXIXth Olympiad, which was held during August 2008, the National Stadium is the largest and most dominant building at the Olympic site. Accommodating 91,000 spectators during the Olympics, the oval-shaped stadium has a roof structure 313 m long by 266 m wide, including a large elliptical opening above the stadium pitch. A retractable roof was originally designed, but omitted at a late stage during the design process. The height of the saddle-shaped top surface varies from 40 m at its lowest point to the approximate height of a 20-storey building – 70 m – at its highest (Figure 2.1).

The rounded vessel-like form comprises two independent free-standing structures: an interior reinforced concrete bowl with its three tiers of sloping seating, and the perimeter and roof steel structure. The bowl structure is itself divided

Figure 2.1
National Stadium, Beijing, China, Herzog & De Meuron, 2008. An elevation of the stadium.

Figure 2.2
The perimeter steel structure
wraps around the inner
concrete bowl (Arup).

into six structurally independent segments separated by 200 mm-wide gaps for seismic and thermal movements. These structures are frame structures, consisting of beams and columns interconnected by rigid joints. Lateral or horizontal loads arising from wind and earthquake are mainly resisted by structural walls forming the two lift cores of each segment. The roof is clad by two tension membranes supported by the perimeter and roof steel structure. An outer transparent ETFE single-layer provides weather protection to the stands, while a lower PTFE membrane offers shade and improved acoustics.

The perimeter steel structure defines the extent and shape of the building as it wraps around it (Figure 2.2). However, unlike most stadiums with exposed structure, from most vantage points both outside and within the structural rationale, if any, is not at all apparent. How does this chaotic assemblage of inclined members that become curved tangles at roof level possibly constitute a roof structure? How can such an apparently irrational configuration of structural members provide a roof that cantilevers over 40 m from its perimeter to the edge of the internal opening? Is this a case where so much structure is thrown into a building in the absence of structural rationality that highly sophisticated structural engineering analyses indicate the structure will somehow stand up? The answers to these questions can hardly be answered without recourse to engineering drawings. They reveal a most unexpected yet conceptually simple structural solution (Figures 2.3 and 2.4).

Perimeter structural chaos effectively conceals a series of twenty-four symmetrically positioned portal frames. Portal frames, just one level of complexity beyond the most basic of structural systems, the post-and-beam, are responsible for supporting the whole roof. Their presence is even more

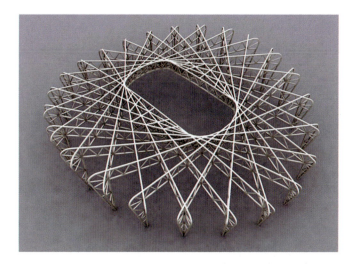

Figure 2.3
A physical model of the perimeter steel and roof gravity-resisting portal frame structure (Arup).

Figure 2.4
The bottom chords of the portal girders can be seen from the seating bowl.

surprising given their general relegation by architects to structure less elegant constructions, like light-industrial buildings. Admittedly, these portal frames are not the normal run-of-the-mill type. Detailed as trusses, and 12 m deep, they interconnect to support each other and form a three-dimensional truss network. Each column, V-shaped in plan, deepens from a pin joint at its base to reach the 12 m depth before bending over to become a portal frame girder (Figures 2.5 and 2.6). This is the roof structure, designed for gravity loads, vertical loads from wind, and earthquake loads.

The horizontal load resistance of the free-standing perimeter and roof structure is also another puzzle inviting resolution. Damage to the portal frames must be prevented during a large earthquake. The stability of the whole roof structure cannot be jeopardized. And yet there are no visible shear walls, bays of conventional cross-bracing or obvious moment frames – the three most conventional seismic force-resisting systems. However, we can discern within the irregularity of the layout of façade members patterns of triangulation, albeit not from any textbook. This irregular triangulated structure, which seems to be a consequence of structural randomization, provides sufficient strength and stiffness to satisfy the demanding engineering design criteria.

Structural elements visually dominate the exterior of this building by their random and dynamic arrangement. Rather than relying upon monumentality conferred by massive structural walls or columns, the modestly sized members exude expressive qualities due to their geometrical configuration. At least on the outer structural layer no vertical nor horizontal members are found. Orthogonality has been

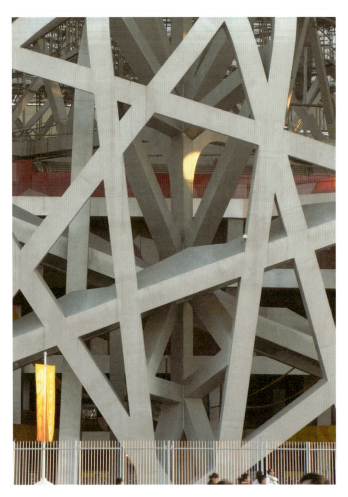

Figure 2.5
A view of a V-shaped truss-column near its base.

Figure 2.6
Horizontal and diagonal members of portal girders are visible beyond the upper curved structure.

Figure 2.7
Columns supporting the concrete bowl are also inclined.

banished entirely from the perimeter structure, but it is still able to fulfil its load-bearing roles (and others). For example, its bewildering number and orientation of members act to screen the seating bowl, whose visual presence is enhanced by red-painted exterior surfaces. The 'screen', up to 12 m deep, is also very porous, if not welcoming. A lack of perimeter structural barriers means there can be many possible entrances.

A potential danger of expressing such dynamic perimeter structure is that more conventional interior structure, by comparison, could be considered an anticlimax. This has been avoided by the inclination of columns around both the perimeter and inner edges of the concrete bowl (Figure 2.7). Steel and concrete members speak the same dynamic language so there is no aesthetic disjuncture between these two structures.

As well as the perimeter structure functioning as a fully load-bearing assemblage and an expressive façade with screening qualities, it hosts most of the stadium's vertical circulation in the form of stairs. The stairs are integral with the least-inclined sloping members which conceal them from view (Figure 2.8). As they rise, the stairs snake around and through the structure. This strategy of embedding circulation within the structural width or depth is observed in other buildings too, such as the Sainsbury Centre, whose perimeter structure along its sides provides space for stairs and other functions (see Figure 5.12).

One of the architectural characteristics of the exposed steel structure that requires comment is its detailing: that is, the form and finishing of the structural members and their

Figure 2.8
A flight of stairs with a visible soffit fully integrated with an inclined perimeter member.

connections. The most significant aspect of detailing is that all exposed members, square steel box sections, have the same external dimension of 1.2 m × 1.2 m. The tremendous variation in forces within members is economically accommodated by adjusting the wall thicknesses of the sections. Plate thickness varies from 10 mm to 100 mm, but the resulting variation in strength is not apparent.

So, not only is there no visual hierarchy of strength or structural importance in the structural members, but since every member, whether primary, secondary or tertiary, has the same dimensions, there is no structural hierarchy *at all*.

Unlike most exposed structure where primary members are larger than those bearing less load, in the stadium perimeter structure even members resisting very little load cannot be differentiated from primary members. This detailing strategy is very effective architecturally. Structural joints are treated the same way. All are fully butt-welded, and although some weld lines are visible due to fabrication inaccuracies, no bolted plates, gusset plates or stiffeners, commonly observed in steel structures, detract from the purity of the exposed structural pattern.

This detailing strategy also conceals an appreciation of materiality. Since the steel structure is painted and there are none of the normal visual clues to indicate steel construction, it is difficult to determine whether members are steel or reinforced concrete without tapping them. Such material ambiguity continues to enhance our experience of the structure since distracting thoughts regarding how such complex construction could ever be built are less likely to arise. It also means that there is no significant difference in appearance between the perimeter steel structural members and those of the concrete bowl. All appear to be the same size and colour, and most are inclined. Such careful and rigorous attention to detailing has unified the appearance of two different structural systems and materials very successfully.

One of the most intriguing issues the perimeter structure of the stadium raises is the question of meaning. Is the structure an example of representation or symbolism? Was the structure really designed to represent a bird's nest? If so, it is very successful. When I first saw the stadium's elevation, the structural pattern reminded me of the enduring game of pick-up sticks. A bundle of fine plastic or wooden sticks is held above a tabletop and released so the sticks fall and create a tangled and random pile. Players then try to extract individual sticks without moving any others in the process.

In fact, 'the original inspiration was from a combination of local Chinese art forms – the crackle-glazed pottery that is local to Beijing, and the heavily veined Chinese "scholar stones"'.[1] These random patterns met the architects' original desire for the perimeter structure to possess a chaotic quality. During the design process the project was nicknamed the Bird's Nest, and the name stuck and was welcomed by the Chinese for the deep positive meaning associated with the image of a nest and the absence of

any negative connotations. The name is certainly very apt given the form of the stadium and its expressive structure. Many other readings of the structure have been made, including: expressing 'the balance of order and disorder in Chinese culture', 'crazy, chaotic structure', 'dizzying interplay of structure and circulation',[2] 'a chaotic thicket of supports, beams and stairs, almost like an artificial forest',[3] 'dynamic', 'sense of movement', 'excitement', and 'gentle curves and lack of rectangular forms also suggest tranquility and harmony with nature'.[4]

Baumschulenweg Crematorium

After proceeding through the gate-house of the Berlin suburban cemetery and following a short walk along a tree-lined forecourt, visitors arrive at the symmetrical low-rise form of the crematorium. An absence of exterior doors and conventional fenestration or other visual clues creates uncertainty in interpreting the building's scale (Figure 2.9). Although the façade composition is read as single storey, up to three storeys are accommodated above the main ground-floor level. Planar concrete elements in the form of perimeter walls, a raised ground floor and a roof slab define the rectilinear form.

Even from a distance, visitors become aware of the roof slab discontinuity. Above the two side-entry portals a roof slot reveals a glimpse of sky that one commentator refers to as 'a harbinger of the end of grief'.[5] These longitudinal slots continue through to the other end of the building. They

Figure 2.9
Baumschulenweg Crematorium, Berlin, Axel Schultes Architects, 1999.
Front elevation.

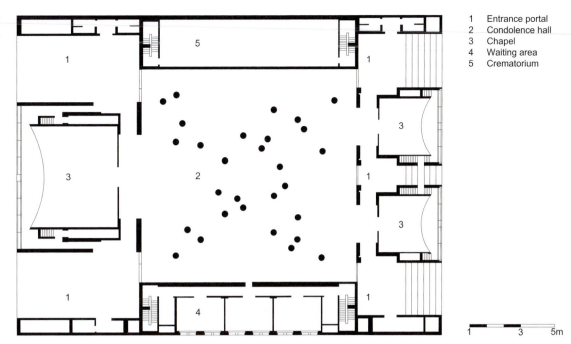

Figure 2.10
Simplified ground-
floor plan.

1 Entrance portal
2 Condolence hall
3 Chapel
4 Waiting area
5 Crematorium

slice the building into three independent structures even though common materiality and consistency of architectural language unite them visually. The outer two zones, to use Louis Khan's terminology, 'serve' the major central area that accommodates three chapels and a condolence hall (Figure 2.10).

Walls dominate the exterior elevations, functioning as both structure and cladding. Side walls initially read as approximately 2 m thick, but in fact they are hollow – doors from the entry portals lead to rooms within the 'walls'. Elsewhere, relatively thin edges of exposed walls and slabs express the dominant structural language of wall, repeated within the interior box-like modules that enclose one large and two smaller chapels. Ceiling slabs over these three spaces are also slotted, allowing light to enter through louvred glazing. Gentle curved ends to the ceiling slabs relieve an otherwise rigid adherence to orthogonality.

A study of the main floor plan indicates tripartite longitudinal subdivision – front and back porticoes and chapel spaces lie at each end of the centrally located condolence hall. Structural walls that are generously penetrated with openings at ground-floor level separate and screen the chapels from the hall. Within each longitudinal zone, structural walls subdivide space transversely. In the middle zone, walls delineate the condolence hall from the side waiting rooms and the crematorium. In the front and back zones, walls play

similar roles by separating circulation space from the chapels. Structural walls therefore dominate the plan, delineating the various functions. Only within the condolence hall have the architects introduced another structural language.

Columns comprise the primary architectural elements of this large interior volume (Figure 2.11). Their presence, together with an unusual lighting strategy, results in a space with a special ambience that is well suited to its function. The 'random' placement of columns recalls the spatial qualities of a native forest rather than an orderly plantation. Scattered large-diameter columns disrupt obvious linear circulation routes between destinations beyond the hall. You must meander. Tending to cluster in plan along diagonal bands, columns subdivide the main floor area into four relatively large spaces, and many others that are smaller and ideal for groups of two to three people. Differently sized and shaped open areas become gathering places.

One of the largest 'places' is located in front of the main chapel. Dwarfed by massive 11 m-high columns, mourners meet to console one another. Columns either facilitate this interaction by virtue of their enclosing presence or provide opportunities for anonymity. They remind visitors of their human frailty, yet might also be a source of reassurance given their physical and symbolic qualities of strength and protection. Their scale instils a sense of awe rather than of intimidation.

Figure 2.11
Condolence hall columns.

Figure 2.12
Annuli of light as column 'capitals'.

The scale of the condolence hall and its columns, as well as its low light levels, recall Egyptian hypostyle construction. But, whereas hypostyle column layout conforms to a rigidly ordered square grid, the crematorium column placement can be described as unpredictable. Here, the grid has disappeared. According to Balmond, with columns free of the grid, space is no longer 'dull and uninspired'. He describes how, during the design process of the Rotterdam Kunsthal, two rows of columns were 'freed-up' in a gallery hall by 'sliding' one row past the other in an 'out-of-phase shift': 'Suddenly the room was liberated. Diagonals opened up the floor plan and the room became one space, not two ring-fenced zones.'[6] By comparison with columns at the Kunsthal, those at the crematorium enjoy far more freedom, even though they remain straight and are vertical.

A masterly introduction of natural light intensifies this powerful and surprising experience of interior structure. At each roof slab–column junction, an area of critical structural connectivity, an annulus interrupted only by a narrow concrete beam allows natural light to wash down the column surfaces (Figure 2.12). Daylight similarly illumines longitudinal side walls. Slots adjacent to walls disconnect the roof slab from its expected source of support. Just where shear forces are normally greatest, the slab stops short, cantilevering from the nearest columns. Light enters through the slots and illuminates and reflects off the structure (Figure 2.13). The conventional grey cast-in-place concrete of walls, columns and roof slab combines with intentionally low light levels to heighten a sense of solemnity and calmness.

Unlike the National Stadium, Beijing, with its random and dynamic structure that borders on the incomprehensible, the crematorium's structural drama and interest result primarily from structural simplicity, generosity of scale and structural configuration. Structural detailing can be described as plain. Columns are of identical diameter with an off-the-form surface finish. As plain cylinders, lacking pedestal or capital other than the annulus of light, they emerge starkly from the stone floor surfacing at their bases to fuse monolithically

Figure 2.13
Light-slot between the side wall and the roof slab.

with the beam stubs and the flat planar roof slab soffit above. Surface textures relieve wall surfaces. Formwork tie holes and regularly spaced positive joints, as opposed to more conventional negative formwork joints, modulate large wall areas. Regular vertical niches spaced along the condolence hall's longitudinal walls play a similar role (Figure 2.14).

Minimalist structural detailing denies any expression of structural actions. Uniform column size belies the different loads supported by each. Columns that are well separated in plan from other columns bear heavy compressive loads while,

due to slab structural continuity, some closely spaced columns experience minimal compression. Although these lightly laden columns could have been removed during the design process, simply by modifying the slab reinforcing layout, an apparent increase in structural efficiency by decreasing column numbers would have diminished architectural aspirations. Similarly, a reluctance to taper the slab depth in those areas where it cantilevers indicates the preciousness of a simple and solemn orthogonal architectural language.

The interior structure of the condolence hall exemplifies the potential for structure to enrich interior architecture both aesthetically and functionally. 'Random' column layout, structural scale commensurate with volume, and interaction of structure and light enliven a large volume, stimulating a variety of reactions and emotions, and actively facilitating its intended use.

Summary

These studies of the National Stadium and the Baumschulenweg Crematorium begin to illustrate the potential of structure to enrich architecture. While the exterior structure of the stadium makes significant aesthetic contributions, interior structure is particularly notable only at the crematorium. Although both structures speak to us in very different ways, the contrast in how we read and experience them is striking. As the relationship between architectural form and structural form is investigated in the next chapter, the diversity of experience that structure offers continues to surprise.

Notes

1. 'The Beijing National Stadium', The Beijing National Stadium Special Issue, *The Arup Journal* 1, 2009, 16.
2. M. Webb, 'Bird's nest bowl', *Architectural Review* 224(1337), 2008, 38–47, at 38 and 44.
3. M. Kwok, 'The National Stadium Beijing', *A+U* 454, 2008, 58–89, at 66.
4. J. Brown, 'Carrying the torch', *Civil Engineering* 78(8), 2008, 48–56, at 50.
5. J. S. Russell, 'Evoking the infinite', *Architectural Record* 5, 2000, 224–31.
6. C. Balmond, *informal*, London: Prestel, 2002, p. 79.

Figure 2.14
Texture and niches of the condolence hall side walls.

three

Relationships between architectural and structural form

Introduction

This is the first of seven chapters that imagine us visiting many buildings and progressively exploring in greater detail the roles structure plays in their various areas and aspects of their architecture. In this chapter we observe and reflect on architectural issues arising essentially on the *outside* of buildings. Viewed from some distance away, the form or massing of a building, rather than any exterior detail, dominates visually and invites an exploration of the relationships between architectural and structural form. But before considering the diversity of relationships between these forms that designers can exploit for the sake of architectural enrichment, the meanings of several terms require clarification.

Architectural form is often used but infrequently defined. Ching breaks from the tradition of using the term loosely by defining it explicitly, yet his definition still remains imprecise. According to him, architectural form is an inclusive term that refers primarily to a building's external outline or shape, and to a lesser degree references its internal organization and unifying principles. He also notes that *shape* encompasses various visual and relational properties: namely, size, colour and texture, position, orientation and visual inertia.[1] Form, in his view, is therefore generally and primarily understood as shape or three-dimensional massing, but also encompasses additional architectural aspects, including structural configuration and form, in as much as they may organize and unify an architectural design.

For the purposes of this discussion, architectural form is

understood as and limited to enveloping form, or shape. This deliberate simplification excludes from architectural form any consideration of interior and exterior structural organization. It acknowledges the possibility that three-dimensional massing may be completely unrelated to structural form. By decoupling structure from the rather nebulous but conventional usage of architectural form, opportunities are provided to examine structure's relationships to specific aspects of architecture included previously within more vague definitions of architectural form. These aspects include such issues as texture, order and spatial organization.

This limited definition of architectural form, exclusive of structural considerations, also reflects both the reality of architectural design approaches and observations of the built architecture discussed in this chapter. In the design process, within architectural practice and buildings themselves, separation between architectural and structural forms is commonplace. Two distinctive structural forms in the Baumschulenweg Crematorium were observed in the previous chapter. Walls that relate closely to the architectural form and columns that do not coexist within the building envelope and contribute richly to its exterior and interior architecture, respectively.

Structural form also requires elaboration. In the context of architectural writing its traditional usage usually conveys the structural essence of a building. For example, the structural form of a post-and-beam structure might be described as skeletal, even though the beams might support planar floor structure and the building as a whole is stabilized by structural walls. In this case the observer perceives the structural

Figure 3.1

Library Square, Vancouver, Canada, Moshe Safdie and Associates Inc., 1995. A typical longitudinal frame and the ends of perimeter transverse frame beams.

framework as the dominant structural system in the building. Perhaps the framework is more visually pronounced than the walls. Visibility of the framework's elements, its beams and posts, is in all likelihood enhanced by an absence of interior partitions, while the walls may recede into the background or are certainly not particularly noticeable.

This book understands structural form as the primary or most visually dominant structural system of a building. Such a structural system is usually in a *vertical* plane, like a moment-resisting frame or a structural wall. The essential *horizontal*

Figure 3.2

Mont-Cenis Academy, Herne, Germany, Jourda & Perraudin, 1999. A glazed box with an entry canopy.

Figure 3.3

Post and beam gravity structure. The beams, detailed as trusses, are continuous over several spans.

structural systems, such as floor or roof diaphragms,[2] which are often concealed, are generally omitted from these discussions for the sake of simplicity.

While most buildings have several primary (vertical) structural systems, some have only one, such as Library Square, Vancouver (Figure 3.1). In the main library building, moment frames, located parallel to each other at regular intervals in plan, resist gravity and longitudinal lateral loads in one horizontal direction. Just two perimeter frames resist lateral loads in the orthogonal direction.

Most buildings contain two or three structural systems – a gravity-load resisting system and one or two systems that resist lateral loads in both orthogonal directions. We can identify two systems at the Mont-Cenis Academy (Figures 3.2 to 3.4). The gravity system consists of a forest of poles supporting continuous wooden trusses that in turn support purlins and the roof. Vertical wooden trusses provide face-load support for the more than four-storey-high walls. Steel tension-only bracing in several bays along each perimeter wall and in the roof plane provides resistance against horizontal loads.

At Exchange House, London, gravity loads and lateral resistance in one direction are provided for by one system, and complemented by another for lateral loads in the orthogonal direction (Figures 3.5 and 3.6). Four arches, two on the exterior, stiffened by diagonal ties, resist gravity and longitudinal loads. The purpose of the arches is to enable the building to bridge its entire length over underground

Figure 3.5
Exchange House, London, Skidmore, Owings & Merrill, 1993. Arches enable the building to span the site.

Figure 3.4
Vertical trusses support the wall. Steel tension-only bracing in the wall planes is not photographed but is similar to that of the roof diaphragm bracing which is visible.

railway lines. Above the arch the columns, as normal, are in compression, but below they are in tension, transferring the weight of lower floors upwards to the arch. Exposed cross-bracing at each end of the building resists transverse horizontal loads.

In buildings with more than one structural system and where it is unclear which system is visually dominant, the concept of *structural form* is unhelpfully simplistic. The term *structural systems* is more appropriate in these cases.

So, having elaborated upon architectural and structural

Figure 3.6
A transverse exterior cross-braced frame.

form, how are they both brought together during the architectural design process? Suckle's study of ten leading architects suggests that architects determine architectural form and interior planning after considering a wide range of factors that usually, in the first instance, do not include structure.[3] Design issues such as integrating the programme or brief within the allowable site coverage and budget, all within an overriding architectural concept, tend to be dealt with first. She finds that while the intensity and importance of an initial design concept vary greatly from designer to designer, structural considerations are not paramount during the initial design stage when determining architectural form. Erickson may speak for many architects when he states:

> Structure is the strongest and most powerful element of form, so much so that if it is not the last consideration in the long series of decisions determining form, it distorts or modifies all other determinants of a building. One finds in fact, that the structure has dictated all the other aspects of the design. The inhabitants should not behave as the columns dictate – the contrary should surely be the case . . . As with all my buildings the structure was not even considered until the main premises of the design – the shape of the spaces and the form of the building – had been determined. Thus, the structure did not preclude but followed the design intent.[4]

It is worth noting that although Erickson postpones structural decision-making in the early design stages, his architecture is notable for its rational and clearly expressed structure. His buildings lack any evidence of conceptual structural design decisions being left too late in the design process, resulting in structure poorly integrated with building function and aesthetics. Consider his Vancouver Law Courts building (Figure 11.14) and the Museum of Anthropology (Figure 12.49) to appreciate the clarity with which structure 'speaks' in his architecture.

Such an attitude towards structure as 'form-follower' rather than 'form-giver' contrasts starkly with the opposing views that have been articulated in various periods of architectural history. For example, Viollet-le-Duc expressed the views of eighteenth-century Structural Rationalists: 'Impose on me a structural system, and I will naturally find you the forms which should result from it. But if you change the structure, I shall be obliged to change the forms.'[5] He spoke with Gothic architecture in mind, where masonry load-bearing walls and buttresses comprise the building envelope. By virtue of its large plan area and its exterior and interior spatial impact, structure so dominates Gothic construction that a close relationship exists between structural and architectural form. However, since the eighteenth century and the advent of high-strength tension-capable materials like iron and then steel, the previously limited structural vocabulary of walls, vaults and buttresses has been extended greatly and often relieved of the task of enveloping buildings. Newer systems like moment frames and cantilever columns are common, and these are used in conjunction with modern non-structural enveloping systems such as precast concrete, lightweight panels and glazing systems. Building enclosure is now frequently separated from the structure to the extent that structural form may be quite unexpected given the architectural form.

Viollet-le-Duc's beliefs in structure as 'form-giver' were reaffirmed just as forcefully in the 1950s by Pier Luigi Nervi:

> Moreover, I am deeply convinced – and this conviction is strengthened by a critical appraisal of the most significant architectural works of the past as well as of the present – that the outward appearance of a good building cannot, and must not, be anything but the visible expression of an efficient structural or constructional reality. In other words, form must be the necessary result, and not the initial basis of structure.[6]

Nervi's view, persuasive only in the context of high-rise and long-span construction, is supported by Glasser: 'as in the case of arenas, auditoriums, and stadiums – it is equally clear that a conceptual design without a rigorous and well-integrated structural framework would be specious'.[7] However, the reality of contemporary architecture – as illustrated later in this chapter and described by Erickson previously – is that architectural form may not be at all expressive of structural form. In fact, intentionally contrasting these two forms offers exciting architectural design prospects.

The following two sections of this chapter illustrate the diversity of relationships between architectural and structural forms. Buildings where the forms are synthesized are examined first. Then the chapter moves to examples where, for various reasons, architectural and structural forms contrast. Note that there are different degrees of synthesis and contrast.

Most buildings, however, do not fall into these categories at all. Their architectural and structural forms neither synthesize nor contrast. Rather, a comfortable and usually unremarkable relationship exists between them. Since several different structural systems usually coexist, a lack of synthesis or a sense of clarity of structural form rules out the possibility of synthesis of architectural and structural forms.

The order in which the two contrasting relationships between forms are discussed does not imply any preference. No single relationship between architectural and structural form, be it synthesis, contrast or none at all, is inherently preferable. What *is* of utmost importance, however, is the degree to which structure, whatever its relationship to architectural form, helps to express the architectural concepts, and contributes to a successful realization of intended architectural qualities.

Synthesis of architectural and structural form

This section discusses eight structural systems that exemplify synthesis between architectural and structural form. These systems define architectural form and often function, at least partially, as the building envelope. We begin with shell structures, which, of all structural systems, can most closely integrate the two forms.

Shell structures

Shell structures achieve the most pure synthesis of architectural and structural forms. Also known as 'surface structures', shells resist and transfer loads within their minimal thicknesses. They rely upon regular two- or three-dimensional curved geometry and correct orientation and placement of supports for their adequate structural performance. Their geometry is determined so that forces are transferred by tension and compression, rather than by bending, which necessitates far deeper cross-sections. When constructed from reinforced concrete, many shells, such as those designed by Isler, a leading European concrete shell designer, reveal smooth curved surfaces inside and out, much like those of a hen's egg.[8] Isler's shells unify architectural and structural

Figure 3.7
Interior of a concrete shell structure. (J. Chilton)

form as they spring from their foundations and continuously curve over to envelop interior space (Figure 3.7).

The shell structures at Cárceres bus station, Spain, also have smoothed surfaces, and a remarkable thickness of only 120 mm for a 34 m span (Figure 3.8). Both the larger shell that shelters buses and the waiting room appear to be formed from a single sheet of bent concrete. Where the shell geometry prevents forces being transferred into the foundations in pure compression, such as at the right-hand side of the larger shell, the shell thickness is greatly increased and the foundations strengthened.

At the Palazzetto dello Sport, Rome, the shell surface does not meet the foundations directly but ends at eaves level

Figure 3.8
Bus station, Cárceres, Spain, Justo García Rubio Arquitecto, 2003. An architecture of two concrete shells. (Stephen Lord)

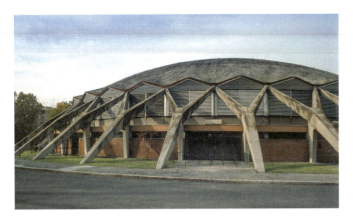

Figure 3.9

Palazzetto dello Sport, Rome, Italy, Pier Luigi Nervi with A.Vitellozzi, 1957. Inclined struts support the shell roof.

Figure 3.10

Interior ribbed surface of the shell.

where inclined struts resist the outward thrusts (Figure 3.9). The shell defines the roof form, functioning simultaneously as structure and enclosure. Its interior surfaces are ribbed (Figure 3.10). Interlacing ribs that evidence its precast concrete formwork segments both increase shell stability and achieve a much-admired structural texture.

Shell structures can also be constructed from straight steel or wood members, as in the cases of geodesic or other braced domes. Although in these cases the many short structural members shape a faceted structural surface which must then be clad, structure nonetheless defines architectural form. The huge greenhouses of the Eden Project, Cornwall, are such examples (Figure 3.11). Hexagons, a geometrical pattern found in many naturally occurring structures, are the building blocks of these shells, or biomes as they are called. Due to the long spans of up to 124 m, the outer primary hexagonal steel structure is supplemented by a secondary inner layer of tension rods (Figure 3.12). By increasing the structural depths of the biomes like this, the diameters of the main hexagon tubes could be more than halved to less than 200 mm, considerably improving their overall transparency. The biomes demonstrate the degree of synthesis of forms possible with shell structures. Although in this project structure acts as building skin in a very minor way, it defines an organic architectural form whilst achieving rational, economic and transparent construction.

Figure 3.11

Eden Project, Cornwall, UK, Nicholas Grimshaw & Partners, 2001. A cluster of interlinked biomes.

Figure 3.12
Biome interior structure consisting of outer primary hexagons and an inner layer of braced rods.

Fabric structures

Fabric or membrane structures represent another type of surface structure. Their tensioned fabric which resists self-weight and wind loads, relies upon three-dimensional curvature for structural adequacy. Fabric form, thickness and strength must match the expected loads, and all surfaces must be stretched taut to prevent the fabric flapping during high winds. Like shell structures, there is no distinction between the architectural and the structural forms. Fabric structures, however, require additional and separate compression members to create high points over which the fabric can be stretched. Arches, with their curved forms, are well suited and aesthetically the most sympathetic to the curving fabric geometry, but masts, flying struts and cables, which are more common, introduce dissimilar geometric forms and materiality. Their linearity, density and solidity contrast with the flowing double-curved, lightweight and translucent fabric surfaces, and can sometimes visually disturb the fabric's overall softness of form.

At the Stellingen Ice Skating Rink and Velodrome, Hamburg, four masts that project through the fabric and connect to it by tension cables provide the primary means of compression support (Figure 3.13). Eight flying-struts provide additional high points. Supported by interior cables tensioned between the four outermost masts, they thrust upward into the fabric to increase its curvature and improve its structural performance. The building interior illustrates clearly the different architectural qualities of the fabric and its linear supporting structure – masts, flying struts and interior steel cables (Figure 3.14).

Figure 3.14
Contrasting architectural qualities of fabric surface and interior structural elements.

Figure 3.13
Stellingen Ice Skating Rink and Velodrome, Hamburg, Germany, Silcher, Werner + Partners, 1996. Overall form.

Catenaries

Catenary structures, like fabric structures, transfer loads to their supports through tension. The simplest example of a catenary is a draped cable spanning between two high points. Catenaries that support roofs are usually designed so that the roof self-weight exceeds the wind suction or uplift pressures that would otherwise cause excessive vertical movement. Reinforced concrete is sometimes chosen as a catenary material for this reason. The concrete encases the tension steel and creates the exterior and interior surfaces. Lighter catenary systems are possible provided that wind uplift is overcome with ballast or a separate tie-down system. Catenary tension members are usually distinct from the cladding and exposed within or outside the building envelope. The Portuguese Pavilion canopy, Lisbon, and Hall 26 of the Trade Fair, Hanover, illustrate these two approaches.

At the southern end of the Portuguese Pavilion, built for Expo '98, a ceremonial plaza 65 m long by 58 m wide is sheltered by a 200 mm-thick reinforced concrete catenary slab. It has been variously described as a 'veil' or 'tent' on account of its remarkable slimness and draped form (Figure 3.15). Two porticoes, one at each end, act as massive end-blocks to resist the catenary tension. Within each portico, nine parallel walls or buttresses resist the large inward pull from the hanging slab. Their weight, plus their strong foundations, prevents them from toppling due to the almost horizontal tension forces acting at roof level. The porticoes are not at all expressive of their important structural roles. Their simple

Figure 3.15
Portuguese Pavilion, Lisbon, Portugal, Alvaro Siza, 1998. The canopy drapes between two porticoes.

orthogonality, which contrasts with the purity of the catenary, would have been compromised if the buttress walls were tapered in response to reduced bending moments with height. The piers of the Dulles International Airport Terminal, Washington, D.C., illustrate a far more expressive approach. Their tapering, as well as their inclination, expresses the strain of supporting a heavy reinforced concrete catenary roof (Figure 3.16).

Undulating waves formed by alternating masts and catenary roofs at Hall 26 of the Trade Fair, Hanover, also demonstrate totally integrated architectural and structural forms (Figures 3.17 and 3.18). In stark contrast to the solid concrete porticoes of the Portuguese Pavilion, the triangulated and trestle-like masts possess architectural qualities of lightness and transparency. Within the main interior spaces the structural steel catenary members, that read as 'tension bands', support the roof and timber ceiling, or, in selected areas, glazed roof panels.

Figure 3.16
Dulles International Airport, Washington, D.C., USA, Saarinen (Eero) and Associates, 1962. Inclined piers support the catenary slab.

Figure 3.17

Hall 26, Trade Fair, Hanover, Germany, Herzog + Partner, 1996. Three catenaries span between masts.

Figure 3.18

A mast withstands opposing catenary tensions at its top and at mid-height. Six pairs of masts are equally spaced across the width of the hall.

Ribbed structures

Ribbed structures can also become almost synonymous with enclosure where they generate and define architectural form, although their skeletal character often necessitates a separate enveloping system. Ribbed structures generally enclose single volumes, rather than multi-storey construction. By restricting the height of these structures effectively to a single (albeit very high) storey, designers avoid potentially compromising a pure architectural language of ribs with additional interior load-bearing structure.

This approach is exemplified at the National Art Centre, Tokyo (Figure 3.19). Ribs, wrapped by continuous lines of glass louvres, define the main undulating façade. It is only from the inside that somewhat of an explanation is offered for its sensuous curves. Two free-standing inverted cones with restaurants atop sit within the full-height atrium. In their vicinity the fullest swelling of the façade occurs. The ribs acknowledge the presence of the cones by their placement in plan and by curving away from them to maintain adequate visual separation (Figure 3.20). The ribs therefore respond to the geometry of the cones within and bring a welcome quality of softness and flow to the façade.

A combination of primary structural ribs and secondary horizontal tubes define the architectural form of the Reichstag cupola, Berlin (Figure 3.21). In this case, ribs lean against each other via a crowning compression ring. An internal double-helical ramp structure supported off the ribs provides them with additional horizontal stiffness through its in-plan ring-beam action (Figure 3.22). A circumferential moment-resisting frame within the dome surface resists lateral loads.

Figure 3.19

National Art Centre, Tokyo, Japan, Kisho Kurokawa and Associates, 2006. Vertical but curved ribs support and define the undulating façade.

Figure 3.21

The Reichstag cupola, Berlin, Germany, Foster and Partners, 1999. Radial ribs and circumferential tubes.

Figure 3.20

The lower of the two cones and nearby ribs. Rib location and their outward curvature respond to the cone.

Figure 3.22

The interior of the cupola. Ramps stiffen the ribs to minimize their dimensions, and horizontal glazing tubes combine with ribs to form a surface perimeter moment frame to withstand horizontal wind loads.

Figure 3.23
Tobias Grau headquarters,
Rellingen, Germany, BRT
Architekten, 1998. Glue-
laminated wooden ribs enclose
the ground-floor interior
concrete structure.

Figure 3.24
Curved wooden ribs behind glass louvres.

Curved wooden members play a similar form-generating role in the two-storey Tobias Grau office and warehouse facility, Rellingen (Figures 3.23 and 3.24). Able to be described as ribs or frames, they wrap around the whole building to define the ovoid-shaped envelope. Where they function as rafters they are placed under the metal roof, but as columns they are exposed outside the skin. Although the wood structure is the form-giver, most of the internal load-bearing structure is reinforced concrete. A first-floor concrete flat-plate overlays a rectangular grid of concrete columns, and several internal concrete walls provide lateral stability. Structure therefore comprises two different materials and four distinctly different structural systems, including the longitudinal steel cross-bracing at first-floor level. Of all these systems, only the curved wooden ribs or frames match the tubular architectural form.

Arches

Arches also offer a potential synthesis of architectural and structural form. They take various shapes, such as semi-circular, parabolic or pointed, but usually have in common a single convex curvature. They usually meet the ground at an inclination to the horizontal, unless they are those of the Paul Klee Museum, Bern (Figures 3.25 and 3.26). Here, the thirty-seven sets of arches that form three 'hills' of slightly different

Figure 3.25
Paul Klee Museum, Bern, Switzerland, Renzo Piano Building Workshop, 2005. Arches form three different-sized 'hills'. (Darrel Ronald)

Figure 3.26
The arches also have a strong presence within the interior. (Darrel Ronald)

spans do not plunge directly into the ground, but change curvature and take the form of smaller concave arches. While the change of curvature introduces more bending and requires deeper members than for conventional arches, their flowing interconnectedness mimics that of the background landscape. While the exterior structure powerfully expresses the nearby gently rolling hills, the arches are partially exposed inside and visually reinforce the curved enclosure.

At the Great Glasshouse, Carmarthenshire, arches take a more traditional form to create a toroidal dome (Figure 3.27). The dome's two constant orthogonal radii of curvature require that the arches distant from the building's centre-line lean over in response to the three-dimensional surface curvature. Clarity of the arched structural form is undiminished by the small-diameter tubes that run longitudinally to tie the arches back at regular intervals to a perimeter ring beam. Apart from supporting the roof glazing, the tubes prevent the arches buckling and deflecting laterally.

Arches are usually orientated in the vertical plane to resist gravity loads; however, at the Pequot Museum, Connecticut, the curved glazed wall of the three–four-storey principal public area is supported by a horizontal arch (Figures 3.28 and 3.29). The semi-circular wall is glazed and roof beams that radiate towards the centre of the roof are supported on

Figure 3.27
The Great Glasshouse, Carmarthenshire, Wales, Foster and Partners, 1998. An arched roof. The thrusts of the arches are resisted by a perimeter ring beam and columns that respond to the arches by their inclination normal to the ends of the arches.

inclined perimeter steel posts. The cross-sectional dimensions of the posts have been minimized by the introduction of a most unexpected structural system – a horizontal arch, but one that synthesizes with the architectural form. Wind load acting normal to the glazing over the centre half of the posts is resisted primarily by this semi-circular horizontal arch, anchored at each end. It functions either as an arch that works in compression or as half a tension ring, depending on the wind direction. The arch, together with its stabilizing ties and connecting members to the steel posts, adds a layer of structure that contributes complexity and interest to the interior space. An alternative to the steel tubular arch would have been to increase the depth of the posts significantly so they could span the whole height of the wall. In this museum, structural form is well integrated with architectural form, which itself draws upon indigenous construction forms.

Figure 3.28
Pequot Museum, Mashantucket, USA, Polshek Partnership Architects, 2000. Exterior view of the curved and sloping glazed walls of main public space.

Figure 3.29
The horizontal arch supports the curved and sloping wall.

Figure 3.30
United Airlines Terminal, Chicago, USA, Murphy/Jahn, 1987. Folded plates span the main entry foyer.

Folded plates

The use of this structural and architectural form is mainly confined to roofs, and sometimes walls. The structural potential of a folded plate can be demonstrated quite simply by taking a piece of paper which is floppy and introducing a fold;

suddenly the paper stiffens and can span as a beam without excessive deflection. In the United Airlines Terminal, Chicago, the folded plates take the form of inclined steel trusses. The top chords, spaced apart to introduce natural light, experience compression while the bottom chords resist the tension from the bending action on the plates (Figure 3.30).

Inclined trusses also form the folded plates at the Riverside Museum, Glasgow, although the structural members are not exposed (Figure 3.31). Although the ends of the folded plates appear to be unsupported, they cantilever beyond a glazed load-bearing wall comprising many very slender steel mullions. This is probably the first building where folded plates are irregular in cross-section and curved in plan. Three straight lengths of folded plates form the S-shaped plan. Given that the folds are exposed inside and out and no other interior structure was allowed, the support of the folded plates in the areas where they bend in plan necessitated very sophisticated and expensive design and construction.

The folded plates of a Hong Kong gymnasium function as structure and full enclosure (Figures 3.32 and 3.33). Reinforced concrete folded plates approximately 200 mm thick span the gymnasium width and then fold down to form walls, effectively creating a folded plate portal frame structure.

Figure 3.31
Riverside Museum, Glasgow, UK, Zaha Hadid, 2011. Front façade showing folded plates in section. (Ray Firskierisky)

Figure 3.32
Gymnasium, Hong Kong, China.
View from above showing the
folded plate construction.

Figure 3.33
Interior of the gymnasium.

Framed structures

Synthesis of architectural and structural form extends beyond
curved and folded forms. Consider the intimate relationship
between orthogonal skeletal structural frameworks and
rectilinear forms. In his discussion of the formative 1891 Sears
Roebuck Store in Chicago, Condit asserts:

for the first time the steel and wrought-iron skeleton
became fully and unambiguously the means of
architectonic expression . . . The long west elevation is
developed directly out of the structural system behind it,
much as the isolated buttresses of the Gothic Cathedral
serve as primary visual elements in its indissoluble unity
of structure and form.[9]

Figure 3.34

Fuji TV building, Tokyo, Japan, Kenzo Tange, 1996. Frames at two different scales synthesize with the rectilinear building form.

Most orthogonal beam–column frameworks integrate well within prismatic architectural forms. The ubiquitous medium- to high-rise office building is a typical example, but even though exemplifying integrated architectural and structural forms, the ensuing architecture may not be meritorious. Three rather unusual, but well-regarded, buildings illustrate the realization of and the potential for synthesizing frames and architectural form.

At the Fuji TV building, Tokyo, the overall rectilinear volume is supported by orthogonal frames of different scales (Figure 3.34). Vertical single-bay three-dimensional frames provide resistance for gravity and horizontal forces. Single-storey moment frames are stacked one on top of the other to form mega-columns. Where the building form is voided they join with horizontal vierendeel trusses (consisting of the same frames joined side-by-side) to form four-storey mega-frames. The qualities of orthogonality, solidity and emptiness of a single-bay

three-dimensional frame therefore reflect the architectural form of the building.

Uncompromising orthogonal rigour characterizes the cubic form and perimeter frames of the San Cataldo Cemetery columbarium, Modena (Figure 3.35). From both architectural and structural engineering perspectives, the exterior surfaces that are penetrated by unglazed openings can also be considered as highly pierced walls, given the relatively small size of openings and an absence of any articulation of individual beam or column members. The frame thickness, exaggerated by the depth of the integral ossuary compartments, reinforces ideas of hollowness and emptiness, reminiscent of empty eye sockets in a skull. This reading corresponds with an understanding of the work as an 'unfinished, deserted house, a built metaphor of death'.[10]

Pitched portal frames, consisting of two columns connected rigidly to sloping rafters, structure innumerable light-industrial and other utilitarian buildings. This structural form, which rarely graces the pages of architectural publications, integrates with architectural form in the Princess of Wales Conservatory, London. In realizing a 'glazed hill' design concept, the architect manipulates

basic multi-bay portals (Figure 3.36). Unlike most portal frames, the side rafters connect directly to the perimeter foundations, successfully reducing the visual impact of the building on its surroundings. The form-generating portals that span transversely are geometrically simple, but subtle transformations that introduce asymmetry and volumetric complexity distance the conservatory from its utilitarian cousins. An uncommon yet elegant structural system provides longitudinal resistance. Roof-plane moment-resisting frames substitute for the more conventional diagonal cross-bracing that is usually associated with portal frame construction.

Walls

The structural wall is another system capable of participating in the integration of architectural and structural forms. As exemplified by the Faculty of Journalism, Pamplona, walls not only dominate its façades but define interior spaces (Figures 3.37 and 3.38). In some areas of the building, horizontal slots

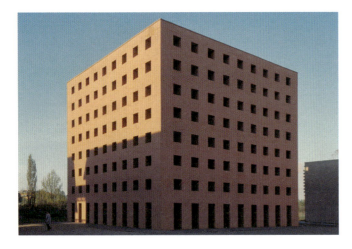

Figure 3.35
San Cataldo Cemetery columbarium, Modena, Italy, Aldo Rossi, 1984. Rigorous orthogonality.

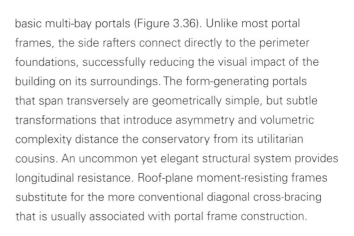

Figure 3.36
Princess of Wales Conservatory, London, Gordon Wilson, 1986. Pitched portal frame variations.

Figure 3.37
Faculty of Journalism, Pamplona, Spain, Vicens and Ramos, 1996. Walls visually dominate the exterior.

Figure 3.38
An interior architecture of walls.

Figure 3.39
Zollverein School of Management and Design, Essen, Germany, SANAA, 2007. (Jeroen Meijer)

force walls to span horizontally and function structurally as beams. Even balustrades read as low walls. Inside and out, walls dominate the architectural experience. Fortunately, any possible blandness arising from this architecture of walls is mitigated by exterior elevational and interior spatial variation, careful attention to surface textures, and the lightening of the concrete colour. The rectilinear form of the walls strengthens the orthogonal architecture they support, enclose and subdivide.

Apart from three small services and vertical circulation cores, the Zollverein School of Management and Design, Essen, is entirely supported by its load-bearing concrete walls (Figure 3.39). The 35 m cube encloses five storeys of unequal height, but none of this is visible due to the irregular square

penetrations on each façade. The degree of irregularity is moderated so that 'columns' and wall panels are discernible.

Traditionally, structural walls are planar and opaque, like those of the Faculty of Journalism, Pamplona, except for relatively small openings. However, it is possible to achieve structural walls with a far greater degree of transparency, yet still able to withstand both vertical and horizontal forces. This capability is celebrated at Prada Boutique Aoyama, Tokyo, with its perimeter diagrid walls (Figures 3.40 and 3.41). Not only does structure allow interior spaces to be flooded with light, the diamond-shaped structural form synthesizes with the five-sided crystalline architectural form. A seismic isolation system located between the two basement levels has facilitated such a slender structural grid. One reviewer comments: 'The architects have noted that this was their first building "to forge structure, space and façade as a single unit"'.[11]

Figure 3.40
Prada Boutique Aoyama, Tokyo, Japan, Herzog & de Meuron, 2003. The main entry and lower floors of the six storeys above ground level. The black glazing lines delineate diagonal structural members, while light-coloured perimeter beams de-emphasize the floor structure.

Figure 3.41
The structural diagrid wall is most clearly visible from within the building.

Contrasting forms

Arches

Architectural and structural forms contrast among a juxtaposition of architectural qualities such as geometry,

materiality, scale and texture. In the examples that follow, geometric dissimilarity between forms is the most common quality contrasted. For example, at Exchange House, London, parabolic arches support a building rectilinear in plan and elevation (Figure 3.5). The contrast between forms arises primarily from the need for the building to bridge over underground railway lines, but even the exposed transverse cross-braced bays at each end of the building are unrelated to the architectural form. The penetration of the two internal arches into the box form leads to difficulties in integrating structure and space planning (Figure 3.42).

An element of surprise is common to buildings with contrasting forms. As you approach a building and become aware of its architectural form you usually expect to discover a certain structural form based on your previous architectural experience. If the actual form is considerably different from what is anticipated, then it is likely that architectural and structural forms contrast. Well-designed contrasting forms

Figure 3.42
Exchange House, London, Skidmore, Owings & Merrill, 1993. An uneasy relationship between an internal arch and a corridor.

Figure 3.43
TGV station, Lille, France,
SNCF/Jean-Marie Duthilleul,
1994. Side elevation.

Figure 3.44
Railway station, Rome, Montuori, Vitellozzi, Calini, Castellazzi, Fatigati & Pintonello, 1950. Curved roof beams over the main concourse.

Figure 3.45
Unexpected interior arches in the TGV station.

provide many opportunities for innovative and interesting architecture. Most examples of contrasting forms can be attributed to designers attempting to enliven their work, but occasionally reasons arise from pragmatic considerations, such as at Exchange House, which functions as both building and bridge.

The architectural form of the Lille TGV station with its gently undulating roof (Figure 3.43) is similar to that of the Rome railway station, with its long-span curved beams that define the roof profile (Figure 3.44). But what you encounter

inside the TGV station is a series of paired steel arches, totally unrelated to the roof shape (Figure 3.45). Disparities between the arch profiles and the roof wave are accounted for by vertical props that support secondary trusses directly under the roof. Because the prop diameters are similar to those of the primary arches, no clear structural hierarchy is established. Consequently, an opportunity for the interior space to be characterized by a visual flow of arches is lost. Nevertheless, the combination of slender compression members and a filigree of stabilizing cables represents the designers' attempt

to realize a vision of a roof structure with as few structural supports as possible, and an appearance of 'fine lace floating above the train'.[12]

Brightly coloured tiled vaults welcome visitors to the Santa Caterina Market, Barcelona (Figure 3.46). These are not traditional masonry vaults, notable for their synthesis of architectural and structural form, but are supported by skeletal steel structure that has little respect for the purity of vaulted geometry. The structural system begins with tangled steel-tube columns at each end of the market that support valley-trusses running its length (Figure 3.47). They in turn carry the tubular steel arches that form the vaults. The limited spanning capability of the trusses required three points of intermediate support, and rather than introducing interior columns, three three-dimensional steel arched-trusses span the width of the market. Visible from both above the vaulted roof and inside, they spring from large perimeter concrete beams, passing over some vaults and penetrating through others. The valley-trusses below hang from them (Figure 3.48).

Figure 3.46
Santa Caterina Market, Barcelona, Spain, EMBT, 2005. Tiled vaults over the main entrance. (Mark Southcombe)

Figure 3.47
Tangled tubular columns support trusses for the tubular arches that form the vaults. (Mark Southcombe)

Figure 3.48
The length-wise trusses and the three penetrating arch trusses that support them. (Mark Southcombe)

Figure 3.49
Novartis Building, Basel, Switzerland, Gehry Partners, 2009. Highly irregular architectural form. (Michela Nolasco)

Other vertical support

Irregular billowing projections define the form of the Novartis Building, Basel (Figure 3.49). Due to a lack of any load-bearing elements on the exterior, structural form is concealed. Surprisingly, given the randomness of the enveloping geometry, the primary structure is a reasonably regular concrete column and slab frame structure, stabilized by three shear cores. However, around an internal atrium, wood-clad columns take a more dynamic configuration that contrasts with the orthogonality of the primary structure due to their variable inclinations (Figure 3.50).

We observe a rather less extreme contrast between architectural and structural form at the LASALLE College of the Arts, Singapore (Figure 3.51; see also Figure 12.62). Here primary structural frames are visible through transparent

Figure 3.50
Less rational structure supporting the floors around the internal atrium. (Alex Learmont Photography)

Figure 3.51
LASALLE College of the Arts, Singapore, RSP Architects, 2007. Irregular faceted walls supported by a regular frame.

Figure 3.52
Stuttgart Airport terminal, Germany, Gerkan, Marg + Partners, 1991. Structural trees.

walls with their faceted geometry. The irregularity of the envelope is achieved by varying the distance that slabs cantilever from beams, and by leaning wall mullions out from their supporting slabs.

Contrasting forms at Stuttgart Airport enrich its architecture and surprise visitors in two ways. First, the structural geometry of the interior is totally unrelated to that of the enveloping form. Second, the meanings inherent in each form are so divergent – an interior structure that exudes meaning by virtue of its representational nature contrasts with the plain architectural form, essentially a truncated wedge. The monoslope roof rises from two to four storeys from landside to airside. Glazed roof slots subdivide the roof plane into twelve rectangular modules, each of which is supported by a completely unexpected structure in the form of a structural tree (Figure 3.52). The trees, all the same height, rise from

floors that step up, one storey at a time. Trunks consist of four interconnected parallel steel tubes, which bend to become boughs, and then fork into clusters of three and four progressively smaller branches. Finally, forty-eight twigs support an orthogonal grid of rafters.

The Regional Government Centre, Marseille, can be read as an amalgamation of at least four distinct architectural forms – two slab office blocks linked by a transparent atrium, and two exterior elongated tubular forms. One, the Council Chambers, stands free, while the Presidential Offices sit on the higher office block (Figure 3.53). The most obvious contrast between forms occurs within the first three storeys of the office blocks where exposed three-storey X-columns are located along each side. They visually dominate the lower storeys, both on the exterior, where they are painted blue, and in the atrium, where they are white (Figure 3.54). One reviewer describes them: 'the X-shaped concrete pilotis line up one after each other, their unexpected geometries ricocheting through the glazed atrium like sculptures by Barbara Hepworth, Frank Stella or the Flintstones'.[13] While their structural form does not relate to any other architectural qualities within the project, they function as transfer structures for gravity loads. They support columns located on a 5.4 m office module at third-floor level and above, and widen to a 10.8 m grid at ground-floor level that is suitably large for the basement car park. The architects deliberately expose the dramatic X-columns on the exterior by moving the building envelope into the building, behind the structure. Unexpected and spectacular, structure enriches both the interior space and the building exterior.

Figure 3.53
Regional Government Centre, Marseille, France, Alsop & Störmer, 1994. A combination of forms.

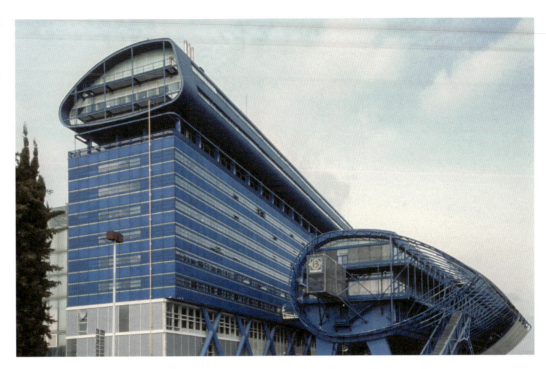

Figure 3.54
The X-columns in the atrium.

Similarly unexpected interior structure greets visitors to Westminster College, London. Raking columns in the entry foyer-cum-café form an impressive series of structurally triangulated frames with vertical columns (Figure 3.55). Raking columns support the main façade, which steps out up its height to form a significant cantilever (Figure 3.56). Usually, columns and horizontal structure such as deep transfer beams support cantilevered or setback façades, but here, inclined columns at odds with the orthogonality of most other architectural elements do the job (Figure 3.57)

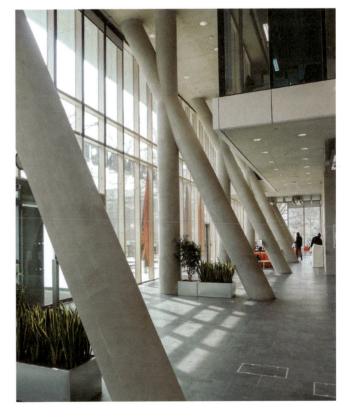

Figure 3.55
Westminster College, London, UK, Schmidt Hammer Lassen Architects, 2011. Vertical and raking columns form triangulated frames that modulate the entry foyer.

Figure 3.56

The front façade cantilevers while the facing façade on the left steps back up its height.

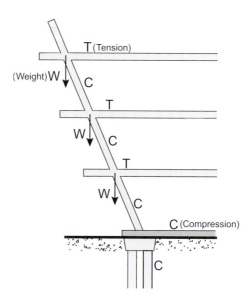

Figure 3.57

A sloping column resists vertical load by a combination of compression in the raking members and either tension or compression in the horizontal floor structure. These horizontal forces need to be resisted by structures that are strong enough to do so, such as, in this case, structural walls around vertical circulation cores.

If the raking columns at Westminster College can be described as unexpected, given the orthogonal, albeit cantilevering, building form, the interior structure of the box-shaped Sendai Mediatheque is mind-blowing. How can such audacious clusters of slender columns support a seven-storey library building, especially in a highly active seismic region? The structure, partially visible through perimeter glazing, is not even remotely similar in plan or section to what it supports (Figure 3.58). Thirteen circular clusters of tubular steel columns constitute the vertical structure. They support relatively lightweight steel stressed-skin floor plates. The four largest clusters are located

Figure 3.58

Sendai Mediatheque, Sendai, Japan, Toyo Ito & Associates, 2000. Exterior view with some structure visible behind the predominantly glazed skin.

Figure 3.59
The structure in the main library area, due to the size and varying inclination of struts, appears to sway.

near the corners of each floor plate, and their many steel columns are triangulated (in different patterns) to make them effective in resisting seismic loads.[14] Each cluster contains either some mode of vertical circulation or services. The remaining clusters not only lack triangulation and therefore lateral stability, but most struts are inclined, in some cases suggesting the cluster has been twisted before being finally welded into place. When viewed at level four, where most of the clusters are visible (Figure 3.59), the structure possesses a high degree of transparency. Also, it appears fragile, like the trunks of young trees swaying, somewhat randomly, in the breeze. This reading of structure is in total contrast to the orthogonality of the building form.

New versus old

All the previous examples in this section are drawn from relatively new buildings. Contrasting architectural and structural forms are part of their intended designs. Yet we commonly encounter other examples of contrasting forms in additions or modifications to existing buildings, particularly given significant age differences between the old and new work. The Reichstag cupola, discussed previously (Figure 3.21), is one of many such examples reviewed by Byard.[15] While architectural and structural forms synthesize in the cupola itself, both contrast with forms of the original building.

A similar situation arises at the Great Court of the British Museum, London. A new canopy covers an irregularly shaped space between the circular Reading Room and numerous neo-classical buildings surrounding the courtyard (Figure 3.60). The canopy, a triangulated steel surface structure, differs dramatically from the buildings it spans between. Greater differences in architectural and structural form, materiality and degrees of lightness and transparency are hardly possible. As expected, the canopy has attracted considerable comment. Reviewers generally admire it. They point to its design and construction complexity, its controlled daylighting, and note its elegance, describing it as 'floating', 'delicate' and 'unobtrusive', at least when compared to an original scheme with heavier orthogonal structure and reduced transparency. However, its billowing form is easier to comprehend from above than from within, where an unsettling visual restlessness arises from the triangulation of the doubly curved surfaces. An absence of structural hierarchy contributes to this reduction of spatial and structural comprehension, further highlighting the contrast between the new and the old.

This structure also serves to remind us that any exposed structure may invite readings that are unintended by its designers. For example, one reviewer observes:

> Grids like this are by their nature non-hierarchical, but it is a Modernist fantasy that this means they are neutral. What the roof does is reinforce the impression that the

Figure 3.60
The Great Court, British Museum, London, Foster and Partners, 2000. Triangulated lattice roof with the circular Reading Room on the left.

Great Court is not a place to linger, but a space to move through; the swirling vortex of its geometry, which Buro Happold wrote its own software to resolve, is curiously restless from many angles of view.[16]

Although the architects did not intend to convey such a sense of restlessness, they would no doubt view this reading as an acceptable price to be paid for a scheme that roofs the courtyard in a most elegant manner.

Summary

In order to discuss the relationships between architectural and structural form an understanding of the term *architectural form* is intentionally narrowly defined as the massing or the enveloping form. The reality of most architectural design practice is that structure rarely generates architectural form, but rather responds to it in a way that meets the programme and ideally is consistent with design concepts. Selected buildings illustrate two categories of relationship between architectural and structural form – synthesis and contrast. No one category or attitude to the relationship between forms is inherently preferable to another. It all depends on the architectural concept. Of vital importance is the degree to which structure, irrespective of its relationship to architectural form, reinforces architectural concepts and contributes to intended architectural qualities. The examples above merely hint at the breadth of potential similarity or diversity of forms that lead to exemplary architecture.

Notes

1. F. D. Ching, *Architecture: form, space & order*, 2nd edn, New York: Van Nostrand Reinhold, 1996.

2. Horizontal structure, like floor and roof diaphragms, is essential to resist horizontal forces from wind and earthquake. Refer to A. W. Charleson, *Seismic design for architects: outwitting the quake*, Oxford: Elsevier, 2008, ch. 4.

3. A. Suckle, *By their own design*, New York: Whitney Library of Design, 1980.

4. Ibid., p. 14.

5. Quoted in P. Collins, *Changing ideals in modern architecture 1750–1950*, 2nd edn, Montreal: McGill-Queen's University Press, 1998, p. 214.

6. P. L. Nervi, 'Concrete and structural form', *The Architect and Building News* 27, 1955, 523–9.

7. D. E. Glasser, 'Structural considerations', in J. Synder and A. Catanse (eds), *Introduction to architecture*, New York: McGraw-Hill, 1979, pp. 268–71.

8. For other examples, see J. Chilton, *The engineer's contribution to contemporary architecture: Heinz Isler*, London: RIBA Thomas Telford, 2000.

9. C. W. Condit, *The Chicago School of Architecture*, Chicago: University of Chicago Press, 1964, p. 90.

10. S. Thiel-Siling (ed.), *Icons of architecture: the 20th century*, Munich: Prestel, 1998, p. 125.

11. Herzog & De Meuron, 'Prada Aoyama Epicenter', *A+U* 7(406), 2004, 78–83, at 80.

12. Quoted in P. Davey, 'The boot and the lace maker', *Architectural Review* 199(3), 1996, 72.

13. J. Welsh, 'Willing and able', *RIBA Journal* 101(4), 1994, 36–47, at 38.

14. Such slender structure is due to a flexible and ductile steel moment frame structure in the basement which reduces earthquake forces induced in the irregular superstructure by 60–70 per cent. Refer to R. Witte (ed.), *Case: Toyo Ito – Sendai Mediatheque*, Munich: Prestel, 2002, p. 46.

15. P. S. Byard, *The architecture of additions: design and regulation*, New York: W. W. Norton & Company, 1998.

16. N. Pople, 'Caught in the web', *RIBA Journal* 108(2), 2001, 36–44, at 42.

four

Building exterior

Introduction

In many urban locations site boundaries and recession planes determine architectural form. Particularly for medium- to high-rise buildings, economic and pragmatic necessity give rise to ubiquitous rectilinear forms. These require architectural approaches other than the manipulation of building massing for them to contribute positively to the urban fabric. With the exception of those buildings completely clad in mirror glass or some other type of opaque cladding, many buildings world-wide share the common feature of displaying some exposed structural elements on their façades.

Arising more from an appreciation of the functional advantages perimeter structure affords than intentionally exposing structure for its own sake, structural members are often exposed. While such structural ordering and patterning of façades often merely reflects that of the surrounding built environment and therefore tends to proliferate architecture of indifferent quality, some architects take a more proactive stance towards exposing structure. They are aware of its potential to enrich exterior architecture.

Before considering in breadth the diverse contributions that structure brings to building exteriors, this chapter begins by examining one building more deeply – the Hong Kong and Shanghai Bank, Hong Kong. A study of the exposed structure on its main façade sets the scene for discussing many of the roles exterior structure plays.

One of the bank's most distinctive features is its exposed structure on the main façade (Figure 4.1). If this structure were to be concealed behind cladding, one of the world's best-known commercial buildings would no longer be recognizable. Devoid of its iconic structure it

Figure 4.1

Hong Kong and Shanghai Bank, Hong Kong, China, Foster Associates, 1986. Main façade.

would merely merge with its neighbours' more conventional architecture.

Development of its unusual structural form arose primarily from the client's insistence on retaining an existing historic banking chamber. Foster and Associates' first sketches for the design competition to select an architect show large, exposed, bridge-like trusses spanning across the building and supporting suspended floors beneath.[1] After being commissioned, the architects continued to develop long-span structural schemes. Although the client eventually decided to trim the budget and demolish the banking chamber, continuing commitment to a long-span structural solution was justified by studies that showed large column-free areas yielded significantly higher rental returns than shorter-span options. The client also appreciated the high level of planning flexibility that long spans provided. After abandoning the relatively crude bridge-truss design, a series of structural iterations that always included strongly exposed structure were continually refined until the final structural scheme emerged.

So, how *does* structure contribute to the exterior architecture of this bank? Beginning with its visual qualities, we note how the structure is located in front of the cladding. Separated from the façade, structure modulates it, providing depth, pattern and order. The vertical structure, namely three hanger-rods and two ladder-like masts, creates a symmetrical and rhythmical ababa composition. On a macro scale, the horizontal trusses subdivide the façade vertically, while beams within the ladder frames, which can also be described as vierendeel masts, articulate individual storey heights at a finer scale. From a distance, structural scale relates well to the overall building scale. Structure, clearly distinguished from other building elements, such as cladding, can be read clearly as such, yet a sense of structural monumentality is avoided. To my eye at least, the scale of structure verges on the minimal, even without allowing for the thickness of protective layers of cladding that encase the steelwork. However, close up, and especially inside the building, those apparently slender façade structural members appear huge. An interior column located within a single-storey space exerts an overwhelming presence due to its relatively large scale in such a confined volume.

As well as structure's contribution to the visual composition of the façade and the way its exposure links the interior and exterior architecture, structure can also be read as playing

several expressive roles – such as expressing structural actions, building function and conceptual issues. The triangulated geometry of the double coat-hanger trusses shows how they transfer loads from their mid-spans and end tension-hangers to the vierendeel masts. At a more detailed level, though, the expression of structural actions is somewhat inconsistent. While the increase in diameter of the tension-hangers towards the underside of each truss accurately reflects the accumulative increase of weight from the suspended floors, the enlargements at the ends of truss members suggests rigid connectivity rather than the reality of large structural pin joints. At a functional level, the mega-frame subdivides the façade to reflect functional and organizational aspects within the building. Masts separate service areas from the main banking hall and offices, and vertical spacing between trusses expresses the five separate corporate divisions within the bank. Overlaying this functional expression, exposed structure articulates the high-tech and state-of-the-art qualities of design and construction.

The following section of this chapter examines the aesthetic quality of exterior structure in more detail. Then, after illustrating how architects use structure to create strong visual connections between exterior and interior architecture, the chapter considers the relationship of exterior structure to building entry. Finally, it concludes by exploring the expressive roles played by exterior structure.

Aesthetic qualities

The exterior character of a building is often determined by how structure relates to the building envelope. Architects frequently explore and exploit spatial relationships between these two elements in order to express their architectural ideas and generally enrich their designs.[2] Structure plays numerous roles in contributing to the visual appearance of a building façade, through modulation, adding depth and texture, and acting as a visual screen or filter. Some of these roles are seen at the Hong Kong and Shanghai Bank, but in all of them the structural scale must relate appropriately to the scales of the surrounding elements in order to achieve the desired outcome.

Modulation

Where beams and columns modulate a façade, they usually visually subdivide the skin vertically and horizontally, creating a rectangular ordering pattern over the building surface. Within these structural modules, secondary structural members, perhaps supporting glazing and themselves an order of magnitude smaller than the primary structural modulators, may further subdivide the surfaces.

Modulation generates patterns that potentially introduce variety, rhythm and hierarchy, and generally increases visual interest. Patterned or textured surfaces are usually preferable to those that are planar and bare. However, as seen on many office building façades, modulation ceases to be attractive if it is too repetitious. Given its ubiquitous nature, modulation hardly requires illustration, but several rather unusual examples are discussed below.

In response to its beach-front marine environment and an architectural concept centred on the beaching of crystalline rocks, a glazed envelope encloses the Kursaal Auditorium perimeter structure at San Sebastian (Figure 4.2). Although not exposed, structure is visible, albeit dimly. The deep external wall structure that rises over 20 m to the roof is sandwiched between two skins of translucent glass panels. Structural framing that takes the form of vertical or slightly inclined vierendeel trusses, tied together by regularly spaced horizontal members, is perceived as shadowy forms from both inside and out. Although considerably subdued visually,

Figure 4.3
Yerba Buena Lofts, San Francisco, USA, Stanley Saitowitz Office/Natoma Architects, 2002. Walls and slabs modulate the front façade.

structure still modulates the large exterior and interior wall surfaces, and on the side walls its geometrical distortions accentuate the building's subtle inclination towards the sea.

A more typical example of structure modulating a whole façade can be observed at the Yerba Buena Lofts, San Francisco (Figure 4.3). Visually dominant primary structural elements – walls and slabs – play two roles simultaneously. While modulating and ordering the façade, they also alter one's perception of the building's scale. Concealment of the mezzanine floor structure behind glazing in each double-height apartment means the ten-storey building is read as

Figure 4.2
Kursaal Auditorium and Conference Centre, San Sebastian, Spain, Rafael Moneo, 1999. Structure behind translucent glazed panels modulates exterior walls.

five storeys. To prevent the repetitive structural elements becoming overbearing, translucent textured glass claddings to half of each apartment divided vertically are set back 'randomly', forming balconies and providing welcome depth to the façade. Four recesses in plan along the building length, including one at each end, introduce even more variety.

The RAC Control Centre, Bristol, concentrates its exterior structural modulation at ground level. Tapering piers emerge through gravel surfacing to follow the outwardly canting glazed skin (Figure 4.4). The piers have the appearance of inverted buttresses. Given that their maximum depth occurs at first-floor rather than ground level, the intensity with which they ground the building onto its site is reduced. Equally spaced around the building perimeter, they punctuate the vertical glazed or louvred walls between them and set up a rhythm that is all the more noticeable due to their large scale. Their main structural function is to support the internal steel posts that follow the slope of the inclined glazed skin and bear the weight of the roof structure. One reviewer observes that the only visible exterior structural elements above first-floor level are fine stainless steel cables, and criticizes the decision not to expose the posts:

> Although this undoubtedly simplifies the technology, the three-dimensional modulation of the building could have been hugely enriched, and the building's horizontals and verticals represented more literally, had these perimeter props remained on the exterior to be seen in association with the brises soleil.[3]

Figure 4.5
New Court, London, UK, OMA, 2011. Along the street frontage, pairs of columns with occasional braces form a colonnade.

While agreeing with an opinion like this for many other buildings, in this case I support the architects' decision. By restricting the exposure of any large-scale structural elements to the base of the building, they have not compromised the clarity of the building's rounded form.

Structural modulation of façades is a theme of New Court, London. Columns and braces, clad in aluminium panels, form a colonnade parallel to the street and contribute depth and texture to the façade (Figures 4.5 and 4.6). Columns create an ababa rhythm and alternate in size. The braces appear to be non-triangulated diagonals which are confined, unusually, between the narrowly spaced columns. Such steeply angled braces are not structurally efficient and perhaps reflect the benign seismicity of the site. They appear randomly placed in elevation, introducing variety and interest to the façade. All this expressed vertical and inclined structure is offset in plan, in front of the hidden horizontal structure necessary to triangulate cross-braced panels. This offset causes twisting at structural joints and may not have been possible had horizontal loads been larger.

The Velasca Tower, Milan, provides the final example of modulation by exterior structure (Figure 4.7). Its attached columns protrude from the building envelope up the height of the tower. They read as the outermost layer of an already visually rich and irregular façade, modulated by fenestration, secondary structural members and vertical infill strips.

Figure 4.4
RAC Control Centre, Bristol, UK, Nicholas Grimshaw & Partners, 1995. Structural piers modulate the base perimeter.

Figure 4.6
Expressed structure modulates the façade with randomly placed braces further enlivening it. On this elevation column loads are resisted by a storey-deep transfer truss. Note that no horizontal structural members of the truss are expressed.

Uninterrupted continuity of the column lines and an absence of similarly deeply projecting horizontal members accentuate verticality. This can be seen as responding to the myriad attached Gothic shafts adorning the nearby Milan Cathedral.

The cross-sections of the exposed tower columns vary with height. Subtle and gradual dimensional changes in depth and width reflect a sculptural approach to column detailing that reaches its climax near the top of the tower stem. Depending on what façade is viewed, either four or six columns angle outwards to support cantilevering floors of the enlarged uppermost six-storey block. In this transition zone, columns become inclined struts, stabilized by horizontal V-braces where they again return to the vertical. Although modulating the surfaces from which they protrude, the

Figure 4.7
Velasca Tower, Milan, Italy, BBPR, 1958. Columns and struts enliven the exterior.

columns and struts contribute aesthetically in other ways as well. The struts visually connect the tower enlargement to its stem. Their fineness and skeletal nature also confer a spatial ornamental quality that softens an otherwise abrupt transition. Struts nearest to the corners of the tower angle outwards towards the corners above, lessening the visual severity of the overhang in that area. In modulating the tower's exterior surfaces the columns and struts also contribute depth and texture, two surface qualities discussed in the following section.

Depth and texture

Although structure can modulate the surfaces around it solely by means of its distinguishing colour or materiality,

Figure 4.8
Notre Dame Cathedral, Paris, 1260. Deep perimeter structure surrounds the chevet.

buttresses contribute an extraordinary depth and texture as a by-product of structural necessity (Figure 4.8).

Modern structural systems usually do not require nearly as much depth, but architects often welcome whatever depth is available for the aesthetic value it brings to a building exterior. For example, deep perimeter structure juts out from Dulles International Airport terminal, Washington, D.C (Figure 4.9). Unlike Gothic buttresses that resist compression thrusts from masonry roof vaults, the terminal's piers resist tension forces from the reinforced concrete catenary roof. The piers are very substantial even though an outward inclination reduces the bending moments they must resist. Their elegant taper reflects both structural actions and the architect's desire to express 'the movement and excitement of modern travel by air'.[4]

From most viewpoints the piers visually dominate the exterior of the terminal. They provide depth and rhythm to the front façade. Even though fully glazed walls butt into the sides of piers and limit the extent of their exposure, additional façade depth is gained by curving the glazed walls between them in-plan into the building. This masterful design move simultaneously dissipates the possible visual severity of

in most buildings, including those just visited, structural depth is a prerequisite for and a major contributor to modulation. Variation of surface depth relieves plainness, and, in conjunction with natural and artificial light, creates opportunities for contrasting bright and shadowed areas that visually enliven a façade. Until the emergence of Modern architecture in the early 1900s, with its flat and thin exterior skins, façades possessed reasonable depth, although that was often achieved through the use of decorative structural elements. The Gothic period, and in particular its cathedrals, is unique for the degree of structural depth associated with its architecture from walls flanked by massive exterior structure. Buttresses topped by pinnacles and supporting flying

Figure 4.9
Dulles International Airport, Washington, D.C., USA, Saarinen (Eero) and Associates, 1962. Piers create deep bays along the façade.

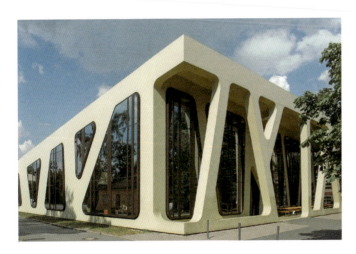

Figure 4.10
Student Canteen, Karlsruhe, Germany, J. Mayer Architects, 2007. On two sides the concrete columns are flush with the glazing, but at the front the columns create a portico of varying depth. The entry is signalled by the cut-out in the exposed ground beam. (Thomas Hess)

planar outward sloping surfaces, echoes the profile of the curved canopy above, and accentuates both points of entry and bays between the piers for people to meet and wait. The curved walls also allow for wind face-loads to be resisted by horizontal arch or catenary action, depending on the wind direction, considerably reducing wall framing member dimensions and maximizing transparency.

The Student Canteen, Karlsruhe, also demonstrates exterior structure providing depth and texture to the exterior of a building (Figure 4.10). The outside of the sculptural columns sit flush with the glazing on two sides of the building, while on the front façade two lines of similarly irregular columns are slightly angled to each other in plan, creating a portico of varying depth. This double layer of irregular columns creates sheltered space for outside dining and prepares visitors for similar vertical and horizontal structural configuration inside.

Although designers usually provide structural depth to façades using ribbed or discrete elements, as in the previous example, continuous structure, like an undulating wall, presents other possibilities. If folded or curved in plan, the structural depth and therefore the stability and strength normal to the wall plane increase. Such a wall can be understood as a vertically cantilevered folded plate when resisting face-loads. In the context of this chapter, shaping a wall in plan presents opportunities for architectural enrichment, as illustrated at the Mönchengladbach Museum.

Figure 4.11
Mönchengladbach Museum, Germany, Hans Hollein, 1982. Curved exterior gallery walls respond to the site contours.

Highly regarded for the qualities of its interior spaces and urban setting, an exterior gallery wall undulates (Figure 4.11). The sinuous wall imbues one gallery interior with special character; and, outside, the wall's serpentine geometry appears as a natural extension of the curvilinear paths and brick walls that lead up the hillside to the museum. The gently curving wall possesses an attractive softness and naturalness.

No doubt the texture of brickwork also enhances enjoyment of this small section of the museum. Texture implies variation of surface depth and is linked to materiality. Each material possesses a unique texture, depending on how it is fabricated, formed or finished. For example, before the introduction of metal arc welding, the texture of steel-plated structural connections arose from overlapping plates and single or multiple rows of rivets. Since the advent of welding, plates can be butt-welded together and the weld ground flush, forming an almost invisible connection and reducing the surface texture. Other steel textures have not changed over time, especially the ribs and stiffening plate sections that prevent large areas of thin steel plate from buckling. At the

Figure 4.12
Mound Stand, Lord's, London, Michael Hopkins & Partners, 1987.
Horizontal and vertical stiffening plates texture a steel beam-wall along the
rear of the stand, below the tension-membrane roof.

Mound Stand, London, this texture contributes significantly to
the texture of exterior surfaces (Figure 4.12).

Due to the planning and construction constraints arising
from placing a new stand over an existing one, some unusual
structural solutions were demanded. Along the rear and
the side walls of the stand, gravity loads are resisted and
transferred to supporting members by one-storey-deep
steel-plate girders. From a distance they appear as walls, but
upon closer inspection we can see vertical and horizontal
stiffening plates, the unmistakable language of thin steel-
plate construction. This texture not only conveys a strong

Figure 4.13
Canopy structure, World Exhibition Centre, Hanover, Germany, Herzog +
Partner, 1999. Attractive textured soffit surfaces.

sense of materiality and speaks of the deep member's
structural responsibilities but enriches the surface qualities of
the building.

Structural texture is even more strongly associated with
timber construction. Consider, for example, a traditional timber
roof with its hierarchical construction. Beginning with primary
members – say, beams – successively shallower members
like rafters and purlins and then sarking progressively build up
the depth of construction as they are overlaid at right angles.

With a structural form far more sophisticated than for
most timber structures, the World Exhibition Centre Canopy,
Hanover, also possesses a much-admired hierarchical
structural texture. Although the main members, the masts and
cantilevering ribs are themselves textured, the fine ribbed-
shell structure spanning between the cantilevers and covered
by a timber lattice and a white water-proof membrane is most
appealing (Figure 4.13)

The degree to which an architect uses structure to
contribute depth and texture should always reinforce the
design concept. So, what if the source of inspiration is a
smooth jewellery box? Toyo Ito's answer is found in the
Mikimoto Ginza 2 building (Figure 4.14). Notable for a
complete lack of texture, this building celebrates surface.
Glimpses through flush-mounted glazing provide the only
indication of depth, and even that is minimal. Imagine if the
wall edges around openings had been chamfered back from
the exterior. The wall would then read as thin as pure skin. Any
sense of wall being structure would vanish.

Figure 4.14
Mikimoto Ginza 2 building, Tokyo, Japan, Toyo Ito & Associates, 2005. The surfaces of the planar perimeter walls are smooth, and the only hint of their depth is where openings are viewed obliquely.

Such a thin and smooth perimeter structure required a special construction method. Panels of steel plates 200 mm apart were positioned, welded, filled with concrete, and the welds ground flush. The steel-plate exterior is completely planar, devoid of texture; one surface wraps the building,

punctured by randomly shaped polygonal openings. Both structure and skin, the thin perimeter walls enable column-free space within, and provide the same experience of structure as surface from outside and within the building (Figure 4.15).

Screening and filtering

Depending on its depth, density in plan and elevation, and its spatial relationship to a building envelope, exterior structure can be read as a screen or filter, contributing yet another set of aesthetic qualities to a façade.

The main façade of the Melbourne Exhibition Centre that faces the Yarra River illustrates this very clearly. A multitude of slender steel posts on a close 3 m × 3 m grid support a wide verandah that slopes away from the main building (Figure 4.16). The posts, two bays deep, tilt away from the building, maintaining orthogonality with the verandah roof above. Their rotation from the vertical introduces a sense of movement that explains why they are likened to reeds along a riverbank. It is difficult to discern the building envelope beyond them, fading into the background behind the sheer numbers of posts that screen and soften it. From inside the centre, building users can appreciate the extent to which the posts diffuse natural light and filter views towards the river. A promenade along the building edge through the posts yields

Figure 4.15
The interior visual qualities of structure (lined with plasterboard) are similar to those of the exterior.

Figure 4.16
Exhibition Centre, Melbourne, Australia, Denton Corker Marshall, 1996. Verandah posts visually soften the façade.

Figure 4.17
A view along the verandah.

Figure 4.18
Luxembourg Philharmonic Hall, Luxembourg, Christian de Portzamparc, 2005. A filter façade surrounds the hall. (Francisco Allegue)

Figure 4.19
Library Square, Vancouver, Canada, Moshe Safdie and Associates Inc., 1995. A gap reveals the cross-section of the screening frame and a glimpse of the main library block behind.

a final delight – their slenderness, close spacing and uniform tilt recall walking through the saplings of a windblown forest (Figure 4.17).

Ideas of forest informed the structural screen around the Luxembourg Philharmonic Hall (Figure 4.18). A total of 823 columns function as a screen and filter. One or two layers of columns lie outside the skin, and one layer inside. The architect wanted the public to enter the building through a circle of tall trees. He explains:

> When I arrived at the site, I saw that we didn't have enough space to plant trees and this gave me the idea of a filter façade made up of this wooded ring, neither opaque nor transparent, forming a cloak of light with the hall as its centre. The rhythm of these parallel trunks in a number of elliptical ranks became mathematical and musical.[5]

At Library Square, Vancouver, an exterior structural frame curves around the main rectilinear library block, wrapping and screening it (Figure 4.19). In two locations, where the frame almost touches corners of the library, gaps open in the

Figure 4.20
Jacob and Wilhelm Grimm Centre, Central library of Humboldt University, Berlin, Max Dudler, 2009. Perimeter columns with varied spacing screen the library collection. (Mal Booth)

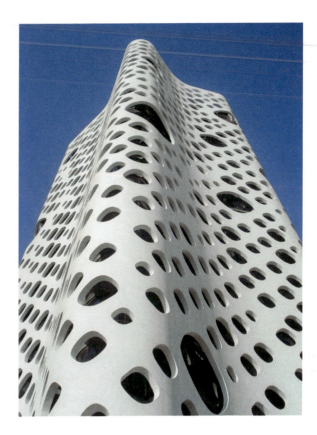

Figure 4.21
O-14 Tower, Dubai, Reiser + Umemoto, 2011. An external structural skin wraps around the building. (Sandra Draskovic)

frame, allowing glimpses of the library behind. Appearing as trabeated construction longitudinally, and vaulted construction transversely, the frame's single-bay-deep structure explicitly references the Colosseum in Rome. An open and arcaded ground-floor structure repeats at roof level as an open framework, and floors at other levels accommodate reading galleries. The openness of the framework provides plenty of natural light for perimeter reading areas and filters light entering the main library.

Less deep screening is provided by the perimeter structure at the Grim Centre, Humboldt University, Berlin (Figure 4.20). The closely spaced columns are load-bearing, although the proximity of interior columns limits the tributary floor area they support. The spacing between external columns varies according to the use of the spaces behind. On upper floors sunlight is limited to avoid damage to the collection, but wider spacing coincides with perimeter work stations located immediately inside the façade.

At the O-14 Tower, Dubai, the perimeter screen wall is a reinforced concrete exoskeleton (Figure 4.21). The reinforcement within the curved walls concentrates in a diagrid pattern around which the circular penetrations are formed. By designing the façade as a load-bearing, braced-tube structure, the central core was reduced in size and internal columns avoided. The floors of this twenty-two-storey building are set back approximately one metre from the skin. Vertical and horizontal forces from floors are transferred to the exoskeleton via many narrow bridges. The separation of the façade from the main building accentuates the sense of screening provided by the exterior structure.

Although diagonal bracing members are expressed on its façades, the uniqueness of Broadgate Tower is the warped plane of buttressing struts at the base of the tower (Figures 4.22 and 4.23). Although this impressive structure appears to be bracing the base of the building against horizontal wind forces, its main purpose is to resist vertical loads from columns on that side of the building. Underground railway lines are located beneath them, so the inclined struts transfer loads to piers adjacent to the railway. A very strong horizontal ground-floor suspended structure completes the triangulation of forces (Figure 4.24). The screening skeletal structure, with its spindle-shaped diagonal members, also provides bracing strength in the direction along the building. While the exposed structure supports half the tower block, it also forms an open canopy which reduces the scale of the urban space, integrating architecture and landscape.

Figure 4.22

Broadgate Tower, London, UK, SOM, 2008. Due to railway tracks running under the right-hand side of the tower, inclined struts transfer forces across to piers underneath the ground plane to the right.

Structural scale

Structural scale strongly influences how exterior structure contributes aesthetically to a façade. The dimensions of structural members can lie anywhere on a continuum between the extremes of mesh-like fineness and massive

Figure 4.23

The inclined structural canopy slices through the space between office blocks.

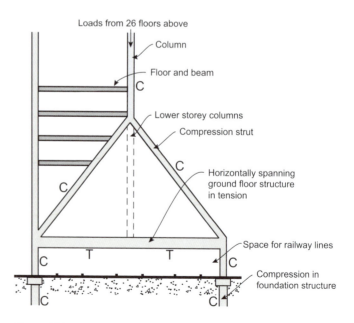

Figure 4.24

A simplified section to explain the transfer structure for vertical loads.

monumentality. Several buildings, beginning with those utilizing small-scale structure, illustrate varied approaches to structural scale.

Where steel is used most efficiently, in tension, members invariably fall into the category of small scale – a consequence of sufficient strength gained from minimal cross-sectional area. At the Cathedral of Notre Dame de la Treille, Lille, stainless-steel rod-and-tube structure, reminiscent of a spider's web, supports a new exterior nave wall (Figures 4.25 and 4.26). This diaphanous steelwork contrasts with both the new post-tensioned stone arch needed to equilibrate the tension within the exposed steelwork, and the cathedral's original masonry structural elements. In this project, the dimensions of the exterior steel members were deliberately minimized by pre-tensioning the steel.[6] Shadows from large structural members would have detracted from the interior visual appearance of the translucent top-hung wall comprising 30 mm thick marble sheets.

The combination of the primary arch with the secondary fine steel structure also illustrates variations in structural scale, usually associated with an expression of structural hierarchy, in a rather extreme manner. As in most situations displaying structural hierarchy, such as the World Exhibition Centre canopy discussed above, primary structural member dimensions exceed those of secondary structure, and so on.

Although not an issue at Notre Dame de la Treille, where we witness a celebration of the filigree quality of structure, small-diameter tension members often belie their critical structural importance. Where exposed on a building façade, perfectly adequate primary tension-only cross-bracing can appear too flimsy or insubstantial. These bracing members are likely to be far smaller than adjacent elements, such as columns or cladding panels. Designers must decide whether or not to expose structure in these situations. If the scale of structure as compared to that of adjacent architectural elements or spaces might lead to undesirable readings, such as the flimsiness mentioned above, perhaps the structure should be either enlarged or concealed.

This issue of structural scale has been handled very well at Cannon Bridge House, London, where underground railway lines have necessitated large column-free areas. The exposed structure of the front wall of the building acts as a simply supported truss spanning almost 70 m; and, if that's not enough, it is cantilevered 21 m from an interior line of support

Figure 4.25
Cathedral of Notre Dame de la Treille, Lille, France, Pierre-Louis Slide Carlier Architecte, 1997. Steel filigree structure supports the nave wall.

Figure 4.26
Horizontal steel structure spans between columns of a pre-stressed stone arch.

(Figures 4.27 and 4.28).[7] The façade truss is not immediately recognized as such due to the fineness and the extensive distribution of the diagonal tension members. The load-bearing role of the structure is also downplayed by maintaining constant member sizes throughout.

We observe the same sensitivity to scale on the cantilever structure layered in front of the side walls. This structure resists the massive force from one end of the front wall truss and transfers it to an interior perimeter support. Whereas just two large diagonal members could have sufficed in combination with the top and bottom horizontal truss chords, widely spaced multi-membered diagonals transfer the forces. By doubling the number of members, their sizes are of similar dimensions to all the other exposed structural members.

At the Law Courts, Bordeaux, exterior structure typifies structure at human scale (Figure 4.29). Exposed five-storey-high columns are relatively slender, given their height and the size of the building behind them. Their modest diameter acknowledges the light loads from the delicate steel trusses they support, and their independence from suspended floors supported by interior columns. On the façades, as in the interior public spaces, structural scale avoids monumentality, consistent with an architectural goal of creating a transparent and non-intimidating environment.

Figure 4.27
Cannon Bridge House, London, UK, Foggo Associates, 2012. The façade-truss structure spans the width of the building and is supported by cantilevered trusses at each end.

Figure 4.28
The cantilever truss diagonals comprise multiple members to reduce their size.

Figure 4.29
Law Courts, Bordeaux, France, Richard Rogers Partnership, 1998. Human scale rather than monumental columns.

Figure 4.30
Cité des Sciences et de l'Industrie, Paris, Adrien Fainsilber, 1986. Scaled-up columns relate to building scale and truss dimensions.

During the conversion of abattoirs to the Cité des Sciences et de l'Industrie, Paris, the reinforced concrete columns were considered under-scaled relative to the long-span roof trusses above them and the overall size of the building. They were subsequently sheathed by masonry walls to bulk them out and create more suitable monumental 'structure' (Figure 4.30). This is an extreme example of the widespread practice of increasing the visual mass of columns, particularly in multi-storey buildings. Often their columns are considered to be uncomfortably slender in comparison to the volume of building they support.

Connecting the exterior to the interior

In contemporary architecture, structure that is exposed on an exterior elevation sometimes bears some resemblance to the interior structure. This may be a consequence of a design process that begins by attending to the interior structure and then letting those decisions, in conjunction with other ideals like transparency, inform the exterior design. However, correspondence between exterior and interior structure may also have deeper roots. There may be a conscious reaction against the practice of façadism, where a façade bears little relationship to the rest of the building; or perhaps a concern for a holistic and integrated architecture with a demonstrable relatedness between exterior and interior. An outside–inside connection need not be literal but might entail external

Figure 4.31
Stansted Airport terminal, Essex, UK, Foster Associates, 1991. Portico 'trees' are an extension of the interior structure.

expression of the interior structural qualities, rather than the exposure of actual members and details.

High-tech architects usually make the interior–exterior connection explicit, as exemplified by the Hong Kong and Shanghai Bank (Figure 4.1). At Stansted Airport terminal, Essex, also designed by Foster Associates, the structural 'trees' that dominate the interior of the building extend from behind the glazed front wall to support a full-length portico (Figure 4.31).

The Mont-Cenis Academy, Herne (Figures 3.2, 3.3 and 4.32), also gives similar advanced notice of its interior structure on the exterior. Timber posts and roof structure that support a full-width entrance canopy are a pure extension of the structure inside the building envelope. Although the exterior posts are as naturally detailed as all others, they have

Figure 4.32
Mont-Cenis Academy, Herne, Germany, Jourda & Perraudin, 1999. The front canopy structure is almost identical to that of the interior.

Figure 4.33
Public University of Navarra, Pamplona, Spain, Sãenzde Oiza Arquitectos, 1993. The pair of exterior columns are precursors to columnar interior architecture.

required slight structural modification. Due to the canopy roof span lengths being longer than elsewhere, steel rod composite-action increases the vertical load-bearing capacity of the posts.

In the buildings considered above, the interior structural system repeats on the exterior. A more subtle approach, perhaps suited to a wider range of architectural styles, entails the exposure of just one structural element that reflects the interior structural qualities of the building. For example, two large columns with haunched capitals that designate entry to the central block of the Public University of Navarra, Pamplona, exemplify this approach (Figure 4.33). Without literally reproducing the interior columns, they set the scene for an almost overwhelming display of columnar interior architecture. Their conical capitals, circular stems and concrete materiality make an unambiguous connection (see Figure 5.21).

Entry

Provision and articulation of entry, very important aspects of architectural design, provide endless opportunities for structural participation. At a basic level, structure might contribute little more than the support of an entry canopy. Yet, in another building, structure might function as *the* architectural element that creates a sense of entry, its expression and celebration. The columns framing the main entrance to the Public University of Navarra, above, fall into this category, and the following examples also illustrate structure playing significant roles in marking and defining entry. Each entrance's structural form is totally different, relating either to the structural layout of its own building or, in the final example, to that of its neighbours.

Eighty-metre-high masts located at its four corners define the main entry points to the Millennium Stadium, Cardiff (Figure 4.34). Spectators enter through structural frames at the bases of the masts supporting outriggers that cantilever inside the stadium and carry the primary roof trusses. The role of signifying entry that canopies usually play is amply fulfilled by these structural elements. Multiple horizontal and inclined structural booms and ties project outwards in a grand welcoming gesture, while the huge beam and mast legs above ground level articulate entry. These mast structures required significant design modifications in order to accommodate entry. The cross-bracing extending down the mast is interrupted above ground level by the deep beam.

Figure 4.35
Terminal 2F, Charles de Gaulle Airport, Paris, Aéroports de Paris, 1999. Semi-circular columns signal entry.

Figure 4.34
Millennium Stadium, Cardiff, Wales, The Lobb Partnership (now HOK Sports), 2000. The main entry is under the beam between the mast legs.

Figure 4.36
A 'split column' viewed from inside.

Together with the mast legs it forms a single-storey moment-resisting frame that avoids the need for ground-level bracing, and simultaneously creates an entry portal. The massiveness of this structural threshold appropriately prepares spectators for the huge enclosure that lies beyond.

Structure also defines entry to the elevated departures area at Terminal 2F, Charles de Gaulle Airport, Paris (Figures 4.35 and 4.36). In this case, pedestrians enter between structural members rather than under them. The entrance locations along the building frontage correspond to the structural organization of the concourse roof – a system of paired primary steel ribs carrying secondary structure that supports the impressive concrete ceiling slabs. V-shaped struts project down from the ribs and bear upon greatly enlarged vertical concrete columns, semi-circular in cross-section. The column orientation and its form offer a dramatic reading. An original

single circular column appears to have been split in half and both halves then moved apart to create an entrance.

Entry between these columns, then, is particularly memorable. As seen from the footpath, the columns clearly signify entry by projecting outside the cladding line rhythmically in step with the roof structure. Although it seems perverse to enter through a massing of concrete when the whole wall cladding is otherwise glazed, upon entry one enjoys pondering the immense physical force required to 'split' and 'move apart' the concrete semi-circles. Given the apparent effort required for its construction, the entrance

Figure 4.37
National Museum of Emerging Science and Innovation, Tokyo, Japan, AMS Architects, 2001. Two sets of posts, one inclined and the other vertical, signal entry. They introduce visitors to the structural language of slender columns, visible from the exterior, that support the curved façade wall.

therefore has special significance. After the experience of passing between the columns you discover that their shapes and materiality complement other curved and exposed concrete surfaces throughout the terminal.

At the National Museum of Emerging Science and Innovation, Tokyo, structure signals entry more subtly (Figure 4.37). The main entry must be searched for between the pairs of opposing inclined poles to the left and the dense cluster of posts on the right. The entry is actually behind the clustered posts which serve as a marker of entry, particularly for visitors walking from the car park to the right. The posts also are an introduction to the six-storey slender columns that, together with horizontal structural brises soleil, support the curved atrium wall.

The Cité de la Musique, Paris, provides the final example of structure articulating entry. An open rectangular framework designates entry (Figure 4.38). Its four closely spaced, two-storey-plus red frames reference the nearby Parc de la Villette follies, less than a hundred metres away. Therefore, rather than reflecting interior structure, which in this building is not particularly evident, the entrance responds to external influences. Unlike the open frameworks of the follies that inspired the canopy design, Portzamparc's entry structure supports two trusses forming an elongated wedge. The

Figure 4.38
Cité de la Musique, Paris, Christian de Portzamparc, 1995. Entrance structure.

trusses, visible through the glazed walls of the wedge that defines a linear circulation spine, visually tie the entrance framework to the main building. Since the trusses bear on the first-storey beams, the structural members above that level are essentially gestural. The open frames of the Cité de la Musique entry structure successfully fulfil common architectural expectations by both marking entry and encouraging it.

Expressive roles

Exterior structure has a long tradition of playing expressive roles. Consider Gothic cathedrals. Their pinnacles, flying buttresses and buttresses express how the horizontal thrusts from masonry roof vaults are resisted and transferred to the ground (Figure 4.8). Load paths become legible through a combination of structural layout, shape and scale. On the other hand, Renaissance exterior structure, such as at S. Giorgio Maggiore, Venice, expresses aspects other than its Romanesque interior or its structural actions. Four giant attached-columns dominate the façade (Figure 4.39). They appear to be supporting a section of pediment thrust up from one that previously spanned the partial width of the church. Framing the main entrance, they express monumentality and the importance of the nave in relation to the aisles.

Figure 4.39
S. Giorgio Maggiore, Venice, Italy, Palladio, 1610. The classical façade does not relate to the Romanesque interior.

Figure 4.40
Fitzwilliam College Chapel, Cambridge, UK, Richard MacCormac, 1991. A chapel side wall with an accommodation block to the left.

Contemporary exterior structure continues this expressive tradition by communicating a diverse range of ideas, architectural qualities and actions. Exterior structure can, to some degree, express any architectural idea. The *clarity* with which such an idea might be communicated is quite another matter. That certainly depends on an architect's skill. In the following examples, structure expresses quite different ideas.

The exterior of Fitzwilliam College Chapel, Cambridge, differentiates itself from adjoining architectural forms to express ideas of protection and enclosure (Figure 4.40). The chapel's distinctive circular geometry sets it apart from the surrounding rectilinear blocks. As an extension to a 1960s accommodation wing, the chapel adopts the same width as the existing construction where it connects. Then, after provision of a circulation area several metres long, perimeter walls begin to form a cylinder, increasing the building width and partially encircling the chapel inside. Like embracing arms, in an understated and simple manner, they protect and enclose, metaphorically as well as physically.

The exterior structure of the Öhringen Business School represents the antithesis of the symmetry and calmness of Fitzwilliam College Chapel. Outside the main entrance, the exterior structure breaks long-established traditions of structural order and rationality (Figure 4.41). In front of a

Figure 4.41
Business School, Öhringen, Germany, Gunter Behnisch & Partner, 1993. The main entrance and the haphazardly orientated buttresses.

Figure 4.42
A horizontal plate passes through the buttress without making contact.

glazed wall, three cross-braced buttresses appear to be quite haphazardly orientated, their alignment relating to neither the building envelope nor the interior structure. A similarly unusual relationship exists between the buttresses and the thin horizontal steel girts they support. The normal hierarchy of mullions supported by girts that are in turn supported by buttresses is subverted. A girt even passes through a buttress without being able to transfer its loads to it (Figure 4.42). Exterior structure in this area of the school appears ad hoc and crude. Blundell Jones notes that this aesthetic is, in fact, carefully developed and a 'confident use of a vocabulary elaborated over decades'.[8] The architect is well known for his colliding geometries and layered spaces. Upon entering the atrium, a fragmented and layered structural language contributes to a light and lively, if not exciting, interior space.

The Peckham Library, in a far less extreme manner, also disregards an ordered and rational approach to design and building, by expressing informality. Certainly, its overall inverted L-shaped form, while unexpected, conforms to typical architectural expectations. Even the structure of the vertical leg of the L that houses vertical circulation, office and study facilities is of reasonably conventional concrete frame construction. Horizontal loads along the building are resisted by precast concrete inverted V-braces, and across the building by several concrete structural walls. Informality is introduced through the casually placed and orientated posts along the main façade (Figures 4.43 and 4.44). Their

Figure 4.43
Peckham Library, London, UK, Alsop & Störmer, 2000. A row of casually placed and orientated columns support the elevated front façade of the lending library volume.

Figure 4.44
The columns exude a sense of informality.

bases appear randomly placed and the slopes of the columns vary within a limited range – informality rather than anarchy! This design strategy avoids the staid and the monumental. It provides a public facility and an urban space that is far from threatening or intimidating. While the irregularity of the column layout is silent regarding its source of inspiration, lacking strong representational or symbolic qualities, the columns are just one coat of brightly coloured paint away from expressing playfulness.

Expressive qualities of new exterior structure at Bracken House, London, an insertion between the end wings of a central demolished block, have clearer and more obvious origins (Figure 4.45). Structural members are not immediately recognizable from a distance due to their relatively fine scale, made possible by the close proximity of the primary columns, located just four metres behind the façade. The exposed structure includes slender secondary columns, mullion-

columns on the exterior bay-window corners and ground-floor piers supporting the columns (Figure 4.46). If an exploration of structural expression begins by considering the slender gun-metal columns, one notes their similarity to the bronze columns of the old building. The scale of both old and new columns, and their fineness, recalls Gothic attached-shafts. At first-floor level, where the columns meet their base-brackets, short cantilevers express structural actions. Tapered arms reflect internal bending moments, and a stainless-steel rod with its enlarged end connection detail expresses its tensile role in preventing the bracket from overturning. Solid stone piers carry and express compression, the dominant structural action. Such a high standard of design is consistent with the client's expectation that the building 'shall offer respect to the great architectural achievements of the past, dominate this century and realize the vision of the next'.[9] Quite a demanding brief!

Figure 4.45
Bracken House, London, Michael Hopkins and Partners, 1991. Main façade.

Figure 4.46
Metal columns, a cantilever bracket and a stainless-steel rod behind a stone pier.

Any discussion on the expressive roles of exterior structure must consider the expression of another important architectural issue: the relationship between a building and its foundations; or, in other words, how a building is grounded. At one end of the spectrum an architect might seek to express a strong sense of grounding where a building is read as being rooted to its foundations and growing from them, but other design concepts might express floating or hovering. Chapter 11 discusses this subject in detail.

Summary

This chapter has illustrated exposed structure enriching the exterior visual qualities of buildings. After over-viewing some of the many contributions exterior structure can make to façades by focusing upon the Hong Kong and Shanghai Bank, the chapter examined the aesthetic impact of exterior structure. Case-studies illustrated how structure modulates surfaces and provides a means for introducing often much-desired depth and texture. Structure also screens façades, and filters light and views. The importance of suitable structural scale is noted where structure plays any of these roles.

Two sections then explored how structure connects exterior and interior architecture and how it marks and articulates entry into a building. Finally, the chapter provided precedents of structure playing expressive roles. Based on the variety of expression evident in the few examples presented, it would seem that exposed exterior structure is capable, to some degree at least, of expressing *any* architectural idea or quality.

Notes

1. S. Williams, *Hongkong Bank: the building of Normal Foster's masterpiece*, London: Jonathan Cape, 1989, p. 85.
2. See, for example, A. Ogg, *Architecture in steel: the Australian context*, Red Hill, ACT: Royal Australian Institute of Architects, 1987, p. 36.
3. A. Gale, 'Not the *Western Morning News*', RIBA Journal 102(8), 1995, 38–45, at 39–41.
4. Quoted in A. Freeman, 'The world's most beautiful airport?', *AIA Journal* 69(13), 1980, 46–51, at 47.
5. C. de Portzamparc, 'Christian de Portzamparc: Luxembourg Philharmonic Hall', *A+U* 10(433), 2006, 60–7, at 63.
6. For technical information refer to A. Brown, *Peter Rice: the engineer's contribution to contemporary architecture*, London: Thomas Telford, 2000, pp. 143–57.
7. For a video explaining the structure and its construction, visit <http://www.thenbs.com/nbstv/architects/programme.asp?refCode=313303&title=Cannon+Place+by+Foggo+Associate> (accessed 17 April 2013).
8. P. Blundell Jones, 'Behnisch in Öhringen', *Architectural Review* 197(1178), 1995, 32–7, at 36.
9. C. Amery, *Bracken House*, London: Wordsearch, 1992, p. 37.

five

Building function

Introduction

In its exploration of the relationships between structure and building functionality, this chapter begins by considering how structure located on the perimeter of a building maximizes spatial planning freedom. A common approach for achieving large structure-free floor areas is to locate primary structure either outside or just inside the building envelope. Next, we analyse how structure can subdivide interior space: first, where the subdivided spaces accommodate similar functions and are perceived as being part of a larger space; and, second, where structure separates different building functions, like circulation and gallery spaces. This leads us to examine how the physical presence of structure, particularly its directional qualities, defines and enhances circulation. Finally, examples illustrate structure disrupting function, both deliberately and unintentionally.

Numerous architectural texts acknowledge the need for thoughtful integration of structure with building function. At a pragmatic level, Schodek explains the concept of 'critical functional dimensions'.[1] This approach requires a designer to determine the minimum structure-free plan dimensions for a given space, or series of spaces. Once these dimensions are decided upon, 'basic functional modules' can be drawn in plan. Spaces between the modules then determine where vertical structure can be located without intruding upon function. Minimum clear spans across modules can then be readily identified and, together with module shapes, can suggest suitable structural systems such as load-bearing walls or moment frames in conjunction with one- or two-way floor- and roof-spanning systems.

Different-sized modules are often required within one building. For example, the office-sized structural module above ground-floor level in the Regional Government Centre, Marseille, is doubled in size through the use of the X-columns in order to accommodate basement-level car parking (Figure 3.53). Schodek also briefly discusses the spatial implications of various structural systems, noting the different degrees of directionality they impose upon the spaces they enclose.

Krier takes a broader architectural approach when discussing structure and function. He emphasizes the spatial qualities of different structural systems and insists upon the integration of structure and function: 'Construction is closely related to function. A clearly defined concept of spatial organization demands an appropriate structural solution. The more harmonious this unity, the closer one comes to the architectonic end product.'[2] He categorizes structure, which he primarily perceives as a spatial organizer, into three different types: solid wall; skeletal construction; and mixed construction comprising both walls and skeletal structure. Each type possesses a different architectural character. For example, solid walled construction, with its introverted and more intimate character, contrasts with skeletal structures that are more open and adaptable. Mixed systems, on the other hand, present opportunities for a hierarchy of interior spaces, greater spatial complexity and 'differentiated tectonic character'.

Whereas Krier emphasizes how interior structure, by virtue of its layout and detailing, affects spatial character and therefore function, this chapter concerns itself more directly with the relationship between structure and the physical aspects of building function. The aesthetic impact of structure upon interior space is discussed in Chapter 6.

Maximizing functional flexibility

Freedom from structural constraints results in maximum flexibility of space planning and building function. A space clear of interior structure can then be ordered by other architectural elements, such as partition walls or screens, if necessary. Clearly, maximum interior architectural flexibility is achieved by positioning primary structure outside the building envelope. Unfortunately, this strategy is often not easily implemented due to possibly excessive structural depths and other architectural implications like cost that are associated with long spans across the whole widths of buildings. A far more common and realistic approach to achieve a high degree of planning freedom involves adopting the 'free plan' – that integration of structure with interior space inherited from the Modern movement. Spaces that once would have been enclosed by load-bearing walls now flow almost completely unimpeded around and between columns that are usually located on an orthogonal grid.

However, the pre-eminence of the grid is being questioned by theorists and practitioners. Worrall, reflecting on Toyo Ito's works, writes: 'The grid, touchstone of flexibility and egalitarianism for its modernist advocates, is for Ito the iron cage of rationality. Architecture's urgent task is thus to dismantle this cage. In this quest, of course, Ito is hardly alone.'[3] One of several examples cited of Ito subverting the grid is the Tama Art University Library. Here, apart from along two sides of the building and one internal gridline, all the bases of the load-bearing arches are located on very gentle curved lines of differing degrees and orientations of curvature (Figure 12.42).

A widespread perception exists of the spatial neutrality of structure that enables the 'free plan'. That is, the impact upon interior architecture by structure, perhaps in the form of columns or short walls, whether assessed by its effect upon function or aesthetics, is considered minimal. However, such structure is far from being spatially neutral. Where located within a building envelope it reduces the net usable area as well as restricting space use in its vicinity. These detrimental effects have been quantified for office buildings. Space loss includes not only the area of the structural footprint itself but adjacent neutralized areas that are inconvenient for furniture and screen arrangements.[4]

More profound disturbances to building function from so-called 'free plan' structure also arise. Consider, for example, the oft-studied Tugendhat House designed by Mies van der Rohe (Figure 5.1). One reviewer suggests uncritically that the architect 'used the columns to help identify places: two of the columns, together with the curved screen wall frame the dining area; two others help define the living area; and another column suggests the boundary of the study area at the top

Figure 5.1
Tugendhat House, Brno, Czech Republic, Mies van de Rohe, 1930. A simplified ground-floor plan.

1	Dining Area
2	Living Area
3	Study Area

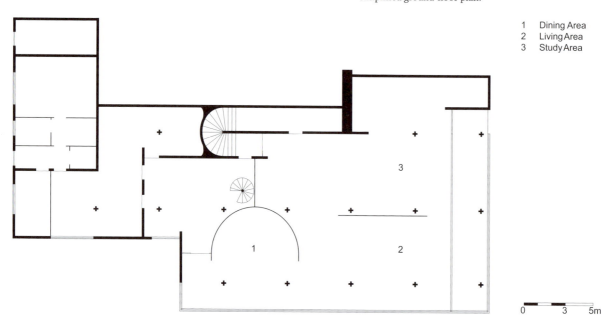

0   3   5m

right on the plan'.[5] However, an alternative reading could view that identification of places as being so unconvincing as to verge on the unintentional. Moreover, after observing the columns positioned close to walls but playing no particular spatially defining architectural roles, and other columns located awkwardly in secondary spaces, one can conclude that the interior architecture would be much improved if the existing walls were to become load-bearing, and as many of the non-perimeter columns as possible were removed!

As already mentioned, maximum planning freedom occurs where vertical structure is located on the perimeter of a building. This option suits single-storey construction better than multi-storey buildings for two reasons. First, perimeter structure inevitably results in long spans, necessitating deep horizontal beams or trusses, and subsequent large inter-storey heights. A deep or high roof structure of a single-storey building does not usually have such severe consequences upon building height as do several layers of deep floor structure. Second, roofs generally weigh far less than suspended floors, so they span greater distances more easily.

There are two categories of perimeter structure. The first comprises exoskeletal structures, where all structural members lie outside the building envelope. In the second category, to differing degrees, structure impinges upon interior space and either potentially disrupts function around the perimeter or else is well integrated with building function. Examples of these two types of perimeter structure are given below.

According to its architect, the need to reduce building bulk was one of the main reasons for choosing a mast structure for the Oxford Ice Rink (Figure 5.2). Primary structure, in the form of two masts, tension rods and a central spine-beam, carry over 50 per cent of the roof weight with the remainder supported by props spaced along each side wall. As a consequence of the substantial overall structural depth, equal to the mast height less that of the roof, and the 15 m intervals between supporting tension rods along its length, the depth of the 72 m-long spine-beam is shallow enough to allow it to be located under the roofing. Roof beams then span across the rink, resting upon the spine-beam and the side props.

The significant penalty associated with the use of perimeter structure – namely, the depth of horizontal members spanning across a building – has been mentioned. Where perimeter structure is required for a multi-storeyed

Figure 5.2
Oxford Ice Rink, UK, Nicholas Grimshaw & Partners, 1985. Exterior masts and projecting horizontal spine-beam.

building, beams or trusses, often at least one storey deep, span the necessary distance. Such horizontal spanning structure resisting loads from more than one storey is termed a 'transfer structure'. An example is found at the Hampden Gurney Church of England Primary School, London. A decision to place the chapel plus assembly hall at the lower ground-floor level meant that most of that floor had to be column free. So, instead of columns, which would render the space unusable for the intended functions, an imaginative roof transfer structure is provided for all the five floors above the assembly hall to hang from (Figures 5.3 and 5.4). There are no columns in the hall, and above that level steel tension hangers transfer the weights of the floors above it to the roof-top trussed arch spanning 16 m.

In another school by the same architects, a totally different structural solution which responds to the complex building form also achieves a large column-free ground-floor gathering space. The main building of Bridge Academy, London, steps down towards the north around a horseshoe-shaped central area (Figure 5.5). From the roof of the main building structure, comprising steel framing stabilized by concrete cores, inclined raking tubular hangers, positioned around the horseshoe, extend down to support the first-floor structure of the Learning Resource Centre (Figure 5.6). As well as mainly acting in tension, the tubes support an EFTE wall and form an exciting light-filled atrium. The combination of the span of the hanging first-floor structure plus the horizontal components of

Figure 5.3
Hampden Gurney Church of England Primary School, London, UK, Building Design Partnership, 2002. The assembly hall. Four pairs of hanger rods transfer forces from the floors above up to the roof-top transfer structure.

Figure 5.4
Inclined tension rods connect into the arched truss which also supports the two high points of a tension-membrane roof canopy.

Figure 5.5
Bridge Academy, London, UK, Building Design Partnership, 2007. From an inclined roof-level horseshoe ring beam, a steeply sloping ETFE wall meets the Learning Resource Centre roof. Inclined tension hangers are visible behind the ETFE.

Figure 5.6
A view through the sloping atrium. The main structure with columns and open balconies is to the left. The raking tension hangers, which also support the ETFE wall, are on the right. The hangers terminate at first-floor level.

Figure 5.7

The column-free ground-floor gathering space. Tension rods supported from the main raking hangers support the black ramp beneath the ceiling.

the raking tension hangers results in the large multi-functional column-free ground-floor area (Figure 5.7).

The exterior structure of the *Financial Times* printing works, London, also facilitates function as well as allowing for flexibility in the future. Perimeter columns line sections of the north and south façades (Figure 5.8). Their location outside the glass skin they support removes from the approximately 100 m-long press hall any internal structure which might

Figure 5.8

Financial Times printing works, London, Nicholas Grimshaw & Partners, 1988. Exterior columns along the main façade.

otherwise disturb movement of personnel or paper within the space. Interior structure defining an internal spine-zone parallel to and behind the press hall is also walled off to avoid any structural protrusions into the hall. As well as its functional suitability, this structure-and-skin combination has won over critics with its elegance of detail and transparency. The nightly drama of printing is now highly visible from a nearby road.

By their very nature, shell structures are supported at their perimeters. Although any associated structural elements, such as ribs that might increase the strength of a shell, are usually constructed inside the exterior skin, their structural depths are so shallow as not to reduce space usage significantly. The Toskana Thermal Pools, Bad Sulza, enclosed by glue-laminated wood-ribbed shells, benefit from planning freedom unconstrained by structure (Figures 5.9 and 5.10). Free-flowing interior spaces surround the main pools. As well as providing openness in plan, the ribbed interior surfaces of the shells contribute to the attractive interior ambience.

The interior portal frames of the Timber Showroom, Hergatz, are representative of most interior perimeter structures whose vertical members intrude into the building plan (Figure 5.11). Sometimes, floor-plan edge-zones whose widths equal the structural depths less the thickness of the external skin can be incorporated unobtrusively into the overall building function. As an extreme example, consider Gothic churches where numerous side chapels slot between deep internal buttresses adjacent to the aisles. At Hergatz, it is of little consequence that structure does not integrate with an edge-zone function. The glue-laminated wooden columns are quite shallow, and the exposed frames possess an unusual attractiveness. Here, a conventional engineering system, the portal frame, often relegated to light-industrial buildings, possesses intrinsic beauty by virtue of its detailing quality. Curves soften the appearance of the frames and invite new architectural interpretations of their form. Member tapering bestows a lightness and elegance, while unobtrusive moment-resisting connections at the eaves joints avoid any discordant notes.

At the Sainsbury Centre, Norwich, the perimeter structure lies completely inside the skin (Figure 5.12). Tubular-steel trusses span between perimeter columns of similar cross-section. Although the 2.5 m-thick structural walls are

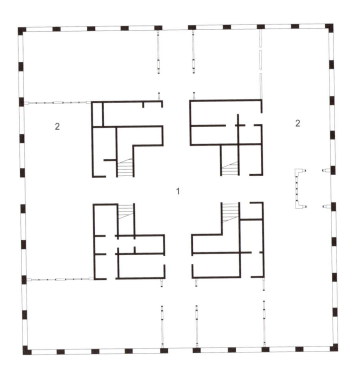

1   Central atrium
2   Gallery

Figure 5.20
Simplified ground-floor plan.

0   5   10m

circulation. The next outer zone, also sandwiched between walls, predominantly houses service areas. Finally, galleries occupy the majority of space between the third ring of walls around the atrium and the perimeter wall-cum-frame. While structural walls and their space-dividing roles are clear in plan, one of the fascinations of this building is that the walls, even though exposed, are not perceived as structure. All wall surfaces are planar and painted white, evoking a sense of simplicity and purity. Such an emphasis upon surface that leaves visitors without any clues hinting at the materiality or the structural significance of walls avoids any potential architectural distractions in the vicinity of the exhibited artworks.

The famous Renaissance architect Alberti perceived a colonnade as a virtual wall: 'a row of columns is indeed nothing but a wall, open and discontinued in several places'.[6] Such a reading can be appreciated when observing the interior columns at the Public University of Navarra, Pamplona. In the main building, columns separate spaces with different functions (Figures 5.21 and 4.33). A row of closely spaced columns runs the length of the two main corridors, dividing each into two unequal widths. The columns, only 1.5 m apart, provide a powerful colonnade experience. Where corridors pass an interior lobby or a waiting area, an extra row of columns separates and screens the two spaces from each other.

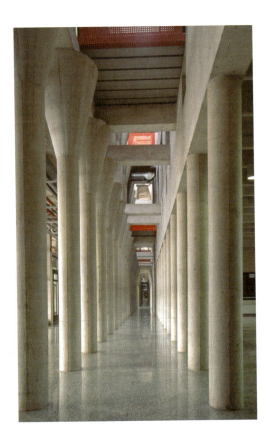

Figure 5.21
Public University of Navarra, Pamplona, Spain, Sáenzde Oiza Arquitectos, 1993. Columns run along the corridor length, and those to the right define the corridor width in the absence of side walls.

Figure 5.22
Terminal 4, JFK Airport, New York, USA, Skidmore Owings & Merrill, 2001. Structure occupies the entry zone. Entrances are to the left.

Figure 5.23
V-struts separate ticketing areas to the left from a circulation area and retail outlets on the floor beneath.

Structure plays a similar screening role and separates different uses of space at Terminal 4, JFK Airport, New York. Immediately inside the main doors to Departures, structure creates an entry zone en route to the ticketing areas (Figure 5.22). Diagonal braces that stabilize the whole terminal, and a series of slightly inclined and inverted chevron braces define the area of the zone. It is unusual to see braces with such a low angle of inclination that potentially reduces the amount of usable space beneath them, but most of the suspended floor below the braces is voided to create a spacious double-storey Arrivals area beneath. A row of vertical V-struts signals

completion of the ticketing process (Figure 5.23) and stairs lead down to a forecourt, retail outlets and departure gates. On the upper level, bridges span towards another permeable structural wall and the airline club lounges beyond. Structure thus delineates the extent of entry in plan and then separates the bulk of the terminal space into three different functions.

A large cone emerges from the turf roof of the Delft Technical University Library, which appears to be embedded within a hill (Figure 5.24). The exposed structure is more than just a virtual projection of the cone surface towards its apex. Near-vertical tension rods support areas of annulus-shaped suspended floors within the cone. The ground-floor area within the cone is therefore left free of structure. Splayed

Figure 5.24
Library, Delft Technical University, The Netherlands, Mecanoo Architekten, 1997. A view of the cone above the turf roof.

Figure 5.26
Law Courts, Bordeaux, France, Richard Rogers Partnership, 1998. A waiting area under a courtroom pod.

Figure 5.25
The circulation desk beneath the cone is surrounded by steel struts.

steel tubes around the circumference of the cone surround the circulation desk area, defining it yet distinguishing it from the other library functions within the main hall (Figure 5.25).

At the main entrance to the Law Courts, Bordeaux, you are confronted by a timber-clad conical pod outside the glazed skin of the main building, and soon you become aware of six others lined up inside. Inclined struts elevate the pods, each housing a courtroom, above concourse level. As well as their structural roles, the struts define informal waiting and meeting areas and separate them from the main circulation route (Figure 5.26). Eight sloping precast-concrete struts under each pod introduce an informal quality to the spaces. From some vantage points any sense of visual order disappears completely. The struts appear to be assembled chaotically, rejecting any aspirations of a formal interior architecture that some people find alienating. Structure can be read as an informal and perhaps visually confused setting that empathizes with the states of mind of those unfortunate enough to visit the courts.

Primary structure at the Art Museum, Bregenz, separates vertical circulation from other space usage, in this case galleries (Figure 5.27). Best appreciated in plan, the vertical structure consists of only three concrete structural walls, the bare minimum to resist lateral loads in orthogonal directions without the building suffering torsional instability (Figure 5.28).

Figure 5.27
Art Museum, Bregenz, Austria, Atelier Peter Zumthor, 1997. The building with the main entrance to the left.

Figure 5.28
Simplified ground-floor plan.

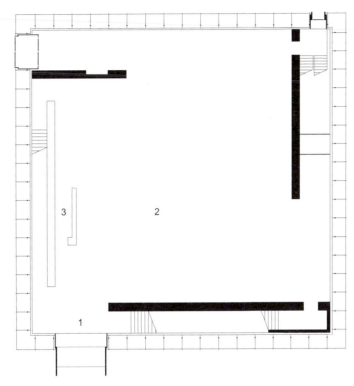

1 Entrance
2 Gallery
3 Reception

0   5   10m

The asymmetrical layout of the walls presents a challenge for the suspended floors that must span most of the building width. From a viewpoint located in the middle of any of the four galleries stacked one above the other, structural walls screen off areas of vertical circulation, and, detailed and constructed with the utmost precision, they become the backdrop on which to display art. Visitors remain completely unaware of another enhancement the structure contributes to the function of the museum – kilometres of piping filled with circulating water are embedded within the concrete structure, transforming it into an environmental modifier.

In the last example of structure subdividing space to facilitate separate functions, concern for the well-being of office workers led to the dominant interior structure of the Centraal Beheer Office Building, Apeldoorn (Figure 5.29). The structural layout provides workers with opportunities to create their own places and feel at home. Within a regular structural grid, spaces or modules 9 m × 9 m in plan connect via short corridors or bridges and are flanked by voids. The layout offers a wealth of three-dimensional spatial variation and experience. Cells merge and interweave. Column pairs articulate thresholds between cells and circulation between them. Each module, square in plan, is supported by two

columns at the third-points along each side, with the clear span between them little more than 2 m. It is the combination of close-spacing between columns and their reasonably large dimensions that enable them to act as screens, introducing a domestic and relatively intimate feel to the spaces. The structure also enhances privacy and the ability for individuality to be expressed and respected. Building users gain a strong

Figure 5.29
Centraal Beheer Office Building, Apeldoorn, The Netherlands, Herman Hertzberber with Lucas & Niemeijer Architects, 1972. Columns subdivide the cafeteria into intimate spaces.

impression of inhabiting the structure and of engaging with it regularly, in contrast to the occasional structural encounter experienced in typical open-plan office accommodation. Even though the building is over thirty years old, according to one staff member, office workers really enjoy working in it.

Articulating circulation

Structure has a long tradition of articulating circulation. Arcades and colonnades have defined circulation for thousands of years. Due its ability to provide order to a plan, structure often functions as the spine that inevitably defines the primary circulation route. As Cook writes:

> Where ceremony is not involved, a central row of columns or a spine-wall is a highly satisfactory way of generating built form. This spine can be formed by a corridor and we then have a brilliantly forceful generator, the spine being the route, the operational generator and also the focus of the structure from which all other parts of the system develop. Stretch the diagram and you have the Gothic nave.[7]

Columns, walls or other structural members can literally and virtually restrict movement to along a single axis. The way the walls within the Contemporary Art Wing, Hamburg, confine and direct movement has already been discussed. Structure can also play less directive roles merely by suggesting a circulation route. Often these more subtle roles are played by horizontal structure, such as beams that exhibit a directional quality. Both of these contributions of structure to circulation are examined below, beginning with examples where structure defines circulation.

The first floor of Teresiano School, Barcelona, provides a most memorable example of structure defining a corridor. The ground-floor plan consists of two spine-walls that create a central corridor with classrooms off either side. At first floor, the load-bearing walls that would be expected to replicate those below are replaced by parabolic arches (Figure 5.30). The combination of a simple repetitive rhythm arising from their close 1.2 m spacing, their roundedness and whiteness, and the quality of light filtering through from central light-wells conveys a remarkable sense of softness and tranquillity.

Although the entrance colonnade to the San Cataldo

Figure 5.30

Colegio Teresiano, Barcelona, Spain, Antoni Gaudí, 1889. The first-floor arched corridor.

Cemetery, Modena, is equally strongly articulated by structure, its aesthetic qualities contrast greatly with those of Teresiano School. Two storeys high and supporting a single-storey columbarium above, concrete wall-like arcade columns are very narrow for their height. They create a processional route, extending the entire length of the building (Figure 5.31). The experience of passing each pair of columns that flank the corridor emphasizes progress along the route, which stretches far into the distance. Unless a deliberate turn-of-the-head reveals views between the columns, the perspective along the main axis is framed by what seems like an infinite

Figure 5.31
San Cataldo Cemetery, Modena, Italy, Aldo Rossi, 1984. The entrance
colonnade recedes into the distance.

Figure 5.32
Canary Wharf Underground Station, London, Foster and Partners, 1999.
The ticket hall with its central columns and spine beam.

number of receding walls. While one reviewer refers to the
colonnade's 'haunted' quality, it certainly fosters impressions
of formality, rawness and joylessness.[8]

Beginning with the Canary Wharf Underground Station,
London, several examples illustrate how the *directionality*
of exposed structure articulates and enhances circulation.
A central row of elliptical concrete columns that register its
length like marker posts visually dominates the ticket hall,
a cathedral-like volume (Figure 5.32). Although the columns
restrict the width of the linear circulation path slightly, their
shape and orientation parallel to the flow of commuters

minimizes this effect and reinforces the primary axis of
movement. A substantial longitudinal spine-beam above
further accentuates directionality. Its attractively rounded
soffit that bears upon sliding-bearings on top of the columns
guides people both into and out of the station. Ribs cantilever
transversely from the spine-beam, hovering like outstretched
wings and modulating the vast area of ceiling. Their relatively
small dimensions and transverse orientation do not detract
from the linearity imposed on the space by the spine-beam.

The roof structure at Terminal 3's departure hall, Hamburg
Airport, also contributes to circulation by clearly reinforcing
the direction of movement (Figure 5.33). Since the roof
dimension in the direction of passenger movement is
considerably greater than the building width – 101 m versus
75 m – one would expect primary structure to span the
shorter distance. However, at Terminal 3, twelve curved
trusses span from landside to airside. They are supported on
two rows of concrete piers spaced 61 m apart and cantilever
beyond them at each end. Breaking with convention again, the
trusses run *between* rather than above the piers, signalling
the direction of circulation between the structural members.
Pairs of elegantly detailed steel struts rise from the piers
to triangulate the roof structure both parallel to and normal
to the trusses, framing the entry thresholds created by the
piers. Departing travellers who approach the terminal by car,
or on foot from a car-parking building across the road, are

Figure 5.33
Terminal 3, Hamburg Airport, Germany, vonGerkan, Marg + Partners, 1991.
Roof trusses emphasize the direction of movement on the departures level.
Looking from airside to landside.

greeted by the ends of the trusses that protrude through
the landside glazed wall. Then, in a gentle curve, the trusses
rise up and over the departure hall with its three levels of
shops and restaurants towards the airside. The introduction of
natural light through glazed strips directly above the trusses
intensifies their directionality.

Immediately after entering the Castelvecchio Museum,
Verona, visitors pass through six interlinked galleries aligned
in a row. Thick walls subdividing the elongated space are
penetrated by arched openings that provide and clearly
articulate a linear circulation route (Figure 5.34). The axis
of movement is further enhanced by the exposed ceiling
structure. Exquisite riveted steel beams that bear on the
cross-walls run the length of the galleries. Beam supports
are recessed into the walls to suggest that the beams are
continuous and pass through them. An elaborate steel bearing
located at the mid-span of each beam, and therefore at the
centre of the gallery, vertically separates the beam from the
ceiling. It supports two shallow concrete beams cast integrally
with the ceiling slab that are orthogonal in plan and cross at
that point. The steel beam, differentiated by its materiality
and richness of detailing from the surrounding construction,
introduces another structural layer that enhances the
experience of circulation considerably.

Figure 5.34
Castelvecchio Museum, Verona, Italy, Carlo Scarpa, 1964. A central beam
under the ceiling helps to articulate the linear circulation route.

Disrupting function

Occasionally, structure disrupts some aspect of the function
of a building. In a few cases an architect may cause this
disruption quite deliberately. More often, though, functional
disruption is like a side-effect of personal medication –
unwelcome but accepted as the cost of achieving a certain
objective. This situation has already been encountered at
the Baumshulenweg Crematorium. 'Randomly' positioned
columns prevent direct circulation through the condolence

Figure 5.35
Research Centre, Seibersdorf, Austria, Coop Himmelb(l)au, 1995. The office block and its irregular columns.

hall, but it would be churlish to complain about it given the wonderful architectural qualities of the space (Figure 2.11).

Hale discusses how some buildings, while of expressive architectural form, function poorly. He gives specific examples of how deliberate structural disruptions, such as columns that are placed in the middle of a house dining room, or in the middle of a lecture theatre, can be read as a means of functional or historical critique.[9]

Similar but less severe disruption occurs at the Research Centre, Seibersdorf. Primary exterior structural elements supporting the building appear to be positioned and orientated randomly, but with sufficient order to allow the building to span the road (Figure 5.35). Interior structure on or near the building perimeter also exhibits disorderly behaviour with respect to other elements. Diagonal braces cut across most windows, but structure most disruptive to function is found in the tiny 'thinking room'. A centrally located column not only dominates the room but severely restricts how it can be used (Figure 5.36). One reviewer describes the room as 'the one truly challenging space' that is consonant with the architects' expressed desire for 'untamed, dangerous architecture'.[10]

It is debatable whether the reinforcement of architectural ideas at the Convent of La Tourette, Eveux, justifies such a high degree of disruption to the use of its interior spaces. The strategy of avoiding perimeter columns by placing them several metres into the building achieves the dual aims of

Figure 5.36
A column dominates the 'thinking room'.

Figure 5.37
Convent of La Tourette, Eveux, France, Le Courbusier, 1959. The western façade and three levels of irregularly spaced mullions.

'floating' the building and freeing up the façade. Apart from the concrete-walled chapel, the remaining blocks 'touch the ground lightly'; and, as viewed from the west, the complex rhythmical composition of window mullions appears to today's viewers like typical barcode patterns (Figure 5.37). Unfortunately, while the building exterior is freed from structure, the spatial functionality of the interior suffers considerably. Circular concrete columns severely limit how seating and furniture can be deployed in many of the rooms (Figure 5.38).

Disruption can also be completely unintended during the design process, but becomes evident when a building is

Figure 5.38
Two columns on the right are set in from the exterior wall and intrude upon a teaching space.

Figure 5.39
Pizza Express restaurant façade, 125 Alban Gate, London, Bere Associates, 1996. Deep window mullions limit the café seating layout.

completed. Two unrelated examples of disruptive structure are encountered at 125 Alban Gate, London. In the first, deep window mullions intrude upon a first-floor restaurant space. Face-loads on the two-storey-high glazed walls are resisted by mullions in the form of innovatively designed vertical trusses. The truss chords consist of stainless-steel rods threaded through glass electrical insulators (Figure 5.39). The combination of the spacing between these mullions and their depth affects the table layout detrimentally. Unfortunately, the mullion spacing is overly generous for one

Figure 5.40
125 Alban Gate, London, Terry Farrell, 1992. A transfer-truss diagonal member poses a potential danger to passers-by.

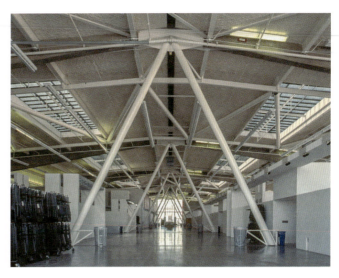

Figure 5.41
California College of the Arts, San Francisco, USA, Tanner Leddy Mantum Stacy, 1999. Light steel frames prevent injuries from the 'nave' brace members.

table, but too close for two, raising the question as to whether the mullions' aesthetic impact justifies the loss of significant usable space.

The second example serves as a reminder of how diagonal members pose a danger to the public. It recalls the full-scale mock-ups undertaken during the Hong Kong and Shanghai Bank design. During development of a 'chevron' structural scheme, eventually rejected by the client, Foster and Associates placed a polystyrene full-scale diagonal member in their office to assess its danger to passers-by.[11] On the first floor of 125 Alban Gate, five one-storey-deep transfer-trusses enable the building to span across a road (Figure 5.40). Truss diagonal tension members, encased in stainless-steel tubes, intrude into the public space. To prevent people from injuring their heads, seats and planters have been positioned to create a safety zone in the vicinity of the structural elements.

A similar situation arises at the Montgomery Campus, California College of the Arts, San Francisco. The architects provide a more permanent solution to prevent structure-induced injuries. The college occupies a former bus maintenance garage constructed in the 1950s that required seismic retrofitting. Steel chevron frames brace the building in both orthogonal directions. Those orientated transversely define a central interior street (Figure 5.41). Known as 'The Nave', it has become a successful venue for exhibitions and other events. Light steel protection frames protrude below waist level from the inclined steel tube braces to prevent accidents.

To conclude this chapter, two buildings illustrate how structure affects building users in unanticipated ways. Within an entry foyer at the Staatsgalerie, Stuttgart, a circular colonnade rings an information desk (Figure 5.42). Due to the large column sizes and their close spacing, they visually form a cylindrical wall that reads more like an attempt to restrict access rather than to encourage it. This reduces accessibility to the desk.

A final, rather quirky example reiterates the potential danger to people from diagonal structure positioned below head height. At the Scottish Exhibition Centre, Glasgow, the main concourse passes under a series of pitched portal frames supporting a glazed skin. The portals consist of tubular steel trusses with clearly expressed pin bases (Figure 5.43). However, an elegant convergence of the three chord members onto a chamfered cylindrical base cannot redeem the unfortunate situation where people sitting in a café area strike their heads against the structure. A more elegant solution than the protective pads might have been the creative deployment of planters as observed elsewhere in the building.

Figure 5.42
Staatsgalerie, Stuttgart, Germany, Stirling and Wilford, 1984. Columns form
a visual barrier around the information desk.

Figure 5.43
Scottish Exhibition Centre, Glasgow, Scotland, Parr Partnership, 1985. Knee
pads on truss-columns.

Summary

In order to explore how structure contributes to and enhances
building functionality, the chapter began by reviewing two
design strategies to achieve it – one based on identifying
and applying 'critical functional dimensions', and a second
more general architectural approach. The question of how to
maximize functional flexibility was addressed with reference
to the 'free plan'. Examples illustrated how perimeter
structures with diverse spatial relationships to their building
envelopes allow the most flexible planning and usage of
interior spaces.

Two groups of buildings then illustrated how structure also
contributes to building function by subdividing space. In the
first group, the spatial subdivision of a large volume enables
similar functions to occur in each small space. Several of the
buildings are notable for the diversity of spatial experience
and architectural qualities they provide. In the second group,
interior subdivision leads to a different space use in each
of the subdivided areas. Typical examples are where the
structure separates circulation from other spaces, such as
waiting areas and galleries.

Circulation is a necessary function of any building and is
frequently defined or articulated by structural elements, such
as arcades and frames. Depending on numerous factors,
including structural spacing, scale, materiality and detailing,

structurally defined routes can be read and experienced very differently. For example, while one corridor exudes tranquillity, another conveys impressions of rawness and joylessness. Even if the physical presence of structure is insufficiently strong to define circulation, it can still enhance it by reinforcing the direction of movement.

The concluding section considered works of architecture where structure disrupts function. In most of these cases where structure frustrates users, architects have given greater priority to the realization of architectural objectives other than function. Examples illustrated causes of disruptive structure, ranging from completely intentional to purely accidental reasons.

This chapter has illustrated the profound influence structure can have upon building function. By virtue of its permanence, structure both defines and limits the activities within a building. The degree of subtlety with which this is achieved depends upon the extent of the physical presence of structure in both plan and section. Whether it is maximizing functional flexibility or disrupting it, subdividing space or articulating function, structure must be thoroughly integrated with both the design concept and the functional requirements of the building.

Notes

1. D. L. Schodek, *Structures*, 4th edn, Englewood Cliffs, NJ: Prentice Hall, 2001, p. 468.
2. R. Krier, *Architectural composition*, New York: Rizzoli, 1988, p. 27.
3. J. Worrall, 'Base and superstructure in Toyo Ito', in J. Turnbull (ed.), *Toyo Ito – forces of nature*, New York: Princeton Architectural Press, 2012, p. 122.
4. G. Davis, C. Thatcher and L. Blair, *Serviceability tools*. Volume I: *Methods for setting occupant requirements and rating buildings*, Ottawa: The International Centre for Facilities, 1993.
5. S. Unwin, *Analysing architecture*, New York: Routledge, 1997, p. 137.
6. Quoted in an extensive analysis of architectural form in F. Ching, *Architecture: form, space & order*, 2nd edn, New York: Van Nostrand Reinhold, 1996, p. 14.
7. P. Cook, *Primer*, London: Academy, 1996, p. 84.
8. Z. Frieman, 'The architect of the city', *Progressive Architecture* 2(91), 1991, 50–63, at 61.
9. J. A. Hale, *Building ideas*, New York: John Wiley, 2000, pp. 87–8.
10. C. Steel, 'Tame at heart', *Blueprint* 127, 1996, 3–6.
11. S. Williams, *Hongkong Bank: the building of Normal Foster's masterpiece*, London: Jonathan Cape, 1989, p. 105.

six

Interior structure

Introduction

Inevitably, some overlap occurs between the previous chapter, which explored the relationships between interior structure and building function, and this chapter. However, Chapter 5 examined how structure subdivides space in order to separate different functions physically and accommodate them in their own spaces, and how it defines and identifies other important functions, such as circulation, whereas this chapter is unconcerned with how structure affects building function in a practical sense. Rather, it considers how structure contributes to the architectural qualities and characters of interior spaces.

Many architects believe that there is far more to the relationship between structure and building function than merely meeting physical spatial requirements. If the design approach of Peter Cook is typical, these practical needs are almost taken as a given, in order that the real architectural challenge can begin.[1] Cook develops the structural strategy of a building by first designing the 'primary elements'. This means adopting a certain structural concept, such as the use of a structural spine, be it a wall or a corridor of columns. As the issue of integrating structure with function is not raised explicitly, it can be assumed the need for fully functional spaces has been attended to during the development of the structural concept. He then turns his attention to 'secondary elements', by which he means individual structural members like beams and columns. Before deciding how to design them, he asks a series of questions:

> Is it a highly rhetorical building with a rhetorical structure? Is the structure to be the muted element? Is the aim for lightness or for a certain emphasis of presence that

may contrast with another part of the building? Is the roof to be 'read' as one or do we want the interval of the elements to be staccato, busy, cosy or symbolic of technicality?[2]

These questions, which suggest but a few of the myriad possibilities this chapter explores, acknowledge the potential for exposed structure to enrich interior architecture visually and conceptually. The extent to which this occurs depends on a variety of factors. Where structural members contrast with adjacent surfaces or architectural elements by means of colour, materiality, depth or texture, or scale, structural exposure is heightened. For example, naturally finished wooden members stand out against a light-coloured background. Sometimes exposed structural elements may not even be perceived as structure if they are unusually shaped, or if they are visually undifferentiated from other non-structural elements, like partition walls. The effectiveness of any degree of structural exposure must be evaluated in terms of how the exposure, or lack of it, contributes architecturally. Visual exposure of structure, if at all, must enhance the design concept and result in compelling and coherent architecture. After all, although bland and monotonous interior environments are required in some instances, such as to achieve a necessary standard of hygiene, they are not generally conducive to human habitation, and are usually anathemas to architects.

As for the content of this chapter, the next section illustrates how structure enlivens interior surfaces. Structure makes similar contributions inside buildings as it does to exterior building surfaces (Chapter 3), such as modulating, patterning and providing texture. The chapter then continues with examples of interior spaces enhanced by spatial rather than surface deployment of structure. In some buildings, structure encourages habitation by its density and small-scaled members. In others, large-sized structural members might tend to overwhelm occupants. It is noted how structure orders plans, creates spatial hierarchy, introduces visual diversity, and injects a sense of dynamism into a space. Finally, the expressive potential of interior structure is examined. Examples include structure expressing a wide diversity of ideas and responding to such issues as site and building function.

Surface structure

This section illustrates how interior exposed structure contributes architecturally by modulating and texturing surfaces. Any interior structure that is connected to or positioned immediately adjacent to the building skin is considered surface structure.

In contrast to most exterior structural elements, the interior exposed structure considered in this book, particularly in low-rise construction, is more likely to consist of wood than any other structural material. Without having to contend with potentially destructive sunlight and moisture, wooden members and their connections are well suited to interior conditions. Consider one of the four roof structures Calatrava designed as set-pieces for the Wöhlen High School. The roof

Figure 6.1
Wöhlen High School, Switzerland, Santiago Calatrava, 1988. Attractive structural framing pattern of the entrance foyer roof.

Figure 6.2
Refined wooden struts connect to the steel rod tension-ring and the rafters with deepened ends.

covers a squat drum at the centre of the school entrance foyer (Figure 6.1). The structure is conceptually simple. Sloping rafters radiate upwards from a supporting concrete ring beam to prop a central lantern. However, articulation of different structural actions, like tension or compression, introduces a constructional and visual complexity that modulates the interior roof surface and forms a most attractive pattern.

Calatrava has separated two of the structural functions performed by the rafters – propping the lantern and the central area of the roof, and, second, transferring the roof weight to each end of the rafters by bending and shear. Wooden spindle-shaped struts perform the propping duties. They fit into conical steel shoes, which at the lower ends of the rafters connect to two elements – the ends of the V-shaped rafters themselves and a circumferential tension-ring consisting of three steel rods (Figure 6.2). The tension-ring absorbs the horizontal component of strut thrusts while the vertical component is transferred upwards through the deep end sections of the glue-laminated rafters. They load short steel stub-columns that bear on the surrounding ring beam and provide enough height for a short, circular clerestory drum. The entry of natural light, restricted to the glazed lantern and the clerestory, accentuates the radiating pattern of the structure. The petal-shaped roof soffit surfaces, and the structure below them, are reminiscent of a flower head.

Saint Benedict Chapel, Sumvitg, offers another very attractive example of interior surface modulation. In this case, structure graces both the roof and the walls. Situated

Figure 6.3
Saint Benedict Chapel, Sumvitg, Switzerland, Peter Zumthor, 1989.
Chapel exterior.

Figure 6.4
Chapel interior, facing towards the altar.

The roof structure of the chapel possesses symmetry and visual simplicity. The ribbed pattern of rafters recalls the ribs on the underside of a leaf (Figure 6.5). Whereas conventional roof framing usually comprises a hierarchical structure, consisting of transverse rafters above a deeper longitudinal spine or ridge-beam, all the chapel roof ribs, including the spine-beam (which in this instance does not span the whole length of the chapel), are of identical depth. Each branches from the spine to bear on a perimeter post. Thin steel plates, welded together to achieve the branching geometry, are interleaved between wood laminates to achieve a two-way structural action. Skilfully concealed, this reinforcement does not detract from the glue-laminated wooden construction. Further evidence of detailing refinement is seen in the shape of the spine-beam itself. Not only trapezoidal in cross-section to soften its visual impact, its width tapers in harmony with the building plan, wide near the front of the chapel and narrow at the rear. These details, which reflect the building form and the designer's aesthetic sensibility, are indiscernible at the first viewing, but contribute significantly to the simple beauty of the exquisite interior structure.

Explicit separation of cladding from structure is also observed at Bodegas Protos, Valladolid (Figure 6.6). Slender steel rods support the tile-clad wooden roof above the glue-laminated wooden arches. The act of physically separating rafters and purlins from the arches has the effect of articulating the arches and emphasizing the sheltering and shading functions of the roof. The gap between arch and roof also helps the flow of cooling air.

on the steep slope of an alpine valley, the chapel is teardrop shaped in plan. On the exterior, timber shingle-clad walls rise to a horizontal glazed and vertically louvred band below the shallow roof. Given the absence of visible support to the roof, it appears disconnected from the enclosing wall below and 'hovers' (Figure 6.3). Inside the chapel, the roof support is revealed. Thirty-six regularly spaced posts are set in from the interior plywood wall-lining (Figure 6.4). Each connects delicately to the wall by three steel pins. The simple move of withdrawing the posts from their conventional location within the walls, and exposing them, affects the interior enormously. Acting as visual markers, they modulate the wall surface, but also increase the shape definition of the interior space and accentuate a sense of enclosure by their continuous alignment with the roof ribs they support.

Figure 6.5
Ribbed roof structure.

Figure 6.6
Bodegas Protos, Valladolid, Spain, Rogers Stirk Harbour + Partners, 2008. Separation of roof from structural arches. (Javier Gutierrez)

Figure 6.7
FDA Laboratory, Irvine, California, USA, Zimmer Gunsul Frasca Partnership + HDR, 2003. The perimeter wall of the library with its internal buttresses.

At the FDA Laboratory library, Irvine, surface modulation is taken to another degree of intensity. Not only does structure modulate the interior wall areas, but due to its considerable depth it plays a spatial subdivisional role around the perimeter of the space. The library is semi-circular in plan, essentially enclosed within reinforced concrete walls. Supporting the ends of beams that radiate from the centre of the semi-circular plan, deep cast-in-place buttresses project into the room (Figure 6.7). They subdivide the wall circumference into six equal segments, each of which has its own sense of partial enclosure. A desk placed in each segment benefits from natural light through a central slit window and a perimeter skylight above.

Ceiling structure, together with inclined columns, considerably enriches the interior space of the Güell Colony Crypt, Barcelona. Rough-hewn stone columns, precisely angled in accordance with Gaudí's catenary analytical study,

Figure 6.8
Güell Colony Crypt, Barcelona, Spain, Antoni Gaudí, 1917. Columns form an inner arcade ring and support the textured ceiling above.

form an inner semi-circular arcade around the sanctuary.[3] This centralized structure focuses attention on the sanctuary and the particularly richly textured ceiling above it (Figure 6.8). Shallow and audaciously thin brick arches support a brick soffit. The construction method, more common in wood than brick, has secondary members bearing on top of, rather than in the same plane as, the primary members. Secondary ribs generally radiate towards the perimeter of the crypt from two circular nodes in front of the altar.

Exposed wooden structure also enriches the interior surfaces of the next two buildings. At the Building Industry

Figure 6.9
Building Industry School, Hamm, Germany, Heger Heger Schlieff, 1996. Lamella wooden vaults span the workshop.

Figure 6.10
Saint Massimiliano Kolbe Church, Varese, Italy, Justus Dahinden, 1994. Interior surface.

School, Hamm (Figure 6.9), seven wooden lamella vaults form the roofs of the workshops. Four vaults cover an interior workshop space, while the other three shelter outdoor activities. Structure contributes a distinctive and attractive ceiling pattern to all the spaces.

Saint Massimiliano Kolbe Church, Varese, exemplifies another building with aesthetically pleasing interior surface wooden structure. Not only is the white hemispherical form unexpected in its northern Italian suburban setting, but so is its interior consisting of timber lining over a triangulated glue-laminated wooden dome (Figure 6.10). The primary triangulating ribs, the horizontal members between them and the lining are all stained white. The structural members with their curved profiles are sympathetic to the enclosing spherical geometry of the main congregational space and modulate its interior surface. Relative to the size of the enclosed volume, the small member sizes are reminders of the structural efficiency of a braced dome.

Most of the connections between structural members are concealed, but the architect has celebrated the joints between primary members (Figure 6.11). The detail possesses similar qualities to Fay Jones's much-admired Thorncrown Chapel connections, where light passes through the joints connecting wooden roof members.[4] Although the exterior cladding of the Varese church prohibits such transparency, the structural connections decorate the interior surface like a setting of widely spaced jewels. The architect has certainly achieved his aim of avoiding 'awe-inspiring and intimidating spaces . . . that

Figure 6.11
A typical joint between ribs.

make a totalitarian impression' and designed a space that is 'sheltering, protective and should inspire trust'.[5]

Whereas most of the previous examples show structure separate from but against interior surfaces, at the Yokohama International Passenger Terminal, the structure itself is the interior surface – in the form of folded plates (Figures 6.12 and 6.13). While the building is best known for its roof-top

landscaping, the roof is supported by steel folded plates that span much of the 70 m building width. The folded plates are supported at each end by box or U-shaped steel girders which themselves appear as if they also have been folded. The interior surface is therefore very highly textured, just like a work of origami. The changing depths of the folds respond to the changing needs for bending strength across the building, such as maximum depth at mid-span. Although steel trusses that are angled to achieve the folded geometry carry most of the loads, some of the surface steel plates contribute structurally. In these areas, surface and structure truly synthesize.

For the final two examples of structure enlivening interior surfaces, we begin by visiting King's Cross Station, London. Although mostly surface structure, the new roof displays spatial characteristics at its central and peripheral points of support. The centrepiece of the roof is a steel diagrid funnel, curved in plan and section (Figure 6.14). It is located close to an existing historic building so can be considered surface structure. Beginning as five V-shaped supports, the structure first transforms into diamond shapes, and where nearly at its maximum height it is fully triangulated by the insertion of radial purlins. The roof structure is semi-circular in plan,

Figure 6.12
Yokohama International Passenger Terminal, Japan, Foreign Office Architects, 2002. Folds of the roof folded plate structure are visible over the main entry.

Figure 6.13

The folded plates as seen looking across the lobby. In some areas, steel truss members are visible behind perforated plates.

with a radius of 74 m. Support is provided by the central funnel structure and sixteen hollow steel columns positioned around the curved perimeter. Rectangular ribs, straight in plan, radiate out from the centre while tubes, curved in plan and section, provide for the shell action that enables the roof to span so far. Apart from both its surface and spatial

Figure 6.14

Western Concourse, King's Cross Station, London, UK, John McAslan + Partners, 2012. The roof structure provides a semi-circular enclosure without loading the historic building to the right.

Figure 6.15

Nicolas G. Hayek Centre, Tokyo, Japan, Shigeru Ban Architects, 2007. Transparent columns and perimeter mullions support the curved and woven roof structure.

nature, the three-dimensional curvature results in a softness of form that is textured by the curved yet triangulated structural framework.

The roof-top structure over a functions room in the Nicolas G. Hayek Centre, Tokyo, is also a fine example of surface structure (Figure 6.15). Like King's Cross Station, its three-dimensional curved form enables much of its self-weight and other loads to be transferred to the two internal, and many perimeter, supports (load-bearing mullions) by shell action. However, the scale here is almost an order of magnitude less than at King's Cross. This is recognized by the reduced spacing of the radiating and curving members and the introduction of several additional orders of complexity. The two primary curved members that form parallelograms each consist of two thin interleaved rectangular sections, and between and above them two similar sections zigzag across. They form a series of triangulated panels, support the short vertical posts connecting to the roof surface and at the same time introduce considerable visual complexity. Unlike Shigeru Ban's other (wooden) undulating roof forms, all these members are steel.[6] Just like his other works, this surface structure exudes geometrical complexity, depth, texture and qualities of interlocking and weaving. Together with its city views, it creates a unique space.

Spatial structure

An underlying premise of this chapter is that spatial structure, such as a free-standing column, has a tangible impact upon the space around it. Ching explains this effect:

> when located within a defined volume of space, a column will generate a spatial field about itself and interact with the spatial enclosure . . . [and] when centered in a space, a column will assert itself as the center of the field and define equivalent zones of space between itself and the surrounding wall planes.[7]

But this is not to say that spatial structure always contributes positively to the making of architectural space. Consider, for example, free-plan column grids. Although they enhance constructability, they do not have the same effect on interior architecture. Such regular structural layouts are unlikely to be read positively. Van Meiss expresses his concern: 'Some spaces have great difficulty becoming places. Let us take the example of the "neutral" spaces of large open-plan offices . . .' He then explains how the Centraal Beheer office structure at Apeldoorn *does* respond to the need for place-making (Figure 5.29).[8] Erickson, also critical of the free plan, writes: 'The open space grids of Mies and Corbu, for instance, are in retrospect both architectural and structural copouts as they do not respond directly to the particular spatial environments and have little to do with the genius of their architecture.'[9]

In spite of the architectural limitations of regular and rectilinear column grids, we must acknowledge the significant roles such structure does play in ordering space. Somewhat ironically, the Centre Pompidou, Paris, a building with extensive floorplate areas that offer almost unlimited planning flexibility, is criticized for its lack of ordering structure. A reviewer bemoans:

> It is even tempting to wonder if columns might have been an asset, or the interruption of circulation or fixed service cores – anything to impose some architectural discipline in the vast interior . . . Yet it does seem that Piano & Rogers have played all their good cards on the highly expressive exterior of the building, leaving themselves not much with which to win our admiration inside.[10]

In many buildings, though, particularly those providing open-plan office accommodation, while column grids may be read optimistically as ordering space, they are more likely to be spatially disruptive.

The influence of spatial structure upon interior spaces of a building can be further appreciated by considering Figure 6.16.[11] Within an identical building envelope very different spatial qualities arise by varying interior structural layouts,

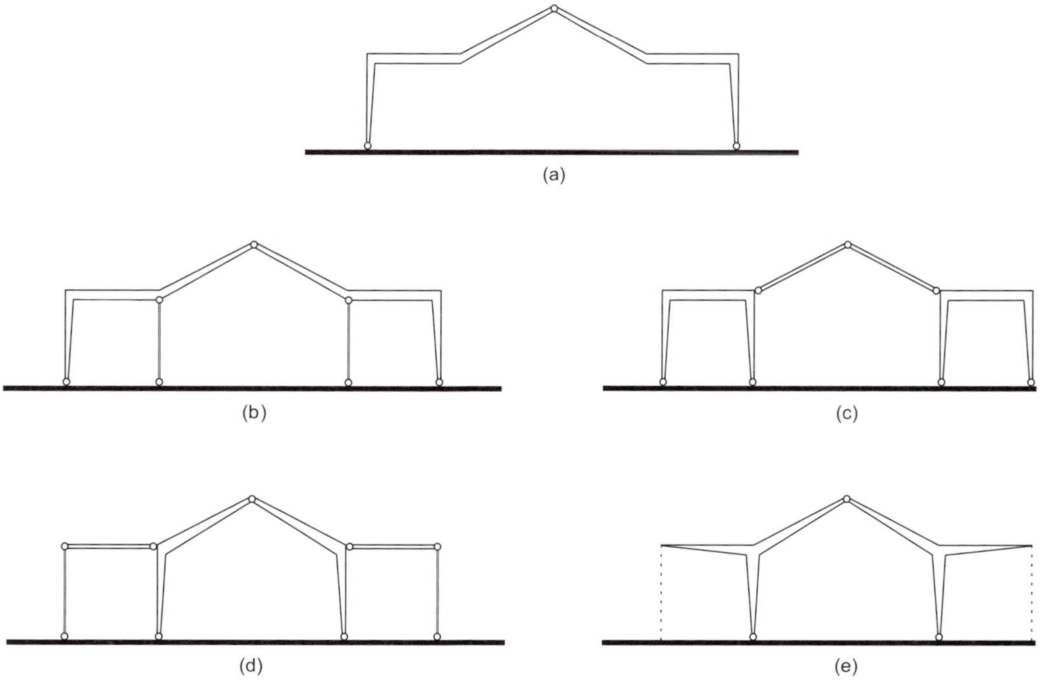

Figure 6.16
Different structural layouts affect how spaces are read.

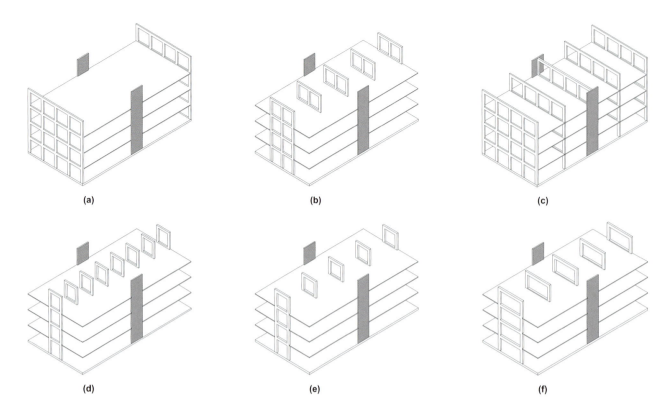

(a)   **(b)**   **(c)**

(d)   **(e)**   **(f)**

Figure 6.17
Alternative structural layouts for resisting transverse lateral loads on a multi-storey building. Gravity-only beams and columns are not shown.

all of which are technically feasible. While the whole internal volume is essentially perceived as one space in options (a) and (b), (c) and (d) each provides two separate and differentiated spatial zones. Option (e) offers the opportunity of creating a closer relationship between the inside and outside.

A similar investigation of alternative structural layouts and their influence upon interior space can, and should, be performed on any building at the preliminary design stage. Figure 6.17 presents different lateral-load-resisting layouts for a regular four-storey building. Variations to moment frames that resist transverse wind and earthquake loads only are shown. In each case the same two structural walls provide longitudinal stability. As in the previous figure, each structural option contributes a unique spatial character to every floor, hopefully reinforcing the design intent. The six options are but a taste of the huge range of possibilities. For example, the next stage of the exploration might involve shifting some or all of the one- and two-bay frames off the building centreline – perhaps placing them on a curved line running between

the ends of the building. While the structural performance is unaltered, such a move could create a particularly innovative and memorable building interior.

The following buildings illustrate the diverse range of architectural qualities achievable with interior structure. We begin with several spaces where structure itself creates a strong feeling of inhabitation. That is, occupants sense they inhabit structure located within a larger volume, rather than the overall volume itself.

First, we visit design studios in two schools of architecture. In both, high spatial structural density and small-scale structural members create human-scale spaces. At the Portland Building, Portsmouth, an orthogonal post-and-beam framework supports the roof and creates a series of subdivided zones (Figure 6.18). Spatial zoning is emphasized by how the framework reads as an insertion into the space, and visually quite distinct from the roof. Although the roof slopes, beams of the interior framework remain horizontal and thereby strengthen their definition of the smaller sub-spaces.

The double-height first-floor studios at the Lyon School of Architecture are broken up far more emphatically by diagonal glue-laminated wooden struts that prop the roof (Figure 6.19). Mezzanine work stations hang from the roof structure and

Figure 6.18
Portland Building, University of Portsmouth, UK, Hampshire County
Council Architects Department, 1996. The wooden framework creates
spatial zones within a studio.

Figure 6.19
Lyon School of Architecture, Lyon, France, Jourda et Perraudin, 1988.
Structure breaks up a large studio area.

create intimate working areas and spatial diversity within the
large volume. Students are never more than a metre or two
away from a structural element, be it a strut or a mezzanine-
floor tension-tie. Although such a dense spatial structure limits
how the studio space can be used, it creates a strong sense
of fostering habitation and of framing activities occurring
within the studio.

Students in the Kanagawa Institute of Technology
workshop, Atsugi, also occupy a dense structural framework.

But unlike earlier examples, the spatial structure these
students inhabit is random enough to suggest they are working
within a forest. The workshop, which is almost square in plan,
with an almost imperceptible mono-slope roof, is supported
by over three hundred columns (Figures 6.20 and 6.21). Most,
even though they are very slender, are embedded deeply
enough in the concrete floor slab to act as vertical cantilevers,
and therefore able to resist wind and earthquake forces.

Figure 6.20
Kanagawa Institute of
Technology (KAIT) workshop,
Atsugi, Japan, Junya Ishigami
and Associates, 2008. The
interior structural forest is
visible behind the glazed façade.

Figure 6.21
Work benches and equipment are scattered around, never far
from structure.

The forest analogy is immediately justified by the
seemingly random and dense layout of the steel posts.
Fourteen functional open spaces, like clearings, can be
identified. If that level of complexity is insufficient, two more
degrees of randomness exist: the cross-sectional dimensions
of the posts vary from the thinnest – 15 mm × 150 mm – to
the squattest – 60 mm × 90 mm – and, finally, the posts

are randomly angled in plan. The introduction of additional
complexity, such as non-vertical columns, other-than-rectilinear
cross-sections, or kinked or curved columns, would probably
have upset the sense of natural serenity that pervades the
space. The structure introduces many architectural qualities
into a volume devoid of distinctiveness. The many possible
readings of the interior structure include diversity, variety,
informality, unpredictability, lightness and delicacy, all of which
totally support the creativity the workshop seeks to nurture.

A sense of the immediacy of structure is also present in
the Wöhlen High School hall. In plan, regular column spacing
articulates a central nave and side aisles. However, in section,
and when observed three-dimensionally, structure takes a far
less conventional form. Free-standing roof support structure
within the enclosing concrete walls dominates the interior
(Figures 6.22 and 6.23). Gracefully curved pedestals support
wooden arches, and the radiating ribs create a delicate and
intricate rhythmical structure. The frequency of ribs, their
spatial orientation with respect to each other and the arches,
and their white stain finish make this structure so appealing.
While timber details lack any elaboration, the precast-concrete
pedestals exhibit strong sculptural qualities. From a functional
viewpoint the interior structure limits the flexibility of the hall,
but on the positive side it creates a wonderful and unique
interior space.

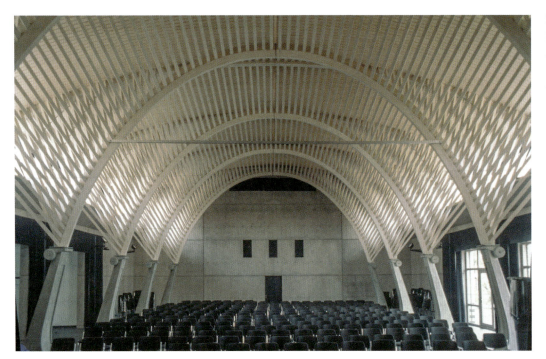

Figure 6.22
Hall, Wöhlen High School,
Switzerland, Santiago Calatrava,
1988. A view towards the rear of
the hall.

Figure 6.23
Looking across the hall.

Building users also intimately experience interior structure within the full-height atrium of the Museum of Contemporary Art, Barcelona. Continuing the theme of layering that is evident on the main façade, the atrium or ramp-hall contains three layers of vertical structure (Figures 6.24 and 6.25). Just inside the façade, a layer of thin rectangular columns supports the roof and the three-storey glazed wall. Next, a free-standing colonnade interspersed with several non-structural vertical elements that also read as structure carries ramps which cantilever from both sides of the columns. Beyond the ramp

Figure 6.24
Museum of Contemporary Art, Barcelona, Spain, Richard Meier Architects, 1995. Exterior glazed wall to the ramp hall with the ramp structure behind.

Figure 6.25
Ramp colonnade to the right and the innermost structural layer on the left.

structure in a direction away from the glazed wall, the third layer of structure takes the form of another colonnade in front of the balconies and supporting beams emanating from the main galleries. The ramp-hall width is therefore defined by colonnades and inhabited by another that supports the ramps. Structure therefore plays a powerful role in spatial modulation. When ascending or descending the ramps, gallery visitors move past and close to these layers of vertical structure. Proximity to the structure and a rhythmical engagement with it contribute to a sense of inhabiting it.

The Stadttor Building, Düsseldorf, provides an example of more dramatic interior structure (Figure 6.26). Two huge tubular-steel towers, located at diagonally opposite corners in plan, resist lateral loads. The architect has separated the gravity- and lateral-load-resisting systems, and chosen to express the latter. The concrete-filled structural steel members are massive by comparison to the light gravity-only columns whose small dimensions increase the building's transparency elsewhere in plan.

Figure 6.26
Stadttor Building, Düsseldorf, Germany, Petzinka Pink und Partner, 1998. An interior braced tower is visible through the glazing.

The braced towers are awe-inspiring in scale. The fact that they occupy voids and are themselves open, their height uninterrupted by floor slabs, mean their entire size can be observed from many interior (and exterior) vantage points. Like giant masts, the structural towers are a defining characteristic of a building already endowed with other special features, such as a vast atrium and extensive glazed façades. In terms of impact upon interior space, the towers with their diagonal braces are visually dynamic, but at the same time their scale is rather overwhelming. Patrons of a ground-floor café situated near the base of a mast look up through the

Figure 6.27
A view up through a tower.

Figure 6.28
GC Prostho Museum Research Centre, Aichi, Japan, Kengo Kuma & Associates, 2010. A spatial wooden three-dimensional grid appears to have been excavated to form interior spaces. (Ken Lee)

Figure 6.29
Regent's Park Pavilion, London, UK, Carmody Groarke, 2009. The pavilion consists of 258 columns and a very lightweight penetrated roof.

mast to the ceiling some 58 m above (Figure 6.27). This is certainly not an intimate and cosy interior space.

The spatial structure within the following two buildings is of a completely different scale. The structural form of the GC Prostho Museum Research Centre, Aichi, was inspired by a traditional Japanese toy, where sticks can be removed from a stick construction merely by twisting them (Figure 6.28). Sixty-millimetre-square wooden members form a 500 mm cubic load-bearing structure. The structure appears as if it once completely filled some of the rooms, but was then hollowed away to create usable space, giving an impression of excavated architecture. Although the structure is far too fine to inhabit, its voids provide opportunities to display artefacts.

In contrast, most of the Regent's Park Pavilion, Osnaburgh Street, London, is habitable (Figures 6.29 and 6.30). Four single seats are provided within the structure and the columns can be meandered through, except in several areas where the 600 mm grid is halved in size. The close spacing of columns and their slenderness invite human interaction. Simple in

Figure 6.30
Three seats amid the forest of slender columns.

concept, the columns are fixed at their bases and rigidly welded to beams of the same cross-section at roof level. The slenderness of the 50 mm-square hollow stainless-steel columns required extensive laboratory testing, structural analysis, and the provision of internal dampers to cope with potential wind vibrations.[12]

The next two examples of spatial structure illustrate how structure in a state of repose plays important spatial ordering roles. Having previously discussed the rounded and

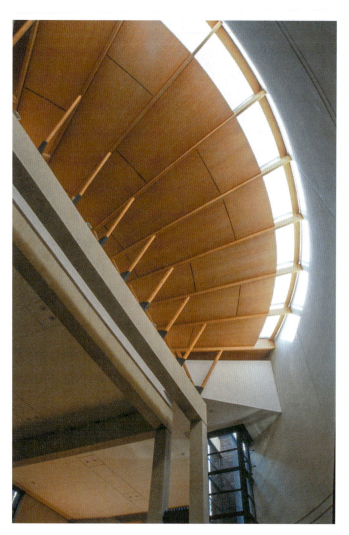

Figure 6.32
The wooden roof is propped off an outer frame.

Figure 6.31
Fitzwilliam College Chapel, Cambridge, UK, Richard MacCormac, 1991. Concrete frames demarcate a central area of the chapel interior.

protective exterior wall structure of Fitzwilliam College Chapel, Cambridge (Figure 4.40), we now consider the impact of a completely different structural system upon its interior space. Three independent concrete frame structures stand within the confines of the chapel walls. The central structure of four columns forms two frames in both orthogonal directions (Figure 6.31). Together with the lowered concrete ceiling slab, the frames demarcate an area square in plan, centred between the walls. Two identical one-way frames flank the sides of this central structure. They are separated far enough from it to be read as independent frames. The four frames that align parallel to the major axis of the chapel therefore read as two sets of layered structure. The outer frames carry most of the weight of the wooden roof that bears on inclined

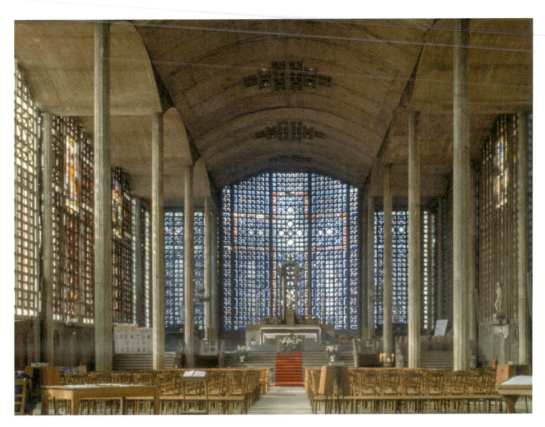

Figure 6.33
Notre Dame du Raincy, Paris, France, Auguste Perret, 1923. Church interior with its four rows of columns.

struts and cantilevers from them towards the curved walls (Figure 6.32).

The interior frames set up a spatial hierarchy. They denote the importance of the liturgical activities by 'enclosing' the space occupied by the altar and sanctuary. The choice of white polished precast concrete for the frames further reinforces the importance of this space. Stairs and side seating occupy left-over spaces to each side of the frames. The space to the rear of the central frames accommodates most of the congregation, the organ and an additional staircase.

The second example, the Notre Dame du Raincy, Paris, also exemplifies structure ordering space (Figure 6.33). Considered by some to be the world's first masterpiece of reinforced concrete architecture, its plan is typical of the neo-Gothic churches of that era. The church is five full bays long with an additional half-bay at each end. Rows of four columns divide the width into two aisles and a central nave. The roof structure reinforces this tripartite order. A vaulted ceiling that relies on hidden transverse upstand-ribs for its support runs the length of the nave, while short aisle vaults are orientated transversely.

The structural layout in plan appears to be based on a previous church design for the site, except that its original bay lengths were doubled by the architect to approximately 10 m.[13] This modification immediately opened up the whole interior, reducing the distinction between nave and aisles, and resulting in a lighter and more subtle ordering of space. Columns modulate both the whole volume and the side walls. Placing columns just inside the skin, rather than incorporating them into the wall, maintains a clear distinction between the structure and the visually arresting precast-concrete and coloured-glass building envelope. This relationship between columns and skin also increases the sense of spaciousness within the church.[14] The columns do not compete with the skin for attention, but rather their slenderness and wide spacing enable them to blend in with it.

Expressive structure

The last section of this chapter focuses upon structure playing expressive roles. The structures of the first two buildings in this section express resistance to external horizontal loads, while those that follow express aspects related to building usage and geometry.

Figure 6.34
Museum of Gallo-Roman Civilization, Lyon, France, Bernard Zehrfuss, 1975. A central row of continuous and sloping columns.

Figure 6.35
Concrete frames extend over the galleries and corridor. The sloping columns express the hill-side embedment of the building.

Five floors of the Museum of Gallo-Roman Civilization, Lyon, are embedded in a hillside adjacent to an ancient amphitheatre. Apart from an uppermost entrance and reception level, the only other visible evidence of the museum is provided by a pair of small viewing galleries that project from the sloping face of the hill to overlook the nearby ruins, and vehicular access doors at the lowest level. Reinforced-concrete frames rise up through the building and support suspended floor slabs (Figure 6.34).

A strong structural presence permeates the underground volume. Large beams and columns project into galleries and modulate the spaces. Fortunately, their sensitive detailing avoids any undue structural severity. Curved junctions between beams and columns, and ceilings and walls, and tapered cross-sections of the beams soften the otherwise visual hardness of the concrete structure. Resistance to the lateral soil pressures acting on the rear wall is expressed by the general heaviness of the frame members, and, more emphatically, by the inclination of the outermost and central columns (Figure 6.35) Their slope, which also reflects that of the hillside outside, expresses the structural buttressing often necessary to resist horizontal soil pressure.

The exposed structure at Westminster Station on the London Underground Jubilee Line also expresses the presence of external soil pressure. In the access tunnels and around the train platforms, curved metal tunnel liners, plates and bolts speak the unique language of underground

construction (Figure 6.36). However, the structure expresses the external pressures most clearly in the main hall (Figure 6.37). Designed to be as open as possible, this huge 35 m-high hall houses seventeen escalators and numerous floors that service the various lines that pass through the station. To add to its spatial complexity, eighteen 660 mm-diameter horizontal steel struts pass across the hall and through a central row of vertical columns interspersed by cross-bracing. Welcome to a Piranesian volume!

Both the surface and the spatial structure express the presence of external soil pressure. The hall side walls are deeply patterned by a vertical grillage of projecting

Figure 6.36
Westminster Station, London, Michael Hopkins & Partners, 1999. Tunnel lining exposed at a platform.

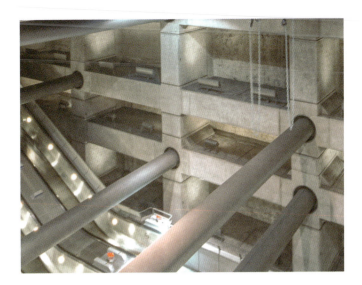

Figure 6.37
Horizontal props between side walls.

Figure 6.38
Props pass through central columns.

piers and horizontal beams. Interior surfaces that are recessed within these members have a rough shotcrete-like finish, often associated with soil retention. This quite massive wall structure, insufficient in itself to protect the hall walls from inward collapse, is propped apart by the circular solid cast-steel struts. The manner in which they are recessed into the wall structure at their ends expresses their role as compression struts. They read as thrusting into the wall and locally deforming it. At the centrally placed columns, projecting collars to the struts express the horizontal continuity required of compression struts (Figure 6.38).

Structure expresses different aspects of functionality in the next four buildings. At the Arts Centre, Rotterdam, structure expresses a number of ideas. First, and at the most basic level, columns that support the auditorium roof slope forward, towards the dais (Figure 6.39). By remaining orthogonal to the inclined plane of the auditorium floor, the sloping columns focus attention to the front of the space, mimicking how people lean forward, eager to hear and see.

In other areas of the building, structure expresses qualities of the unexpected nature of the art it contains. Within the Hall 2 gallery roof-plane, what appear to be irregular red-coloured bracing elements flash overhead as they pass between translucent truss cladding (Figure 6.40). These members form an unrecognizable pattern, raising the question as to whether they are structural. Balmond, the structural engineer, explains:

Figure 6.39
Arts Centre, Rotterdam, The Netherlands, Office for Metropolitan Architecture, 1992. Columns in the auditorium lean towards the dais.

Figure 6.40
Unusually configured roof-plane bracing.

In Hall 2 of Kunsthal a thin red line runs through the roof space. It is a small structural tube that follows, in plan, the path of an arch; and the curve intersects the roof beams to pick up lateral loads being delivered along those lines. Two pairs of ties reach out to prevent the arch from buckling in its plane of action. As the lines of the structural system of arch and tie become interrupted by the beams, it is not clear what the thin red line means. Is it structure? Is it pattern? Or, is it architectural device? The answer is: all three.

Structure need not be comprehensible and explicit. There is no creed or absolute that dictates structure must be recognized as a basic functional skeleton or the manifestation of a high-tech machine. It can be subtle and more revealing. It is a richer experience to my mind if a puzzle is set or a layer of ambiguity lies over the reading of 'structure'.[15]

Other unconventional interior structure in the Kunsthal also expresses the ambiguity mentioned above. Chapter 2 discusses how the two lines of columns 'slip' out of phase in Hall 1, and in a circulation space a thick slab appears to be propped near its end by a tension-tie hung from a truss above (Figure 6.41). But what is supporting what? The slab depth appears sufficient to cantilever without being propped. Perhaps the truss is being held down to counter wind uplift? The ambiguity is unexpected and unsettling, like the modern art being exhibited.

Figure 6.41
An ambiguous relationship between a cantilevering slab and a tension-tie from the roof.

Within the Channel 4 Headquarters entrance atrium, London, stainless-steel cables visually express the dominant structural action – tension (Figure 6.42). A tensile system, chosen for its transparency, supports curved and glazed atrium walls. Above the atrium roof, steel tension and compression members cantilever out from primary concrete structural elements to carry the weight of the entire glazed wall. Glass panels hang in tension from those above, with the uppermost panels transferring the accumulated weight to the main structure via shock-absorbing coiled springs. This load-path is virtually invisible, even when compared to

Figure 6.42
Channel 4 Headquarters, London, UK, Richard Rogers Partnership, 1995.
Atrium interior.

Figure 6.43
Oxford University Museum, UK, Deane and Woodward, 1860.
Courtyard interior.

the diminutive prestressed cable-net components that resist horizontal wind pressures on the glazed façade. The horizontal cables that follow the semi-circular plan shape of the glazed wall are stressed against vertical cables spanning between ground floor and the substantial roof cantilevers.[16] Slender horizontal steel tubes connect each glazed panel junction back to the taut cable-net. Precision-engineered connections signify state-of-the-art technology. The many cables, horizontal and vertical, as well as the tubes, result in visual as well as structural complexity.

As well as expressing structural actions, the structure seems to express the stressful atmosphere pervading the building. The atrium space adjacent to the curved wall is one of the least visually restful spaces I have ever experienced. The cables, all highly tensioned, trace out taut spatial patterns that are not immediately recognizable or understood. This is a very visually busy structure, which, as I read it, expresses the tension and stress associated with TV performance – an architecture of tension, in more ways than one.

We can find a more literal example of structure expressing an aspect of building use in the glazed courtyard of the Oxford University Museum. Surrounded on three sides by heavy neo-Gothic masonry wings, the cast-iron framework supporting the courtyard roof is a remarkably lightweight

Figure 6.45
Sloping columns of three suspended pods also express informality.

Figure 6.44
Peckham Library, London, UK, Alsop & Störmer, 2000. The exterior columns below the main library space move through it to support the roof and introduce an informal quality.

structure usually maintains a rigid adherence to orthogonality. However, there are exceptions, such as the Peckham Library. The informal exterior structure (Figure 4.44) pierces through the floor of the lending library to support the roof. In so doing the sense of informality expressed on the exterior breaks into the interior (Figure 6.44). Informality is even multiplied by the sloping columns of the three pods raised above the main floor level (Figure 6.45). In this building, interior structure expresses the ethos of the library which is in stark contrast to traditional notions of orderliness and formality.

structure (Figure 6.43). Its skeletal qualities are augmented by wrought-iron detailing that complements the natural history exhibits on display. Haward acknowledges its expressive qualities when he reads the structure as a forest. He also sees it playing a didactic role, describing it as 'the central feature in the iconographic scheme for the Museum to be read as a "Book of Nature"'.[17] Structure visually dominates the interior to such an extent that it may detract from the prehistoric animal skeletons on display. The metallic and animal skeletons possess similar visual properties of complexity and delicacy.

In most buildings, orthogonally configured structural members both respond to and express the rectilinear structural systems and architectural forms they support. Even where forms take on more complex geometries, primary

Summary

Interior structure can transform otherwise nondescript interior spaces by contributing architectural qualities and character. This chapter has presented three modes by which structure visually and conceptually enriches interior architecture – surface, spatial and expressive.

In the exploration of *surface* structure, the buildings discussed illustrate the architectural potential for enriching spaces using exposed structure located on interior surfaces. In several examples, quite elaborate structure creates attractive surface patterning. In others, exposure of structural elements that are normally concealed, coupled with a design approach characterized by simplicity and rigour, proves more than sufficient to transform spaces.

With respect to structure's *spatial* impacts, others have explained how structure generates a spatial field around it, affecting how a space is perceived and creating opportunities for 'place-making'. A simple study illustrated how, within the same volume, changes in structural layout can greatly affect how a space is read. Relatively small-scale structure that forms domestic-sized spatial units also affects our spatial experience. It instils an impression of being inhabited, and of framing activities within it. Where larger in scale, interior structure also offers many diverse spatial and visual experiences. At the extremes of structural scale, structure either all but disappears visually or else its massiveness may be overwhelming. Structure also plays important roles ordering spaces and, in other cases, imposing a sense of spatial hierarchy.

The *expressive* potential of interior structure is boundless. The examples provided above only begin to indicate the extent to which structure can express all manner of issues. Two structures illustrated expression of externally acting soil pressure. In another building, structure expresses concepts related to breaking conventions and 'the unexpected'. We also saw structure mirroring the intensity of the emotional climate of one set of building occupants. Finally, interior structure visually reinforces the qualities of the exhibits it encloses.

Notes

1. P. Cook, *Primer*, London: Academy, 1996.
2. Ibid., p. 85.
3. R. Zerbst, *Antoni Gaudí*, Köln: Taschen, 1991, p. 115.
4. R. A. Ivy, *Fay Jones*, Washington, D.C.: The American Institute of Architects, 1992, p. 35.
5. D. G. Brigatti and J. Dahinden, *Spazi Evocanti il Mistero – la Chiesa S. Massimiliano Kolbe in Varese*, Barasso: Grafiche Quirici, 1997, p. 114.
6. Although all the members of the roof structure are steel, the two outer curved layers of the columns are only light-gauge hollow sections, and therefore are decorative. They partially conceal straight steel members within.
7. F. Ching, *Architecture: form, space & order*, 2nd edn, New York: Van Nostrand Reinhold, 1996, p. 122.
8. P. Van Meiss, *Elements of architecture: from form to place*, New York: Van Nostrand Reinhold, 1990, p. 138.
9. A. Suckle, *By their own design*, New York: Whitney Library of Design, 1980, p. 14.
10. S. Abercrombie, 'Evaluation: Beaubourg already shows its years', *Architecture* 72(9), 1983, 62–71, at 70.
11. After A. Ogg, *Architecture in steel: the Australian context*, Red Hill, ACT: Royal Australian Institute of Architects, 1987, p. 49.
12. R. Gregory, 'Osnaburgh Street Pavilion', *The Architectural Review* 227, 2010, 78–83.
13. A. Saint, 'Notre-Dame du Raincy', *The Architects' Journal*, 13 February 1991, 26–45.
14. See, for example, K. Frampton, *Studies in tectonic culture: the poetics of construction in nineteenth and twentieth century architecture*, Cambridge, MA: Massachusetts Institute of Technology, 1995, p. 132.
15. C. Balmond, *informal*, Munich: Prestel, 2002, p. 64.
16. For a more detailed description of the system's complexity and action, refer to W. Addis, *Creativity and innovation: the structural engineer's contribution to design*, Oxford: Architectural Press, 2001, pp. 113–15.
17. B. Haward, 'Oxford University Museum', *The Architects' Journal* 190(13), 1989, 40–63, at 40.

seven

Structural detailing

Introduction

Exposed structural detailing can contribute significantly to the architecture of a building. Detailing can transform ordinary or purely utilitarian structural members and connections into objects of aesthetic delight, as well as communicate design ideas and concepts. This chapter begins by illustrating how architects express a wide diversity of design ideas through structural details. It then demonstrates the breadth of architectural qualities that such expressive detailing contributes to architecture.

For the purposes of this discussion, we will define *structural detailing* as determining the form of and the shaping and finishing of structural members and their connections. Structural detailing, as a design process, comprises the design of the cross-section, elevational profile and the connections of a structural member, in order to achieve the engineering requirements of stability, strength and stiffness. Detailing begins after we have settled on the structural form for a given design. For example, if we decide to adopt an exposed timber post-and-beam system, as shown in Figure 7.1, we can select details from many possible combinations of differently detailed beams and columns, or design something different. Then we can select from the range of standard joints and finishes, or else exercise our own creativity to design a more innovative solution. Similar ranges of alternatives are suggested for the detailing of structural steel and reinforced-concrete members (Figures 7.2 and 7.3).[1]

The architectural design concept should drive detailed design. Before attending to the specifics of structural details a designer should begin by revisiting his or her concept and interrogating it. How might it inform detailing decisions?

Only then is it possible to achieve an architecture where all its structural members are integrated with architectural elements and all work together towards reinforcing the design concept. Such an outcome is improbable if a designer uncritically permits detailing choices to be constrained by typical or conventional practice. That will deny clients and building users opportunities for architectural enrichment. As Louis Khan writes:

> A building is like a human. An architect has the opportunity of creating life. It's like a human body – like your hand. The way the knuckles and joints come together makes each hand interesting and beautiful. In a building these details should not be put into a mitten and hidden. You should make the most of them. Space is architectural when the evidence of how it is made is seen and comprehended.[2]

Where detailing is hidden from view, however, any design considerations beyond structural performance, economy and buildability are wasted. A pragmatic approach to detailing is quite sufficient.

As well as reflecting or expressing the architectural design concept, as noted above, structural detailing must be structurally adequate and consistent with the structural engineering assumptions. For example, a connection assumed pinned in the structural analysis should be detailed as such. Therefore, at least in buildings large enough to require professional structural engineering expertise, successful structural resolution, including detailing, requires close collaboration between architects and structural engineers. Structural detailing should therefore satisfy both the architectural design concept and structural necessity.

Figure 7.1

Several alternative structural member options for wooden post-and-beam construction.

Pin joint

Structural model (stability provided by structure elsewhere in plan)

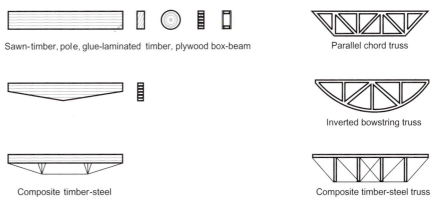

Sawn-timber, pole, glue-laminated timber, plywood box-beam

Parallel chord truss

Inverted bowstring truss

Composite timber-steel

Composite timber-steel truss

Beam and truss options

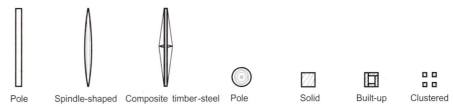

Pole   Spindle-shaped   Composite timber-steel   Pole   Solid   Built-up   Clustered

Post options

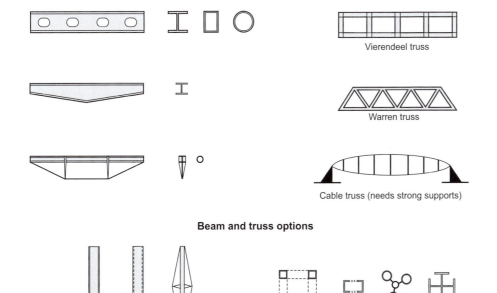

Vierendeel truss

Warren truss

Cable truss (needs strong supports)

Beam and truss options

Composite columns

Figure 7.2

Several alternative structural member options for steel post-and-beam construction.

Post or column options

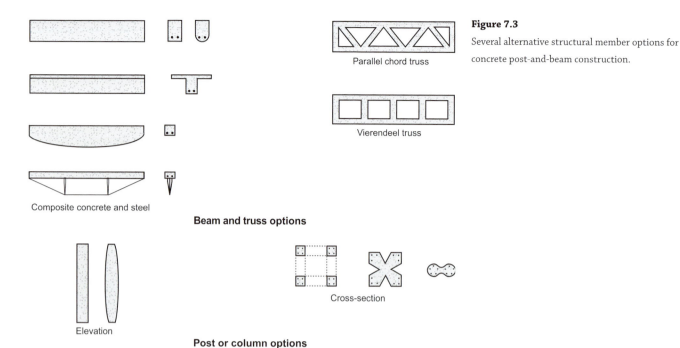

Parallel chord truss

Vierendeel truss

Composite concrete and steel

Beam and truss options

Elevation

Cross-section

Post or column options

Figure 7.3
Several alternative structural member options for concrete post-and-beam construction.

Expressive and responsive detailing

Structural detailing expresses or responds to a wide variety of influences. In most cases, details are inspired by some aspect *within* the building being designed. Typical sources of inspiration include architectural form, function, materiality and construction, or structural actions. Examples of each are discussed in the following sections. Several buildings are then examined whose details reflect ideas or issues arising *outside* the building – perhaps an event, an aspect of technology, vernacular architecture, an aspect of culture or even an historical period.

Architectural form

This detailing strategy adopts some feature of the architectural form to guide the development of structural details. If not laboured unduly, such an approach can bring a sense of harmony to a project, unifying otherwise possibly disparate elements. Where implemented successfully, the resulting details appear to have a sense of rightness or inevitability about them. As architect Fay Jones, a widely acknowledged

exponent of synthesizing the detail and the whole (architectural form), explains:

> Organic architecture has a central generating idea; as in most organisms every part and every piece has a relationship. Each should benefit the other; there should be a family of form, and pattern. You should feel the relationship to the parts and the whole . . . The generating idea establishes the central characteristics, or the essence, or the nucleus, or the core; it's the seed idea that grows and generates the complete design, where it manifests itself from the large details down to the small subdivision of the details.[3]

Well-integrated relationships between structural detailing and architectural form are found at the Grand Louvre, Paris, and the Suhr office building. In the underground foyer of the Louvre Gallery, detailing of the coffered suspended ground-floor slab reflects the precision and the geometrical purity of the iconic glazed pyramid above (Figures 7.4 and 7.5). The truncated pyramidal geometry of the coffer voids within the slab unifies the different construction materials through common forms. Detailing of the central column also exhibits the same theme of geometrical purity (Figure 7.6). Full-height triangular incisions into each side of an otherwise square column form a complex cross-section. The square and

Figure 7.4

Grand Louvre, Paris, France, I. M. Pei, 1989. Louvre pyramid.

Figure 7.5
Coffered slab soffit.

triangular shapes integrate with those of the coffers in the immediate vicinity, and with the pyramid above.

Structural detailing of the Suhr office building takes its cue from an essentially rounded floor plan (Figure 7.7). Geometrically complex paddle-like ground-floor struts approximate circular cross-sections at their bases and widen smoothly to become thin blades at their tops (Figure 7.8). The main stairway, tucked into a service core behind the primary circular form, also incorporates rounded details. The rounded top and bottom surfaces of the precast-concrete stringer are also consistent with the architectural form (Figure 7.9).

Figure 7.6
Triangular recesses within the central column relate to the pyramid above.

Figure 7.7
Suhr office building, Switzerland, Santiago Calatrava, 1985. The building is circular in plan, with an attached service core behind.

Figure 7.8
Perimeter blade-like strut.

Figure 7.9
Rounded precast-concrete stair stringer.

Figure 7.10
Everlyn Grace Academy, London, UK, Zaha Hadid Architects, 2010. A structural wall reinforces the dynamic expression of other architectural elements in the school.

Usually concrete structural walls are rectilinear in elevation, but at the Everlyn Grace Academy, London, a primary exterior wall is shaped in response to the building form, notable for its often reoccurring but identically angled columns, walls and façade. In spite of its large surface area and its concrete construction, the action of angling the ends of the wall immediately introduces a sense of movement (Figure 7.10). The visual inertia of the wall is greatly reduced, to the extent it contributes along with other sloping elements to the dynamic quality of the school.

Building function

In the following two examples, a commercial building and an art gallery, structural detailing both expresses and contributes positively to aspects of their functions. In the first case, the detailing is highly refined, while in the second it has been deliberately designed to appear relatively crude. Structural detailing responds to and reinforces the distinctive purpose of each building.

The Tobias Grau office and warehouse facility, Rellingen, illustrates a clear relationship between detailing and building function (see Figure 3.23). The company designs and manufactures high-quality light-fittings which have been incorporated extensively into its new facilities. In this setting, structural detailing maintains an equivalently high aesthetic standard. The structural details are more readily

Figure 7.11
Tobius Grau KG office, Rellingen, Germany, BRT Architekten, 1998. Structure in the office interior.

comparable to those of furniture design than to typical building construction. The attractiveness of the main curved glue-laminated portal members is surpassed by two lines of slightly inclined wooden posts that delineate circulation from office area (Figure 7.11). Spindle-shaped, the slender posts are capped top and bottom by conical steel shoes. The two bays of tension-only bracing are also far more elegant than usual. They avoid repeating the simple and conventional diagonal cross-braced solution where straight members connect to diagonally opposite joints. Structural refinement in the form of two additional rods that extend from the upper corners of the bays avoids the ubiquitous pair of diagonals. This structural complication yields a more visually interesting arch-like shape, increases the width available for circulation underneath the bracing, and helps raise the level of structural sophistication to that of its surroundings. Even in the warehouse, fine rod cross-bracing has been so carefully designed and integrated with the portals, the wall-lining and the structural horizontal members that it reads more like sewing stitching than conventional bracing (Figure 7.12).

Structural detailing also expresses aspects of building function at the Arts Centre, Rotterdam, which was discussed in the previous chapter (see Figures 6.39–6.41). When visitors approach the building from street level their aesthetic sensibilities are assaulted by two structural details. First,

Figure 7.12
Fine diagonal bracing reads as 'stitching'.

Figure 7.14
Two of the three differently detailed columns.

Figure 7.13
Arts Centre, Rotterdam,
The Netherlands, Office for
Metropolitan Architecture,
1992. Ungainly exterior beam.

a large, brightly painted, unrefined I-beam projects crudely above the roof (Figure 7.13). Second, adjacent to the main entry, three columns within close proximity to each other are detailed completely differently. The front two columns that form a steel rod cross-braced bay comprise a square concrete column and a castellated steel I-section (Figure 7.14). The third column, behind, is a standard steel I-section. This deliberately inconsistent detailing expresses the nature of the unexpected and nonconformist art exhibits within. Structure, by flouting convention, expresses the ethos of this museum of modern art. The structural engineer for the project, Cecil Balmond, explains why these and other interior columns 'disturb the air' and their personalities clash:

> Imagine the same material and form for all the columns – there would be less impact. Imagine a regular spacing to the columns and the dynamic vanishes. Imagine further the different conflicts of plan resolved by some 'hidden' structural gymnastic, with one column coming through ultimately in a pretence of neatness – the reduction would be complete. There would be nothing left, no animation, no off-beat pulse. The juxtaposition brings in its own drama, and the mix urges entry, to bypass the inconsistency for more settled regions within. These columns signal the experience of the building itself, with its schisms, its interior slips and jumps and separate materialities.[4]

Materiality and construction

Some architecture is characterized by a strong expression of structural materiality and construction. Each structural material possesses features particular to its own materiality. For example, thinness of section, flanged cross-sectional shapes, potential for extreme slenderness in both compression and tension, and the ability to accommodate significant penetrations in members are characteristics unique to steel construction. Concrete, in a plastic or even completely fluid state while still fresh, can harden in moulds of almost any shape and display many different surface textures. Other signatures of concrete include negative details at construction joints and form-tie recesses. Wood materiality, on the other hand, is best expressed by its natural grain and colour, typical

Figure 7.15
Mossbourne Community Academy, London, UK, Rogers Stirk Harbour + Partners, 2004. Conventional timber hierarchical construction: flooring supported by secondary beams over primary beams. Continuous (not simply supported) primary beams rest on blocks bolted between continuous paired columns.

rectilinear cross-sectional shapes, and connection details that respond to its relative softness and anisotropy. Other structural configurations, such as vertical and hierarchical layering of horizontal joists and beams, and relatively closely spaced beams and posts, are also trademarks of wooden construction (Figure 7.15).

This section – which illustrates structures whose detailing not only expresses building materiality and construction but celebrates it – begins by considering a structural steel building whose materiality becomes apparent at first glance. The structure of the United Airlines Terminal concourse and departure lounges, Chicago, utilizes a limited vocabulary of two steel sections – the I-beam and the tube (Figures 7.16 and 7.17). Highly penetrated I-sections form the irregularly shaped beams of portal frames that articulate and modulate the concourses. Tubes function as purlins, and also as clustered columns for each portal-frame leg. In several spaces the two sections combine to form a composite beam with a conventional top I-beam flange but a tubular lower flange.

The architect has mostly used off-the-shelf sections, yet, through varied structural form and consistent and refined detailing, has facilitated a sense of liveliness, lightness and materiality. The high-quality detailing of the exposed structure

Figure 7.16
United Airlines Terminal, Chicago, USA, Murphy/Jahn, 1987.
The main concourse.

Figure 7.17
Innovative steel construction.

is largely responsible for this exemplary architecture that could have otherwise been a featureless and elongated space. A reviewer observes:

> Terminal 1 is not a project in which it is possible to hide a poor symbiosis of architecture and engineering disciplines; it is obvious that Jahn [the architect] and the structural engineers at Lev Zetlin Associates worked well together in an understanding of what the result should be. It has been noted that the structural expression so prevalent in the project – rounded forms, exposed ribs,

and structural members with punched webs – recalls the structural parts of aircraft; this layer of meaning, says Jahn, was unintentional . . . the assembly shows elegance in every detail. Steel connections and finishes could be the subject of a whole photographic essay in themselves. Joints, brackets, and end conditions have been taken past that point where they merely work, to become abstract sculpture.[5]

A far simpler approach to the detailing of two steel lift-towers is taken at Evelina Children's Hospital, London (Figure 7.18). Enclosed by a steel diagrid conservatory roof that rises five storeys above floor level, the towers service the lifts and support the ends of concrete bridges spanning from the main hospital block. In contrast to the sleek, all-welded joints of the diagrid, the lift-tower detailing expresses the process of fabrication and erection, as well as its stability. The language of steel fabrication speaks through the welded plates with their external stiffeners, an unmistakable sign of structural steel (Figure 7.19). Then the method of erection is expressed by the doubling of horizontal plates where sections of the towers are joined – bolted together not by ordinary nuts and bolts, but by stainless-steel bolts and elegant cap nuts. Double-cantilever beams are some of the vertical sections bolted into place (Figure 7.20). By resisting the overturning moment of the weight of the bridge slab by the tensioned-

Figure 7.18
Evelina Children's Hospital, London, Hopkins Architects, 2005. A steel lift-tower within the conservatory.

Figure 7.19

Towers express steel construction through the use of steel plates and stiffeners.

Figure 7.20

Bolts clamp tower sections together and a double-cantilevered beam supports a concrete bridge slab at one end and is held down at the other by a tensioned rod anchored in the foundations.

Figure 7.21

Hazel Wood School, Southampton, UK, Hampshire County Council Architects Department, 1990. The hall roof structure is typical of that for the whole school.

down rod attached to the other end of the cantilever, simple and minimal bolting between the sections of the tower was possible.

Exposed structural detailing also plays a dominant architectural role at Hazel Wood School, Southampton. Throughout the building, circular wooden columns support a glue-laminated lattice roof (Figure 7.21). While exhibiting the layering so typical of wooden construction, the roof structure takes that characteristic a step further by interlacing the beam chords and spacing them apart with timber blocking. The transverse beams spanning the school hall read as shallow vierendeel trusses. Additional structural layering occurs locally above the columns where short glue-laminated beams cantilever either side of column centrelines to receive loads from the two-way lattice beams. These beam–column details recall the wooden brackets of vernacular Japanese construction (Figure 7.22).

Wooden construction is also strongly expressed in a building at Hedmark Museum, Hamar, that protects historic ruins (Figure 7.23). While the post-and-beam structural form of this building is conventional, the structural detailing is very innovative. The posts and beams, rather than typical single rectangular members, are V-shaped, constructed from two 90 mm-wide glue-laminated wood members. Their unusual cross-section is very advantageous architecturally. First, posts and beams are almost as wide as they are deep (approximately

Figure 7.22

Short beams transfer loads from the lattice roof to a column.

Figure 7.23

Hedmark Museum, Hamar, Norway, Sverre Fehn, 2005. A simple protective building structured and largely clad by V-shaped posts and beams. (Camille Cladouhos)

Figure 7.24

FABRICA (Benetton Communication Research Centre), Treviso, Italy, Tadao Ando & Associates, 2000. Concrete construction and materiality are clearly expressed in the structural elements defining the sunken courtyard.

1200 mm). This results in roof and walls consisting of just structure and narrow glazed strips. The absence of cladding and lining materials increases the simplicity and clarity of construction. Second, deeply textured surfaces line both inside and out.

Whereas timber construction dominates the interior architecture of Hazel Wood School, concrete structure plays a similarly strong aesthetic role at the Benetton Research

Centre, Treviso. Exposed concrete dominates the interior of this almost entirely underground project. In typical Tadao Ando fashion, detailing expresses the construction process (Figure 7.24). Precisely spaced form-tie recesses, precision alignment of formwork joints, and a high standard of concrete finish reflect the care devoted to structural detailing. Surface finishing is especially important here because of the plainness of all other column and wall details.

By restricting himself to circular and rectangular formwork, Ando does not exploit the plasticity of concrete like Santiago Calatrava. Several of Calatrava's works, such as the cast-in-place concrete Stadelhofen Railroad Station underground mall, Zürich (Figures 12.33 and 12.34), display comprehensively the extent to which the plasticity of concrete can be expressed. These buildings are essays in the architectural exploitation and expression of cast-in-place concrete as a structural material.

In comparison to cast-in-place concrete, the typical characteristics of precast concrete – thin and compact cross-sections, relatively complex forms and repetitive member layout – are exemplified in the ferry terminal and office building, Hamburg (Figure 7.25). Thirty-three pairs of precast-concrete A-frames define the 200 m-long building. Generally placed just inside the exterior skin on each side of the building, each pair of frames supports simply supported beams and suspended floor slabs that span between them.

Figure 7.25
Ferry terminal and office building, Hamburg, Germany, Alsop and Störmer, 1993. Partially exposed precast-concrete A-frames.

Figure 7.26
Precast bracket and frame junction.

Several frame bases are exposed within the ferry terminal waiting-room. They support precast-concrete cantilever brackets, similarly detailed as the main frames, to extend the terminal area beyond the main building line (Figure 7.26). Given their skeletal form, blue-painted finish and smallness of cross-section, the brackets could actually be mistaken for steel construction. The architect clearly articulates the pin connections between the A-frames and their brackets, and therefore emphasizes the site-jointed nature of the precast components. In both their forms and connections, the brackets and frames are consistent with and expressive of the materiality of precast concrete.

The first of the final two examples where structural materiality and construction are expressed clearly is the Guggenheim Museum, Bilbao. Just enough structure is exposed to explain the construction of the building (Figure 7.27). Although the structure of this remarkable building lies mainly hidden within its billowing and twisted sculptural forms, in several locations its skeletal steel structure is exposed. The most accessible and informative area of this exposure occurs at the tower (Figure 7.28). In conjunction with the long gallery, the tower 'holds' the La Salve Bridge to the main body of the museum. The exposed tower structure, visible from the bridge, explains how other building exterior surfaces are structured. Rather unexpectedly, a conceptually simple triangulated steel framework supports the geometrically complex skins. Compared to the audacious titanium-clad three-dimensional curved surfaces, the adjacent structural details of nuts and bolts and standard steel sections appear crude. Their ordinariness disguises the extent of the underlying structural analytical and design sophistication.

On a far smaller scale, and more overtly than at Bilbao, Frank Gehry expresses the nuts and bolts of structure *inside* the Fisher Center, Annadale-on-Hudson. Curved steel ribs and bent horizontal girts are the means of achieving the dramatic sculptural walls that form a protective skin around the main theatre (Figures 7.29 and 7.30). Steel I-sections, their flanges welded to curved web plates, rise from their foundations and span a four-storey volume to gain support from the concrete walls enclosing the theatre. Braced within their planes, the entire construction of these ribbed walls – the inside surfaces of the stainless-steel cladding sheets, the girts, ties, braces, cleats and even the heads of self-tapping screws that connect the different components together are exposed in a rare architectural move.

Figure 7.27
Guggenheim Museum,
Bilbao, Spain, Frank O. Gehry
& Associates, 1997. View
of the museum from the
La Salve Bridge.

Figure 7.28
The tower structure and its exposed braced framework.

Figure 7.29
Fisher Center, Bard College, Annadale-on-Hudson, USA, Frank O. Gehry &
Associates, 2002. Side elevation with the main entry canopy to the right.

At the Carpentry Training School, Murau, exposure of
structural detailing extends beyond 'informing' to 'educating'
(Figure 7.31). The wooden roof structure can be envisaged
playing an important pedagogical role in the life of the school.
Given that the structural members of the workshop-spanning
trusses are ordinary straight lengths of glue-laminated wood,
their visually prominent connections awaken interest in
structural detailing. The deep roof structure relies upon steel
plates to join its members together. The plates, inserted into
and fixed to the wood by pressed-in steel dowels, are then
bolted together (Figure 7.32).

Figure 7.30
Exposed construction of an exterior wall that curves towards the theatre roof.

Figure 7.32
Web members connect to a truss bottom chord.

Another more elegant detail, but less visible due to its height above ground, occurs at the level of clerestory glazing (Figure 7.33). Stainless-steel plates are bolted to wooden studs to extend their height to eaves level. This unusual detail enables the combined wood–steel studs to span vertically between the floor slab and the roof diaphragm to which they transfer wind face-loads. Importantly, the detail expresses the fact that the exterior walls do not provide vertical support to the roof – the thin vertical plates are weak in compression. Under lateral loads, however, they bear horizontally against

Figure 7.31
Carpentry School, Murau,
Austria, E. Giselbrecht, 1992.
End elevation.

Figure 7.33
Face-loads only are transferred through the vertical plate-rod connection.

a steel rod that passes through their vertical slots. This detail simultaneously allows horizontal load transfer and unrestrained vertical movement between the plates, studs and roof structure.

Structural actions

Detailing that expresses structural actions within members and connections also provides opportunities for architectural enrichment. According to Collins, Soufflot, the eighteenth-century Rationalist architect who reacted against the ornamental embellishment of structural details, advocated 'simply limiting aesthetic effects to those which logically followed from the nature of the structural component, and designing those components in accordance with rational criteria'.[6] But the pendulum has swung since the 1700s. Now, architects such as Louis Kahn react against bland concrete and wooden members muted by their rectilinear shape in both

cross-section and longitudinal elevation, and 'off-the-shelf' steel sections that satisfy nothing other than the outcome of engineering calculations. Referring to the pervasive use of steel I-beams, Khan criticized structural engineers who used excessive factors-of-safety in conjunction with steel beam standardization. In his view, this led to overly large member sizes 'and further limited the field of engineering expression, stifling the creation of the more graceful forms which the stress diagrams indicated'.[7]

Two distinct types of expression are found in the following examples where detailing expresses structural actions, including bending moment or stress diagrams. In the first, detailing expresses the variation of structural actions, and nothing else. In the second type, to use Stanford Anderson's words, 'The functionally adequate form must be adapted so as to give expression to its function. The sense of bearing provided by the entasis of Greek columns became the touchstone of this concept.'[8] In other words, designers utilize elaborate detailing in order to clarify the expression of structural action. First, then, we begin with unelaborated structural detailing.

The exposed first-floor beams at Jussieu University, Paris, express their internal structural actions. Steel box-beams, curved both in elevation and plan, express the relative intensity of their bending moments (Figure 7.34). The beams are simply-supported and their elevational profiles take on the parabolic forms of their bending moment diagrams. We note in passing that the architect has privileged the

Figure 7.34
Jussieu University, Paris, Edouart Albert, 1965. Beam geometry expresses the bending moment diagram.

articulation of bending stress, rather than shear stress. The latter, which usually increases linearly from a value of zero at a mid-span to reach its maximum value at the ends of a span, is rarely expressed. Certainly, the floor trusses at the Centre Pompidou, Paris, are an exception (Figure 12.26). Their diagonal web members increase in diameter as they approach the truss supports in response to the increasing value of shear force.

By varying the beam flange width in plan at the university, the beams narrow at their ends to match the diameter of the tubular steel columns into which they frame. The level of transparency provided by these small-diameter columns is especially appreciated given the 'sagging' beam profiles. Zannos suggests that designers should avoid this type of structural detailing:

> If it is indeed true that we dislike forms that appear weak because their shape is deformed or seems to have been deformed by loading, it is quite natural that we prefer forms that are in contrast to that shape. We may thus propose the following law of aesthetics: a form . . . agrees with our aesthetic intuition – and, hence, satisfies us aesthetically – if its shape contrasts the shape that would have resulted if the form had been deformed by loading.[9]

In this building, rather than the sagging beam soffits creating the sense of oppression that might be experienced in a more enclosed space, they lead the eye away from any potential visual heaviness towards the light and the open space on either side of the building.

The Stadelhofen Railway Station, Zürich, comprises a number of steel and concrete structures, all of which illustrate to some degree detailing that expresses structural actions. For example, consider an escalator entrance structure (Figure 7.35). Like all other cantilever beams in the station, the cantilever tapers to a point, approximating the shape of its bending moment diagram. Near its end, it supports an unusually configured and orientated two-pinned frame whose member profiles also match their bending moment diagrams. The form of this hanging lower structure recalls the dynamic form of a swimmer diving. Under each of the two canopies of the escalator entrance, smaller interior beams cantilever from tubular torsion-resistant beams. The circular bolted plates express the transfer of torsion into the main members (Figure 7.36).

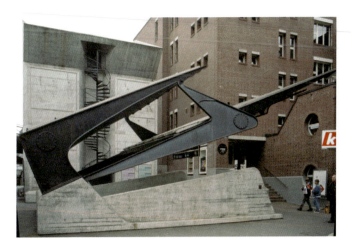

Figure 7.35
Stadelhofen Railway Station, Zürich, Switzerland, Santiago Calatrava, 1990. Escalator entrance structure.

Figure 7.36
Upper cantilever-to-torsion-beam connection, with smaller canopy cantilevers in the background.

At another railway station, the Stratford Regional Station, London, structural actions similarly inspire expressive detailing (Figure 7.37). Although the focus here is upon just one detail, the base-connection of the portal frames, other details, such as how the primary curved frames taper to points where they are propped, equally express structural action. Each frame base-connection joins the frame rigidly to a concrete substructure. This base rigidity helps the frame resist gravity and lateral loads, and minimizes its depth.

High-strength bars tension the base-plates down to the concrete via cast-steel bases. Rather than adopt usual construction practice whereby a column base-plate connects

Figure 7.37
Stratford Regional Station, London, UK, Wilkinson Eyre, 1999. Curved columns spring from cast-steel bases.

Figure 7.38
Lyon School of Architecture, France, Jourda et Perraudin, 1988. A cast-steel shoe expresses the compression load-path.

directly to a concrete foundation by vertical bolts whose shafts are concealed, this detailing expresses the clamping of the base-plate. Not only are the bolt shafts visible, but their inclination aligns them parallel to the lines of stress within the frame member. The shaping and roundness of the base exemplifies the 'adapting' of form, as mentioned by Anderson, above. The base expresses and elaborates how tensions from the embedded bars compress the base-plate against the concrete, and how this compression stress that acts upon the base is dispersed uniformly at the steel-base–concrete interface.

Connections of wooden members at the Lyon School of Architecture present a more overt example of elaborating structural details for the sake of improved clarity of expression. Delicate cast-steel shoes provide the transition detail at both ends of the inclined struts and vertical columns (Figure 7.38). The elaboration of these details takes the form of four ribs that fan out from the steel-pin housing, and spread over the member depth, expressing the flow of compression force just as effectively as do the attached shafts of Gothic piers. The ribs illustrate how force is transferred from a relatively large and soft wooden cross-section and channelled into a far smaller and harder steel pin.

The detail is adapted for beam–column connections, although the expression of (shear) force flowing from beam to column through the castings is less obvious (Figure 7.39). What *is* clear, however, is an expression of clamping action – of the timber beam being clamped between castings that

are fixed to the wood by screws top and bottom. Rather than expressing load paths, the clamping nature of the connection mechanism is communicated visually. This detail is a reminder of Chernikhov's seven constructivist joints, each of which expresses a different nature of connection.[10] Before leaving this connection detail, note that its unusual form allows a down-pipe to pass through it, just millimetres from the end of the beam. This is a simple example of how the necessity for structure and services integration frequently gives rise to inventive and expressive structural forms and details.[11]

The final example where detailing is inspired by structural action expresses another form of connectivity – clasping.

Figure 7.39
A beam–column connection that allows for a down-pipe to pass through where required.

Figure 7.40
Palau Güell, Barcelona, Spain, Antoni Gaudí, 1880. Cantilevering brackets clasp the oriel floor.

Figure 7.41
Glasgow School of Art, UK, Charles Rennie Mackintosh, 1899. Truss forms inspired by medieval construction.

An oriel on the main façade of Palau Güell, Barcelona, projects over the street and is supported underneath by short cantilevers (Figure 7.40). Their rounded profiles are mirrored by a row of similar members above the roof. Both sets of cantilevers appear to be doing more than just supporting gravity loads. Their tips wrap around and against the horizontal slabs as if to prevent them from sliding towards the street. Taking the form of bent fingers holding a mobile phone, they read as clasps – like those restraining jewels in their settings, holding the oriel back against the main building.

Other sources of inspiration

To conclude this study of expressive and responsive detailing, two examples are noted where structural details are inspired by sources from outside the building or its programme. First, the eclectic structural detailing of the Glasgow School of Art roof structures, where above the main stair and surrounding exhibition space decorative timber trusses evoke images of medieval construction (Figure 7.41). In another space, a roof bracket detail indicates a Japanese influence.

Figure 7.42
Post-Modern Art Museum, Stuttgart, Germany, James Stirling, Wilford & Associates, 1984. Classical detailing of a post-and-beam entrance structure.

Figure 7.43
Mushroom reinforced concrete columns in a gallery.

At the Post-Modern Art Museum, Stuttgart, structural details also draw upon a diverse range of external sources (Figures 7.42 and 7.43). The columns and lintel that frame an exterior entrance clearly express their classical origins. Inside the building, concrete mushroom columns are exposed in several spaces. They evoke images of the flat-slab columns that were introduced in the early 1900s and, in particular, those columns that support the roof of Frank Lloyd Wright's 1930s Johnson Wax administration building, Racine, Wisconsin.

Summary

Having defined structural detailing as the configuration, shaping and finishing of members and their connections, this chapter explored how detailing makes significant architectural contributions to buildings by its expressive nature. An analysis of observed structural details suggests that most express or respond to some aspect of the building of which they are part.

Examples illustrated details that relate to architectural form, building function, materiality and construction, and structural actions. Detailing that expresses structural actions can either express states of stress within members or articulate structural connectivity, like clamping or clasping. Sources of detailing inspiration also lie completely outside the building and its programme.

The multiplicity of examples, the sheer diversity of expressive and responsive details, and the different aesthetic qualities of details all indicate the enormous potential for exposed structural detailing to enhance architecture.

Notes

1. A. Ogg, *Architecture in steel: the Australian context*, Red Hill, ACT: Royal Australian Institute of Architects, 1987, p. 44.
2. Louis Khan, quoted in K. Frampton, *Studies in tectonic culture: the poetics of construction in nineteenth and twentieth century architecture*, Cambridge, MA: Massachusetts Institute of Technology, 1995, p. 227.
3. F. Jones, *'Outside the Pale': the architecture of Fay Jones*, Fayettville, AR: Department of Arkansas Heritage, 1999, pp. 48 and 54.
4. C. Balmond, *informal*, Munich: Prestel, 2002, p. 88.
5. J. Murphy, 'A grand gateway', *Progessive Architecture* 68(12), 1987, 95–105, at 104.
6. P. Collins, *Changing ideals in modern architecture 1750–1950*, 2nd edn, Montreal: McGill-Queen's University Press, 1998, p. 127.
7. Louis Khan, quoted in Frampton, *Studies in tectonic culture*, p. 210.
8. Anderson is quoted in the essay 'Towards a critical regionalism: six points for an architecture of resistance', in K. Frampton (ed.), *Labour, work and architecture: collected essays on architecture and design*, London: Phaidon, 2002, p. 88.
9. A. Zannos, *Form and structure in architecture: the role of statical function*, New York: Van Nostrand Reinhold, 1987, p. 162.
10. Joint types such as penetration, clamping, embracing, mounting, interfacing, coupling and integration are defined and discussed in J. Reno, 'Constructing beginnings: a role for building technology in architectural design education', *Journal of Architectural Education* 45(3), 1992, 161–70.
11. A. W. Charleson, 'Aesthetics of architectural structural and services integration', *Proceedings of the 32nd Annual Conference of the Australia and New Zealand Architectural Science Association*, 1998, 145–50.

eight

Structure and light

Introduction

Following the view that architectural space exists when it is experienced by the senses, particularly sight, Van Meiss considers architectural design to be 'the art of placing and controlling light sources in space'.[1] He understands light sources to include actual light sources such as a windows, as well as illuminated objects like enclosing surfaces or other architectural elements that could include structural members. From this perspective, structure is potentially an important architectural element – both as a source of light, where light passes through it, or illuminates and reflects off it, and as a controller of how and where light enters a space.

When stone and masonry load-bearing wall construction dominated previous periods of architectural history, openings for light could be considered the absence of structure. Millet's description of the relationship between structure and light is particularly applicable to that former era. Focusing more on structure's potential to control light than function as a source of light itself, she writes: 'Structure defines the place where light enters. The structural module provides the rhythm of light, no light. Where the structure is, there is no light. Between the structural elements there is light.'[2] However, since the introduction of metal skeletal structural forms during the nineteenth century, it is no longer a case of *either* structure *or* light in architectural space – both can coexist. Slender structural members have a minimal impact upon the amount of light entering a space. Whereas the former prevalence of masonry structure, in plan and elevation, necessitated its penetration in order to introduce light, in current architectural practice daylight requirements are more often achieved by choice of structural form and detailing.

Contemporary structure, with its relative slenderness, and small plan 'footprint', can usually meet the need for natural light.

Depending upon its configuration, structure either inhibits or facilitates the ingress of light. In a building with perimeter structure that does not exclude natural light, structure relates to light in one of four modes: as a source of light, where, for example, light passes through a roof truss to enter a space; to maximize light, by minimizing the shadow effect of structure; to modify light, by reflecting and diffusing it; and, occasionally, for light to affect our perception of structure.

The following sections of this chapter discuss each of these modes, but before moving on to them, Louis Kahn's contribution to the integration of structure and light must be acknowledged. Consider one of Kahn's developments – light-filled columns:

> As early as 1954, he had the idea that the column could be hollowed out so that its periphery became the filter for light entering the column . . . In 1961 Kahn began the Mikveh Israel Synagogue Project in Philadelphia. Here he inserted hollow columns into the exterior walls at intervals. These nonstructural cylinders act as diffusion chambers. Daylight shines through their exterior openings, ricochets around the inside of the columns, and filters subtly through openings into the synagogue . . . Kahn was beginning to use the hollow column as a sophisticated light-regulating device.[3]

Kahn went on to use structural columns as light-regulating members in the National Assembly Building at Dacca, but the Kimbell Art Museum is perhaps the best-known building to illustrate his aphorism 'Structure is the giver of light.'[4] Daylight penetrates through longitudinal slits in the vault-like shell roofs only to be reflected up against their concave surfaces. Light that is uniform in intensity and diffuse in quality illuminates the artworks. Structure also functions as both source and modifier of light in some of his other buildings. The Philip Exeter Library is a notable example. Roof light entering the full-height central atrium reflects off two-storey-deep concrete beams that span from diagonally opposite corners:

> The giant X beams are visually scaled to the height of the space, they also act as baffles and registers for the clerestory light . . . In the central space of Exeter, a sober, grave, and noble character is realised, not only by the interaction of the indirect *lumière mysterieuse*, filtering down the grey walls from above, but by the sombreness and ashlar-like articulation of the concrete screen walls.[5]

Source of light

This section explores examples where structure functions as a primary source of direct light, rather than as a source of modified or reflected light, as exemplified by Kahn's works. While the sun is clearly the source of all natural light, the term *source of light* is to be understood as describing the method of admitting natural light into a building. After noting how some structural forms facilitate entry of daylight into a building, we observe how open structural forms like trusses, and even areas where structural members are normally connected, admit light. Several examples then illustrate a common situation where structural members define the ingress of natural light. Finally, attention turns to artificial light sources that are fully integrated with structure, in contrast to the usual practice of simply mounting or hanging them from structural members.

Some structural forms are far more suited than others to allow daylight to penetrate into building interiors. For example, the skeletal quality of moment or rigid frames is more conducive to the passage of light than opaque structural walls. However, other less common structural forms also provide opportunities to admit light. These tend to occur where different structural systems within the one building meet, as in the case of the catenary and mast system at Hall 26, Hanover (see Figures 3.17 and 3.18). Light penetrates the roof where

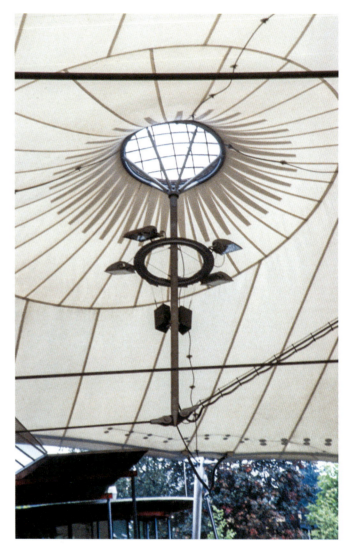

Figure 8.1
Stellingen Ice Skating Rink and Velodrome, Hamburg, Germany, Silcher, Werner + Partners, 1996. Daylight enters the junction between the flying strut and the fabric membrane.

the catenaries connect to the masts. In another example, at the Stellingen Ice Rink, Hamburg, the junctions between points of compression support and the fabric roof serve as direct light sources. Even though the translucent fabric admits a small percentage of external light, openings in the fabric beneath the mast-tips and above the flying-struts explicitly invite daylight into the space (see Figures 3.13, 3.14 and 8.1).

The most common situation where structure functions as a primary light source occurs where light passes through an open or skeletal structure, like a truss, while being excluded from surrounding areas by opaque cladding. Architects utilize

Figure 8.2
San Francisco International Airport, USA, Skidmore Owings & Merrill LLP, 2000. A side two-dimensional truss transforms into three dimensions over the central span of the terminal.

the width, and occasionally the depth, of open structural members as primary daylight sources. Structure rarely acts as a longitudinal conduit for daylight. Well-known precedents are limited to Kahn's hollow columns and some of the tubular lattice-columns at Toyo Ito's Sendai Mediatheque (see Figures 3.58 and 3.59).[6]

Daylight is introduced into the central area of San Francisco International Airport through specially shaped trusses. While narrow skylights are positioned immediately above the top chords of the two-dimensional trusses located near generously glazed side walls, the trusses in the middle of the building's plan widen to become sources of light (Figures 8.2 and 8.3). Although still maintaining the elevational profile of their neighbours that are adjacent to the walls, these internal trusses have a lenticular geometry introduced in plan. Their entire upper surfaces are fully glazed but direct sunlight is excluded by tautly stretched translucent fabric. On a sunny day, the space under these trusses is more brightly illuminated than the side areas that gain light directly through the adjacent walls. Whereas the diagonal members in the side planar trusses consist of both steel tubes and tension-rods, the central three-dimensional trusses use fine rods only to maximize the intensity of light.

At the Dome Leisure Centre, Doncaster, triangular roof trusses project above the roof plane that attaches to the truss

Figure 8.3
San Francisco International Airport. Light passes through a three-dimensional truss.

Figure 8.4

Dome Leisure Centre, Doncaster, UK, FaulknerBrowns Architects, 1989. A glazed truss-to-column connection.

Figure 8.5

Kew Swimming and Recreation Centre, Melbourne, Australia, Daryl Jackson Architects, 1990. Light penetrates the truss that defines the step in the roof.

bottom-chords (Figure 8.4). Where the trusses are glazed, their sloping sides function as skylights. The Carpentry School, Murau, displays a similar approach (see Figure 7.31). Here the roof plane meets the primary truss half-way between the top- and bottom-chords. The upper half of the sloping sides of the truss are glazed. Light also enters from perimeter clerestory glazing.

A stepped roof form at the Kew Swimming and Recreation Centre, Melbourne, provides another alternative to conventional surface-mounted light sources, such as roof skylights. The step in the roof becomes a near-vertical glazed surface. It also creates a more interesting exterior form and

interior space compared to a horizontal roof and skylight (Figure 8.5). The truss depth (rather than its width) determines daylighting levels. Natural light passes through the truss that spans the length of the building, into the main pool area. Given its overall lightness, the fineness of its tubular members and neatly welded joints, the truss itself is an attractive architectural element.

Structure also acts as a light source, albeit infrequently, where light passes through an area of structure normally regarded, at least by structural engineers, as a critical joint region. The Baumschulenweg Crematorium, Berlin, where light audaciously enters the condolence hall first through annuli at the column–roof-plate junctions and, second, at the longitudinal wall–roof connections, was visited in Chapter 2. Both structural junctions, usually important from the perspective of gravity and lateral loads, have had their load transfer mechanisms modified for the sake of light (see Figures 2.12 and 2.13).

Other cases of light passing through structural joints are exemplified in two sporting facilities. At the Stellingen Ice Rink, Hamburg, mentioned previously, areas in the vicinity of the fabric and its supports are well suited for introducing light. The need for the fabric–steel interfaces to be dispersed rather than be concentrated, in order to avoid puncturing or tearing the highly stressed fabric, provides such an opportunity (see Figure 8.1).

In the second example, light passes through joints into the Sant Jordi Sports Hall, Barcelona (Figure 8.6). The unique feature of these joints is that they express the hinge or fold-lines necessitated by the Pantadome system of roof erection. In this construction method the roof structure is first assembled on the ground and then raised by hydraulic jacks. As the roof rises, hinges allow the central dome and peripheral areas to fold relative to each other. When the roof is in its final position, additional structural members lock the hinge zones to stabilize the structure before de-propping.[7] Although many small skylights over the central dome also contribute to the lighting levels, the temporary hinged-joint regions, later made rigid, are the primary light sources.

While designers arrange for light to pass through open structural systems or connections between structural members, the reality is that most light enters a building through penetrations in the external walls and roof cladding. These are usually positioned and shaped to respect the layout and geometry of the internal or external supporting structure. Windows and skylights are normally positioned between structural members. The Burrell Gallery restaurant, Glasgow – a wooden and glass 'lean-to' that wraps around the south-east corner of the gallery – provides a simple yet attractive example (Figure 8.7). Natural light entering the fully glazed enclosure passes between closely spaced 330 mm × 100 mm glue-laminated wooden posts and rafters. While a strong yet simple rhythm of structure and light characterizes the space, structure not only limits the daylight but to some extent modifies it. Given that the posts and rafters are spaced at little more than twice their depths, the members create shade and also reflect light off their vertical surfaces.

Light enters far more dramatically between structural members of the reinforced-concrete catenary of the Portuguese Pavilion, Lisbon (see Figures 3.15 and 8.8). An unprecedented design decision led to the removal of a narrow strip of concrete at the northern end of the catenary that would normally cover the tension-rods. Consequently, above the podium where visiting dignitaries to Expo '98 were publicly welcomed, sunlight filters between exposed stainless-steel rods. Striated shadows pattern the

Figure 8.6
Sant Jordi Sports Hall, Barcelona, Spain, Arata Izosaki & Associates, 1990. Light enters through constructional fold-line joints, as in this corner of the roof structure.

Figure 8.7
Burrell Gallery, Glasgow, UK, Barry Gasson Architects, 1983. Repetitive yet attractive glass and timber restaurant enclosure.

Figure 8.8
Portuguese Pavilion, Lisbon, Portugal, Alvaro Siza, 1998. Light passes though the slit in the concrete slab, and between the stainless-steel tendons.

buttress walls that withstand the catenary tensions. The project's structural engineer, Cecil Balmond, describes the effect poetically:

> Made out of concrete, the curve flies seventy metres without apparent effort – from afar it looks as if it is made of paper. And at the last moment of span, just before the safety of the vertical anchors, the form is cut. Lines of cables cross the void instead, pinning themselves to strong abutments. This de-materialisation is both a denial and a release. Weight vanishes and the mass hovers. Like the underbelly of some flying saucer the canopy floats. It is a trick of the light.[8]

The railway station at Satolas Airport, Lyon, is the final example where structure defines the extent of penetrations for natural light. Two rows of skylights run the length of the train platforms. Each diamond-shaped area of glazing reflects the geometrical pattern of the underlying structural ribs (Figures 8.9 and 8.10). In section, structure reads as a series of portal frames, but not of the type found in most buildings. Each frame, skewed to the main axis, expresses a sense of lightness and elegance with its outwardly inclined columns and cambered beams. The intersections and bifurcations of the frames create the attractive and flowing skeletal framework into which the skylights are so well integrated.

The Satolas Airport structure also integrates artificial lighting effectively – in a far more sophisticated manner than merely providing a means of support for surface-mounted or hung light-fittings. Lights that illuminate the ribs soaring over the outer two station platforms are recessed within sculptured stub-columns (Figure 8.11). Located between the perimeter diagonal struts and the roof ribs, the lighting details recall Calatrava's similar but less ghoulish integration

Figure 8.9
Railway station at Satolas Airport, Lyon, France, Santiago Calatrava, 1994. Glazing centred over the main concourse.

Figure 8.10
A view across the concourse. Glazed areas are integrated with the pattern of ribs.

of structure and artificial light at the Stadelhofen Railway Station, Zürich (Figure 8.12). At several locations in the underground mall, the light sockets that are recessed into rounded concave concrete surfaces read as teardrops. The floor structure above the lights is treated just as sensitively by being pared back to elegant tapering ribs with glass-block pavers admitting natural light.

Figure 8.11
Recessed lights in stub columns.

Figure 8.12
Stadelhofen Railway Station, Zürich, Switzerland, Santiago Calatrava, 1990. Integration of structure and artificial lighting.

Maximizing light

Where requiring high levels of daylight or transparency through the building skin, architects adopt a number of stances towards structural detailing. Maximum daylight implies reducing the silhouette or shadow of structural members. The two most common methods are either to minimize structural member sizes or to penetrate typically sized members. Transparent structural members are also becoming increasingly popular.

Detailing to minimize structural size

Chapter 7 discussed how the dual architectural qualities of complexity and lightness arise where structural dimensions are minimized. Simple calculations show that if one tension-rod is replaced by two smaller-diameter rods with a combined strength equal to the original, the area of the structural silhouette is reduced by approximately 30 per cent. With four rods this reduction in silhouette reaches 50 per cent – the more members, the more light, but also more visual complexity.

At 237 m long, 79 m wide and 28 m high, the vaulted Trade Fair Glass Hall, Leipzig, was the largest single-volume glass building of the twentieth century. The steel exoskeletal structure consists of ten primary trusses that stabilize a grid-shell (Figures 8.13 and 8.14). Triangular in cross-section, the arched trusses are fabricated from relatively small-diameter steel tubes whose varied wall thicknesses reflect the intensity of structural actions. A resolute strategy to achieve maximum transparency excluded potentially large-scale members from consideration. As Ian Ritchie, project architect, explains:

> Transparency was a key design objective. We wanted to minimize the structural silhouette, and in fact the total area covered by structure in any radial view met our adopted criterion of no more than 15 per cent. (This percentage, arrived at by analysing many of the glass structures we have designed, represents the maximum interference which allows the overall design to have a strong feeling of lightness.)[9]

Even though completed back in 1986, the three glazed conservatories known as Les Serres on the south façade of the Cité des Sciences et de l'Industrie, Paris, still represent a fine example of structure designed to maximize light (Figures 8.15 and 8.16). Finely detailed horizontal cable-beam girts span 8 m between vertical steel posts to support face-loads acting on the 2 m-square glass panels. An enlarged version of the girts transfers horizontal loads from the intermediate vertical

Figure 8.13

Trade Fair Glass Hall, Leipzig, Germany, Ian Ritchie Architects, 1996. Exterior trusses support the vaulted grid-shell.

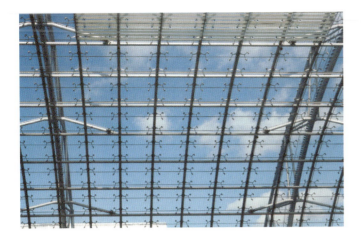

Figure 8.14
Trade Fair Glass Hall, Leipzig. Trusses and the grid-shell as seen from within the hall.

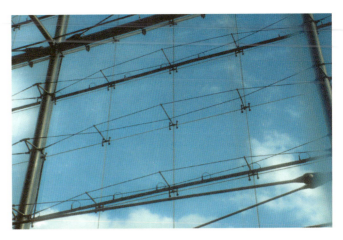

Figure 8.16
Cité des Sciences et de l'Industrie, Paris. A hierarchy of prestressed cable-beams resist face-loads on the glazed walls.

posts to each side of the 32 m-wide bays. Prestressing the catenary cables to limit the number of structural members acting in compression has enabled this type of detailing to approach the limit of achievable transparency. Glass plays an important structural function by supporting its own weight, hanging from the uppermost tubular steel beams. The transparency of the system is described by one author:

> The tension trusses sit some distance behind the plane of the glass, and the connections to the glass are so light that they seem almost not to touch the glass. This fact, and the lightness of the tension supporting structure,

enhance the feeling of transparency which Fainsilber [the architect] was so keen to achieve. The resulting structure is light and almost ephemeral: the boundary between inside and out is sensitively and lightly defined.[10]

Although not pushing technological boundaries as hard as at Les Serres, the school at Waidhausenstraße, Vienna, also exemplifies structural detailing to maximize daylight. A fully glazed circulation spine and two halls, one for assembly and another for sports, link the southern ends of three conventional concrete classroom blocks. Glazed mono-slope roofs rise from the ground floor to enclose

Figure 8.15
Cité des Sciences et de l'Industrie, Paris, Adrien Fainsilber, 1986. Les Serres or conservatories on the main façade.

Figure 8.17
School at Waidhausenstraße, Vienna, Austria, Helmut Richter, 1995.
Composite steel walkway beams.

Figure 8.18
Triangular cantilever trusses support the mono-slope glazed roof.

the halls and the four-storeyed walkways. Walkway beams
of composite construction reduce individual structural
member sizes to small I-section beams acting as compression
chords, and steel rods below them resist the tension
component of the bending moments (Figure 8.17). The
assembly hall roof structure cantilevers from a rigid support
base to the roof of the classroom blocks. In this case

structural lightness is a consequence of generously deep
three-dimensional trusses and their relatively fine tubular
members (Figure 8.18).

The Carré d'Art, Nîmes, is the final example of detailing that
minimizes structural size to maximize light. In order to respect
the height of the surrounding buildings in its historic city,
half the library and contemporary art museum is built below
ground. Although the lower three basement floors are not
daylit, a six-storey central atrium allows natural light to reach
deep inside the building. The problem of channelling light
through a space containing the main stairway is solved by
the choice of glass stair-treads (Figure 8.19). As one reviewer
comments: 'The purpose of the glass staircases becomes
clear in descent to the lower levels. Daylight transforms what
would otherwise have been a gloomy pit into a magical grotto.
It is like standing under a waterfall.'[11]

Having successfully brought light down into the atrium, as
much light as possible then needs to be moved horizontally
into the surrounding spaces. Structural detailing and modifying
structural configuration enhance this process, more than by
reducing structural size. In order to maintain planar concrete
ceiling soffits, upstand beams span between columns. The
difference in depth between the beams and slabs creates a
space for services under the raised floors. Where the beams
on each storey frame the perimeter of the atrium and also
the perimeter walls, they are offset from the columns in plan,
and their sides facing the light are bevelled (Figure 8.20).

Figure 8.19
Carré d'Art, Nîmes, France, Sir Norman Foster and Partners, 1993. Glass stair-treads and the supporting structure in the atrium.

Figure 8.20
Bevelled and set-back beams.

This arrangement not only visually slims the floor system but, more importantly, significantly increases the quantity of daylight entering interior spaces.

Penetrations in structural members

Although penetrations through structural members are normally considered aspects of structural detailing and could have been discussed in the previous section of this chapter that considered structure as a source of light, such a common and significant response to the need for daylight warrants specific discussion.

Before considering several contemporary examples, two cases of historic interest deserve mention – first, Henri Labrouste's stackroom at the Bibliothèque Nationale, Paris. Giedion describes the highly penetrated floors that are located under a glazed roof:

Cast-iron floor plates in a gridiron pattern permit the daylight to penetrate the stacks from top to bottom. Floor plates of this open design seem to have been used first in the engine rooms of steamships . . . Nevertheless, observing them in our day, we recognize in the manner in which light penetrates the grillwork of the iron floor the germ of new artistic possibilities.[12]

Since the popularity of stiletto-heeled shoes, steel-grating floors have limited application, but as observed at the Carré d'Art, glass flooring is now a well-established substitute.

The other notable historic example of light-enhancing structural penetrations occurs in Frank Lloyd Wright's Usonian House, Mount Vernon. Concrete blocks, L-shaped in plan, are placed and stacked vertically to form U-shaped columns. Both faces of blocks on one side of the U are penetrated and glazed. Objects displayed on glass shelves within the column are illuminated by daylight.[13]

Returning to contemporary examples of structural penetrations maximizing light, we revisit the United Airlines Terminal, Chicago (see Figure 7.16). Circular penetrations through beam webs appear to contribute to its well-lit spaces, but given that the lighting designer does not mention them in his lighting strategy, their contribution to overall lighting levels is probably quite low.[14] At the Schools of Geography and Engineering, Marne-la-Vallée, webs of steel beams are perforated by small-diameter holes (Figure 8.21). This method of introducing light through steel sections is likely to be more widely exploited in the future due to its greater subtlety. But as in the United Airlines Terminal, its true value might lie in making the structure *appear* lighter, rather than measurably increasing the intensity of daylight.

Windows invariably penetrate concrete structural walls, but smaller and more numerous penetrations may be appropriate when daylight rather than views is sought. Behind the striking façade of the Mexican Embassy, Berlin, sits a circular atrium,

Figure 8.22
Mexican Embassy, Berlin, Germany, González de León and Serrano, 2000. A penetrated circular wall forms part of the atrium.

its exterior wall essentially a partial concrete drum (Figure 8.22). 'Capped by a massive skylight and punctured on its curved walls by cylindrical portholes, the drum is all about natural light. It evokes the "lightness" of concrete, its dual character, simultaneously delicate and weighty.'[15]

Figure 8.21
Schools of Geography and Engineering, Marne-la-Vallée, Paris, France, Chaix & Morel, 1996. A finely perforated web of a steel beam.

Transparent structure

Secondary and tertiary transparent structural elements in the form of glass window mullions and glass blocks have been

Figure 8.23
Broadfield House Glass Museum, West Midlands, UK, Design Antenna, 1994. Interior of the glass extension.

Figure 8.24
Town Administrative Centre, Saint-Germaine-en-Laye, Paris, France, Brunet and Saunier, 1995. Glass columns support roof beams.

used for many years. The Sainsbury Centre for Visual Arts, Norwich, with its full-height glass mullions, was completed in 1977 (see Figure 5.12). However, only recently has designers' improved knowledge of glass technology led to it undertaking primary structural roles. Although glass is currently the preferred transparent structural material, no doubt alternative materials will be developed in the future.

A lean-to extension at Broadfield House Glass Museum, UK, relies entirely upon glass structural elements (Figure 8.23). Laminated glass plates form vertical posts in glazed walls and support glass rafters at glued mortice and tenon joints.[16] Wall and roof glazing provides in-plane bracing resistance.

In the Town Administrative Centre, Saint-Germaine-en-Laye, in what is considered a world first, laminated glass columns designed for an axial load of 6 tonnes support atrium roof beams (Figures 8.24 and 8.25). The columns, cruciform in section, possess a greenish hue. Any greater degree of transparency would render them almost invisible and therefore hazardous to building users. In this public space the columns delineate circulation and waiting areas from staff work stations. The structure subdivides and orders space without significantly reducing visibility and security. The columns slightly obstruct daylight passing through the glazed walls of an internal garden, but such a potentially small shadow effect is of no consequence given the transparent roof. Excessive glare and thermal gain are likely to be far more serious.

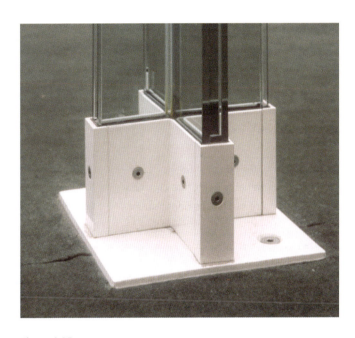

Figure 8.25
A glass column base detail.

During the conversion and refurbishment of a 1920s post office into the Apple Store, New York City, the architects maximized lightness, transparency and a sense of spaciousness with the provision of a central glass staircase supported by glass load-bearing walls (Figure 8.26). The space under the stairs remains a void except for the glass fins that provide transverse stability and enhance the vertical load-carrying capacity of the glass walls. Below the levels of the stair-treads the wall thickness comprises three layers of

Figure 8.26
Apple Store, New York, USA, Bohlin Cywinski Jackson, 2002. The central glass staircase.

Figure 8.27
Stair-treads connect to the glass wall.

glass. Two laminated panes support the handrail. The glass landing and stair-treads are laminated from four layers of glass. Elegant circular stainless-steel fixings connect the glass panes together to achieve a truly transparent structure (Figure 8.27).

In the previous examples, glass structural elements are either in compression or function as simply supported beams. However, the Yurakucho subway glass canopy, located within the Tokyo International Forum complex, cantilevers (Figure 8.28). Simple but inventive, the canopy begins cantilevering from a horizontal torsion beam. Each rib begins with four glass plates, and when the next set of plates cantilevers

Figure 8.28
Yurakucho subway canopy, Tokyo International Forum, Tokyo, Japan, Rafael Viǧnoly Architects, 1996. Diminishing numbers of triangular glass plates in each rib cantilever from each other to form the structural glass canopy.

from the first set, the number of plates is reduced to three. Just one plate forms the tip of the cantilever. As well as the number of plates reducing due to less bending stress towards the tip, each plate is triangulated in elevation. Its shape expresses the pattern of bending stress caused by being loaded at one end and supported both at the other end and at mid-length.

Modifier of light

While structure acts as a source of light and is frequently designed to maximize the quantity of light entering a building, it also modifies the intensity and quality of light. As well as excluding or blocking light by virtue of its opaqueness, structure also filters and reflects light.

Filtering

Numerous closely spaced and often layered structural members filter light. Where structural layout and density evoke the trees of a forest, as in the Oxford University Museum courtyard, daylight is experienced as if filtered through a canopy of tree branches (see Figure 6.43).

Roof structure within the Wöhlen High School auditorium also plays a strong light-filtering role (see Figures 6.22 and 6.23). Daylight enters the hall through clerestory windows above the interior structure. The closely spaced ribs that

Figure 8.30
Shade-structure arches and ribs.

radiate from the primary arches act as light filters. A white-stain finish increases the reflectance of the wood under both natural and artificial lighting.

Santiago Calatrava's fascination with ribbed structures also finds expression in an exterior structure known as L'Umbracle, in the City of Arts and Sciences precinct, Valencia (Figures 8.29 and 8.30). As well as enclosing car parking at ground level, the roof of L'Umbracle functions as a tree-lined garden. An arched and ribbed shade structure encloses the whole area, and while its ribs are more slender and spaced further apart than those at Wöhlen High School, one strongly experiences its light-filtering qualities. Plants growing over the ribs in some areas increase the level of shading.

The interior structure of the Seed House and Forestry Centre, Marche-en-Femenne, also filters light and provides shade (Figures 8.31 and 8.32). Bentwood arches that span the building width support the completely glazed ovoid form. Longitudinal arches provide stability in the orthogonal direction. The combination of closely spaced arches and 100 mm-wide members leads to significant areas of shade, especially where the timbers are lap-spliced. Strong striped patterns of sunlight and shadow enliven the interior spaces.

Reflecting

Structural members screen direct sunlight, but also provide surfaces off which it reflects and then diffuses

Figure 8.29
City of Arts and Sciences, Valencia, Spain, Santiago Calatrava, 1998. L'Umbracle with its garden shade-structure.

Figure 8.31
Seed House
and Forestry
Centre, Marche-
en-Femenne,
Belgium, Samyn
et Associés, 1996.
Exterior view.

Figure 8.32
Shading increases at the splice positions of the transverse arches.

into surrounding space. In these situations structure may be considered a secondary, or even the primary, source of light. The deep atrium beams of Louis Khan's Philip Exeter Library, already mentioned in this chapter, exemplify this interaction between structure and light, even though some

commentators query whether the beams achieve sufficiently high light levels at ground-floor level. They point to the small quantity of direct light admitted through the partially shaded clerestory windows, and the low reflectivity of the grey concrete beams. We have also already observed the light-washed columns in the Baumschulenweg Crematorium, Berlin (see Figure 2.11). The reflected light from these columns can be considered secondary light sources.

Roof beams in the Mönchengladbach Museum receive significantly more direct light than those at the Philip Exeter Library; also, due to their lighter colour, they play a more influential role in screening sunlight and reflecting it into the gallery (Figure 8.33). A similar approach is taken in the Business School gymnasium, Öhringen (Figure 8.34). The white-stained glue-laminated wooden beams that span the width of the hall *reflect* rather than *screen* light. North-facing translucent glazing slopes from a lowered ceiling and up and over the beams that project above the roof line. Their raised location with respect to the roof eliminates any possibility of their screening direct sunlight at the end of a day when the sun's rays are almost horizontal, but the reflectivity of the beams increases the effective width of the glazed

Figure 8.33

Mönchengladbach Museum, Germany, Hans Hollein, 1982. Beams screen and reflect light into the gallery below.

Figure 8.34

Business School, Öhringen, Germany, Günter Behnisch & Partner, 1993. A primary beam with the skylight above and the roof below.

Figure 8.35

Library Square, Vancouver, Canada, Moshe Safdie and Associates Inc., 1995. An uplit vaulted ceiling.

roof areas and therefore the intensity of illumination within the gymnasium.

Surfaces of structural members also provide opportunities for reflecting artificial light. The Vancouver Public Library is typical of many buildings where a comfortable level of background lighting is reflected from suspended floor soffits (Figure 8.35). Uplights illuminate the vaulted concrete slabs whose shallow coved surfaces are well suited to achieving appropriate levels of indirect and diffuse light.

Fabric structures are well known for their ability to reflect and diffuse light. Their conventional white-coloured and shiny surfaces (dark fabrics are prone to severe solar overheating) guarantee a high degree of reflectivity which responds well to uplighting. The ability of the fabric to diffuse light is best experienced on a sunny day. Fabric translucency, which varies according to thickness and type of fabric, provides relatively low-intensity light that is even and soft. The Mound Stand, London, is a typical example (Figure 8.36). Although the PVC-coated polyester fabric primarily provides shade, a pleasant quality of diffuse light filters through the canopy.

Figure 8.36
Mound Stand, Lord's, London, Michael Hopkins and Partners, 1987. Underside of the fabric roof.

Modified by light

Although structure often controls light – its intensity and quality – the relationship between structure and light is not entirely dominated by structure. For light not only reveals structure but modifies our perceptions of it. Millet explains how in two churches of very different character, one Bavarian Rococo, and the other contemporary North American, glare from relatively intense and well-controlled daylight dematerializes their structures and has structural members perceived as luminous lines.[17]

Dematerialization occurs where an area of structure that is illuminated far more intensely than the surrounding ambient light levels seems to disappear or at least loses its sharpness of definition in a bright haze. For example, the lengths of columns that pass through a display window in the Timber Showroom, Hergatz, are so brightly illuminated when exposed to strong sunlight that they merge into the glary background (Figure 8.37). The unlit lengths of columns

Figure 8.37
Timber Showroom, Hergatz, Germany, Baumschläger-Eberle, 1995. Glare dematerializes the base of the portal legs. They appear to terminate at the top of the display window.

Figure 8.38
Mönchengladbach Museum, Germany, Hans Hollein, 1982. Geometric patterns of light subvert the sense of inhabiting an orthogonal structural grid.

therefore read as not being grounded, appearing to stop above the window opening, thereby increasing the visual complexity and interest of the building. It is unlikely that this visual effect, which may go unnoticed on a dull day, was intended by the designers. Their focus of attention would have most likely been on the provision of adequate fenestration to display the company's products. A similar effect is observed at Saint Benedict Chapel, Sumvitg (see Figures 6.3 and 6.4). Where interior posts pass in front of the clerestory, glare from their surfaces reduces their clarity and the starkness of their silhouettes against the sky, and intensifies the perception of the roof floating.

Intentional dematerialization of structure by light characterizes the work of the contemporary architect Juan Navarro Baldweg. According to one reviewer, Baldweg develops the theme of light and structure in a completely new way:

> Here light prevails over shade, homogeneity over contrast. A diffuse and even light that descends from above can be obtained by removing every last trace of shadow: thus the roof is transformed into a combined system of V-shaped girders and skylights, becoming a luminous mechanism . . . Just as the girders are given a triangular cross-section to eliminate every remaining cone

of shade, so too the pillars acquire a triangular section, so as to obtain, through the play of light, an effect of dematerialization of the wall.[18]

Artificial lighting can also be used to modify our perceptions of structure. For example, where ground-floor exterior columns are singled out for illumination by down-lighting, they are transformed into cylinders of light. Illumination of the Tokyo International Forum interior roof structure produces a considerably more dramatic effect: 'At night, light reflecting off the surface of the roof truss ribs transforms the structure into a monolithic floating light source illuminating the glass hall and assuring the visual presence of the building in the Tokyo skyline.'[19]

In the final example where structure appears to be modified by light, light disrupts the perception of an orthogonal structural layout. At the Mönchengladbach Museum, an approximately 6 m-square column-grid is imposed upon the irregular-shaped main gallery. Rather than visually reinforcing the grid geometry by means of beams or other elements, lines of artificial lighting achieve the opposite effect. Lengths of fluorescent tubes that are surface-mounted on the plain ceiling create polygonal patterns of light that break down our perception of inhabiting a grid (Figure 8.38). Drawn to the light, the eye follows the lines of brightness.

Their patterning provides a welcome visual alternative to that of the orthogonal structural layout.

Summary

Structure and light are both indispensable and interdependent elements of architecture. While structure may control light – its locations of entry into a building and its quantity and quality – the need for daylight inevitably determines structural form and detailing. Although during the design process structural decisions may be subservient to those concerning light, once built, roles reverse and structure controls light.

After acknowledging Louis Kahn's innovative integration of structure and light, this chapter explored how open structure can act as a source for light to enter a building. Structural form, members and even structural connections all participate in this role. Readers were also reminded of how structural layout often delineates the shapes of transparent areas in the exterior skins of buildings.

The integration of structure and both transparency and the ingress of daylight is achieved by a variety of approaches. These include detailing structure with more small rather than fewer large members, penetrating solid structural members, and using glass or other translucent materials.

Since sunlight is unwelcome in certain spaces, structure plays light-modifying roles. Structure filters and reflects, producing even and diffuse qualities of light. Finally in this chapter, examples illustrated how light modifies our perception of structure. Light dematerializes structure, has structure read primarily as a source of light, and subverts awareness of structural rationality.

Depending upon our design concept and the desired qualities of light in the spaces of a building, we should consider one, some or even all of the above design approaches to light, perhaps using structure as a source of light, to maximize light, to modify it, or even to have it change our perceptions of structure.

Notes

1. P. Van Meiss, *Elements of architecture: from form to place*, New York: Van Nostrand Reinhold, 1990, p. 121.

2. M. S. Millet, *Light revealing architecture*, New York: Van Nostrand Reinhold, 1996, p. 60.

3. A. Tyng, *Beginnings: Louis I. Kahn's philosophy of architecture*, New York: John Wiley, 1984, p. 145.

4. Ibid., p. 146. Comments by Louis Kahn compiled in N. E. Johnson, *Light is the theme: Louis I. Kahn and the Kimbell Art Museum*, Fort Worth, TX: Kimbell Art Foundation, 1975, p. 21.

5. R. Dimond and W. Wang (eds), *On continuity*, Cambridge, MA: 9H Publications, 1995, p. 188.

6. R. Witte (ed.), *Case: Toyo Ito – Sendai Mediatheque*, Munich: Prestel, 2002.

7. For a pictorial explanation of the construction sequence, see M. A. Branch, 'Internationally styled', *Progressive Architecture* 72(4), 1991, 87–93.

8. C. Balmond, *informal*, Munich: Prestel, 2002, p. 316.

9. I. Ritchie, *The biggest glass palace in the world*, London: Ellipsis, 1997, p. 34.

10. A. Brown, *Peter Rice: the engineer's contribution to contemporary architecture*, London: Thomas Telford, 2000, p. 73.

11. C. Davies, 'Norman Foster: portfolio of three buildings', *Architecture* 82(9), 1993, 106–9, at 109.

12. S. Giedion, *Space, time and architecture*, 5th edn, Cambridge, MA: Harvard University Press, 1978, p. 224.

13. Millet, *Light revealing architecture*, p. 63.

14. S. R. Shemitz, 'Lighting the way', *Architectural Record* 175(13), 1987, 148–55.

15. A. Bussel, 'Great expectations', *Interior Design* 72(7), 2001, 297–301, at 300.

16. For construction details, refer to S. Dawson, 'Glass as skin and structure', *The Architects' Journal* 210(10), 1995, 32–4.

17. Millet, *Light revealing architecture*, p. 66.

18. M. Zardini, 'Light and structure in Juan Navarro Baldweg's work', *Lotus International* 98, 1998, 56–9, at 58.

19. M. Toy (ed.), 'Light in architecture', *Architectural Design Profile* 126, 1997, 43.

nine

Representation and symbolism

Introduction

This chapter explores how exposed structure enriches architecture when structural forms and details contribute meaning by virtue of their representational and symbolic qualities. *Structural representation* is understood as structure typifying a physical object, like a tree or a crane, while *symbolic structure* recalls an idea, a quality or a condition. Like beauty, representation and symbolism lie in the eye of the beholder.

Both representational and symbolic structure encompass different degrees of explicitness. While some examples of representation are almost universally recognized, others are not. The situation is even more pronounced in the case of symbolism. When discerning symbolic meaning in architecture, as in any object, we bring our whole life to bear upon it. Our imagination, upbringing, education, life experiences, sense of well-being and professional expertise all influence how we perceive meaning in architecture in general, and in exposed structure in particular. It is little wonder, then, that many symbolic readings are completely unimagined by designers.

Architect Sverre Fehn illustrates the deeply personal nature of human response to structural representation and symbolism. He sensitively imagines an individual's reaction to an exposed structural member, a column:

> In the church the fisherman enters his pew. From his seat he recognizes that the column has the same dimensions as his mast. Through this recognition he feels secure. He sits by his column, a form also acknowledged by the gentle touch of his fingers. On the open sea, the tree was a symbol he trusted, as it brought him safely home. The same representation assists him now in turning his thoughts towards prayer. Within his spirit the sea is calm. In his search for the stars, the column offers him a personal dialogue.[1]

This passage exemplifies structure, in this case a column, playing both representational and symbolic roles. Although both roles may be played simultaneously when a structure is read, the following sections discuss each role separately.

Representation

Examples of structural representation can be divided into two unevenly sized groups. In the far larger group, sources of representation include objects and processes found in the natural world. Artefacts, those that comprise the smaller group, also become sources of design inspiration and invite attempts at representation.

The few examples that this chapter describes are but a fraction of all possible structural representations. Plant forms that recall the shapes of well-developed trees are by far the most common. Only in the Eden Project (see Figure 3.11), whose hexagonal structured biomes are scaled up versions of bumblebee eye structures, is structure based on natural microscopic or molecular forms. This is not to deny the potential for other sources of inspiration from the natural world. Forms from plants, the worlds of mammals, birds, insects and marine life, and forms from naturally occurring solids like metals and crystals are all latent sources of representation.[2]

Natural world

In the context of discussing the designs of young Finnish architects, Antoniades suggests that 'one may classify as a uniquely Finnish obsession, the introduction of tree-form elements into architecture'.[3] He illustrates numerous examples where tree and forest have inspired and generated structural form in recent architecture, and he includes some conceptual explorations of trees as generators of high-rise building structures. However, while many examples of arboreal columns are to be found in Finland, articulation of column as tree occurs in many, if not most, countries.[4]

Of all natural forms, trees and forests are by far the most likely to be represented structurally, and their popularity among architects is reflected in the case-studies that follow. After exploring a number of different structures that manifest tree forms, several buildings are considered where the structure is more likely to be read as forest, and then the chapter moves on to examples that exhibit the geological process of erosion and various anthropomorphic and zoomorphic features.

Structural trees dominate the main façade at the Palais de Justice, Melun (Figure 9.1). An entrance canopy that extends across the building frontage rests upon six tree-like columns.

Apart from the small fins radiating from the perimeter of the trunk bases to deter graffiti artists, these columns are literal steel replicas of trees. Like real trees, they possess trunks and forked branches. There are even twigs, located immediately underneath the canopy. Only the leaves are missing. Such explicit representation raises the question: how do the trees relate to the building's interior? Once inside, do you promenade along a tree-lined avenue? Unfortunately, in this building no connection exists between its exterior and interior architecture – the trees are little more than an architectural gesture, albeit one that is rather grand.

At Tod's Omotesando Building, Tokyo, the zelkova trees along its street frontage are represented more abstractly (Figure 9.2). They are treated as a two-dimensional pattern in contrast to the previous, more literal, example. Here, the criss-crossing concrete wall piers of the perimeter load-bearing structure form a dramatic surface pattern both inside and out. The surfaces of the structural members are emphasized by glass mullions behind flush glazing, and the cream colouration of the wall thickness and other elements uphold their visual clarity. The structural challenges associated with designing such a unique gravity- and lateral-load-resisting structure in a highly active seismic zone were lessened by incorporating seismic isolation. The six-storey superstructure rests on rubber bearings above the basement.

Figure 9.1
Palais de Justice, Melun, France, Jourda & Perraudin Architectes, 1998. A tree-supported canopy on the main façade.

Whereas in the previous two examples the trunks and branches are formed by linear members, the branches of the structural trees at the Oriente Station, Lisbon, are elegantly curved. Their arboreal representation is equally explicit. The station platform canopy appears lightweight and very delicate by comparison to the heavy concrete-arched structure housing the main concourse and other facilities upon which it rests (Figure 9.3). Recalling the pointed Gothic arches of Oxford University Museum's courtyard structure (Figure 6.43), the steel ribbed canopy bears a strong resemblance to a grove of palm trees – an association reinforced by its detailing. Apart from its square fabricated-steel column-bases, other members of the roof canopy comprise I-sections. The main arch members not only curve but taper. The haunched and rounded rib–arch connections and the use of sharp-edged and thin sections recall similar properties of palm fronds and strengthen the botanical analogy (Figures 9.4 and 9.5).

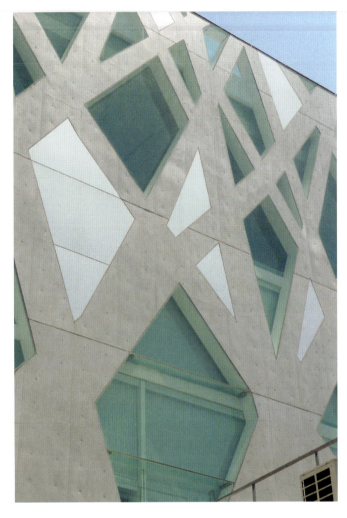

Figure 9.2
Tod's Omotesando Building, Tokyo, Japan, Toyo Ito & Associates, 2004. A portion of the rear façade with its exposed perimeter concrete structure of abstracted tree trunks and branches.

Figure 9.4
A view along the canopy structure.

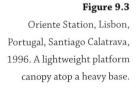

Figure 9.3
Oriente Station, Lisbon, Portugal, Santiago Calatrava, 1996. A lightweight platform canopy atop a heavy base.

Figure 9.5
Palm tree frond-like ribs connect to a primary arch.

By comparison to the previous examples, the level of literal representation at the Stansted Airport terminal, Essex, is somewhat muted. As discussed in Chapter 4, the structural trees link the exterior and interior architecture of the building. Their trunks consist of four steel tubes on a square grid, joined together with beams above head height to form two-way moment frames. Well-integrated services and information pods are located within the trunks. Tubular struts branch diagonally in both section and plan from each corner of a trunk to support lattice-dome roofs (Figure 9.6). The wide (36 m) spacing between the trees means that they are perceived more as individual elements than as members of a forest.

Where the structural representation of the tree is less explicit, large numbers of columns can evoke the notion of forest or plantation. For instance, we identify more with the concept of the forest than with the tree, where 'Rows of rough hewn columns of ancient pine march through the cavernous space in regimented, arboreal splendor' at the Mont-Cenis Academy, Herne (Figure 3.3).[5] The forest, rather than the tree, is again communicated in the Baumschulenweg

Figure 9.6
Stansted Airport terminal, UK, Foster Associates, 1991. A typical interior structural tree.

Crematorium, Berlin (Figure 2.11). Its plain cylindrical columns are devoid of branches. Although a similar column on its own could hardly be considered to represent a tree, the sheer numbers of columns and their collective 'random' placement evoke a forest.

Another variation on the forest theme is expressed strongly at the Aluminium Centre, Houten (Figure 9.7). The building is propped on 368 tubular aluminium columns 6 m high and between 210 mm and 90 mm in diameter. The column diameters are related to the span of the beams they support. Some columns that are inclined provide horizontal stability through their triangulation.

Figure 9.7
Aluminium Centre, Houten, The Netherlands, Micha de Haas, 2002. The building is supported on a forest of aluminium posts. (© Paul Rotheroe)

Figure 9.8
Outdoor Activities Centre, Portsmouth, UK, Hampshire County Architects, 1995. Where the building is approached from the car park in the background, the partial or full disappearance of the wall panels suggests a process like erosion.

Figure 9.9
Wöhlen High School entry canopy, Switzerland, Santiago Calatrava, 1988. Ribs cantilever from the main arch.

Whereas the previous buildings in this section exemplify structure representing either trees or forest, the structure at the rear of the Outdoor Activities Centre, Portsmouth, suggests a natural process – erosion. Although the centre's exposed wooden construction and metal fasteners deny the hostility of its coastal location – only several metres from the sea shore – the western side of the building, facing inland yet subject to prevailing winds, incorporates masonry and concrete construction (Figure 9.8). When approaching the building from the car park, you pass two bays of externally buttressed masonry walls that 'break down' and eventually become a colonnade of free-standing buttresses closer to the main entrance of the centre. Given the disappearance of sections of wall panels, a geological process like erosion springs to mind, even without overt signs such as crumbling bricks and jagged or worn surfaces. This example of representation is certainly not explicit, and in fact nothing in the architect's account of the building supports this reading.

Anthropomorphic and zoomorphic sources are also represented by structural form and detailing. Chapter 7 commented upon the elegantly detailed metal castings at the Lyon School of Architecture (Figure 7.38). Their ribs not only express the flow of internal forces but are expressive of the visual characteristics of human fingers. Also, consider the 'feet'-shaped base-plates under the entrance canopy to Wöhlen High School (Figures 9.9 and 9.10).

Figure 9.10
Feet-like base-plates to the window mullions behind the canopy.

Figure 9.11

Glass Hall, Tokyo International Forum, Tokyo, Japan, Rafael Vignoly Architects, 1996. The full-height glazed wall facing the other sections of the Forum complex.

Figure 9.12

The roof structure as seen from the main concourse. It spans from the column on the left to the column near the other end of the hall.

Around the perimeter of the Palazzetto dello Sport, Rome, inclined exterior struts that resist compression loads from its ribbed-shell roof resemble athletes with arms extended, stretching their calf muscles by pushing against a wall (Figure 3.9).

For the final example of zoomorphic representation, we visit the Tokyo International Forum Glass Hall roof. Given the architect's intention for the roof structure to express its flow of forces, the representational aspect of the design is probably unintended but has resulted in a much-lauded architectural outcome (Figures 9.11 and 9.12).[6]

The roof structure spans the length of the atrium, supported near each end by a large column. Usually, for reasons of minimizing structural depth and economy, designers prefer to span the shorter of two directions, but here the roof structure spans a distance many times the building width. By so doing, the sizes of the vertical structural elements in the main 46 m-high wall are minimized. They have been relieved of any need to resist gravity forces which would cause them to buckle. This has had a great impact on the transparency of the walls, but, equally significantly, has provided the opportunity to design a roof structure of rare elegance and complexity.

The form of the structure echoes the lenticular shape of the building plan and thereby achieves a gentle flow of forces to the two supporting columns. The many rods that comprise the truss tension reinforcement curve in section and elevation (Figure 9.13). This so-called truss is far from being a typical truss. It is more like an inverted tied arch (Figure 9.14). The curved ribs simultaneously maintain the three-dimensional curved geometry of the tie rods and apply loads to them.

Viewed from below, the force paths are barely discernible. Due to the fineness of the tension-rods, the far larger dimensions of the curved ribs dominate visually, and they also partially hide the four large steel compression tubes above them. Expression of structural action is therefore overshadowed by the exposure of the structural ribs themselves that, together, resemble a giant ribcage. Other readings of the roof structure are possible as well, of course, such as the ribs defining the shape of a boat hull.

Figure 9.13

Closer to the roof, the tension rods become more visible. As they approach mid-span they curve downwards and inwards.

Artefacts

Architectural books and journals contain many examples of structural representation originating other than from the natural world – areas such as aeronautical, nautical and automotive engineering, and industrial and historic structures are but a few sources.

Several buildings where structure represents different types of artefact have already been encountered. For example, under the Némausus Apartments, Nîmes, uniformly distributed slender columns in the basement create the impression of the building floating. Structural walls that read as rudders, given their location at the rear of the 'ship' and their rudder-like elevational profile, provide longitudinal stability for the ground floor (see Figure 5.18).

The nautical theme surfaces again at the Armenian School Library, Los Angeles, an addition to an already cramped site. Raised one storey above the ground, four large red elliptically-clad columns and some slender steel tubes are the library's only footprint (Figures 9.15 and 9.16). The 'Ark', as it is known, is intended to recall the biblical Noah's ark, which is important in Armenian culture, as well as to symbolize aspects of Armenian immigration to countries like the USA. Its clear ark-like form, with elliptically plan-shaped walls, a rounded hull and an expressed keel, is held aloft by two different structural elements. Large columns placed under the centrally located keel are assisted by secondary props whose main task is to ensure transverse stability. Even then the ark appears quite precariously balanced. Although the props are symmetrically and regularly placed, because the outer props support the intersections of the faceted planes that form the ellipse, and due to their inclination to the vertical, they read as randomly

Figure 9.14

The roof structure can be thought of simply as a tied arch (a) that is inverted with the arch then functioning as a catenary and the tie as a compression member (b).

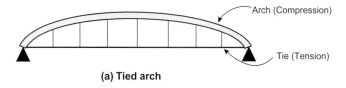

(a) Tied arch

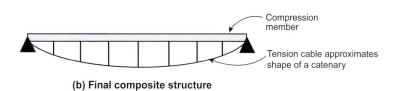

(b) Final composite structure

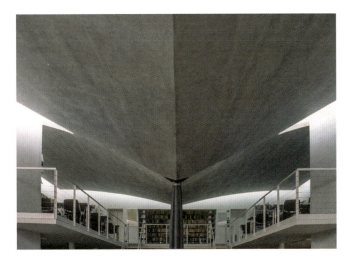

Figure 9.21
Wöhlen High School library roof, Switzerland, Santiago Calatrava, 1988.
A central column supports the roof shell which 'shelters' the mezzanine
galleries to the rear.

of an open soft-covered book, or the outstretched wings of
a flying bird (Figure 9.21).[8] The completed roof consists of
a folded and curved concrete shell. Its weight is supported
by a tubular steel post, reinforced by curved ribs that give
rise to its spindle-shaped profile. Horizontal stainless-steel
rods located on the perimeter of the roof in several locations
stabilize it by tying it back to structural walls. Daylight

washes down the walls through gaps between the roof and
the walls. The enfolding presence of the curved concrete
roof surfaces immediately above the mezzanine reading
galleries provides a strong sense of enclosure and protection.
These emotions, evoked by the combination of the structural
form and the perimeter lighting, reinforce a reading derived
from the natural world – that of the wings of a bird sheltering
its offspring.

The Church of the Autostrada, Florence, contains the final
example of structure possibly representing objects from
the human world. Situated on the outskirts of Florence,
adjacent to the motorway, the church commemorates
those workers who lost their lives building Italy's modern
motorway system. Both architect and reviewers agree that
the church's tent-like form simultaneously acknowledges the
nomadic life of the ancient Israelites and the travelling public
driving past the church (Figure 9.22). However, opinions
pertaining to the interpretation of its dramatic interior
structure remain divided.

I refer to the amazing array of irregular struts that support
the roof and also differentiate the sanctuary from the nave,
frame the main altar, and screen off a passageway (Figures
9.23 and 9.24). One reviewer suggests that the structural
forms allude to 'the calcified bones of a skeleton, and to
desiccated stems'.[9] While a preliminary cross-sectional

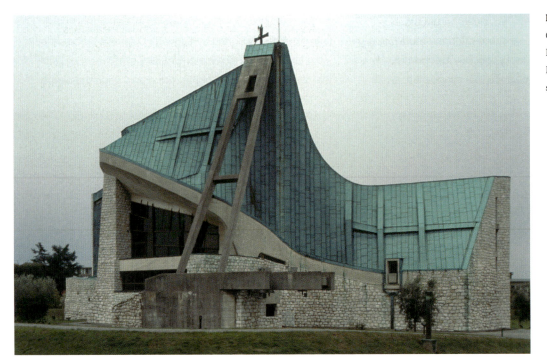

Figure 9.22
Church of the Autostrada,
Florence, Italy, Giovanni
Michelucci, 1968. The church as
seen from the motorway.

Figure 9.23
Dramatic interior structure with the main altar to the left facing the rows of seats. (Courtesy F. Amadei)

Figure 9.24
Details of the concrete structure.

sketch by the architect, Giovanni Michelucci, suggests tree-like supports, Michelucci denied any intention of naturalistic representation. Instead, he referred to his desire to introduce fantasy, variety and surprise into his architecture, and acknowledged how forms inspired by trees contribute to that process.[10] He insisted that no particular representation or symbolism was intended, other than allowing 'fantastic' structural shapes to invite a variety of readings. Perhaps the church's programme as a monument to the human cost of civil engineering construction suggests another reading? To me, this unconventional and intriguing structure, in terms of both its form and its exquisite, irregularly modelled surfaces, reads as an abstraction of construction scaffolding, props and temporary bracing, and other construction equipment like derricks and cranes.

With this building fresh in our minds – a building whose structure defies categorization, which can be interpreted in multiple ways, and which possesses a palpable and tantalizing

sense of both representation and symbolism – we next consider examples where structures play more obvious symbolic roles.

Symbolism

As discussed in Chapter 1, the practice of people imbuing structure with meaning is commonplace, both outside and inside the architectural community. Several examples, drawn from quite different sources, including two from the world of vernacular architecture, illustrate this activity.

Kenneth Frampton's *Studies in tectonic culture* includes an analysis of an Algerian Berber house by the sociologist Pierre Bourdieu:

> In addition to all this, at the center of the dividing wall, between 'the house of human beings', stands the main pillar, supporting the governing beam and all the framework of the house. Now this governing beam which connects the gables and spreads the protection of the male part of the house to the female part . . . is identified explicitly with the master of the house, whilst the main pillar on which it rests, which is the trunk of a forked tree . . . is identified with the wife . . . and their interlocking represents the act of physical union.[11]

A very different and religious symbolic meaning is attached to the exposed interior structure of the Rangiatea Church, Otaki, New Zealand: 'The ridge-pole, fashioned from a single tree, symbolizes the new faith and a belief in only one god. The ridge-pole is supported by three pillars symbolizing the Christian Trinity.'[12]

Exposed interior roof structure seems particularly amenable to symbolic interpretation. Lance LaVine writes of house ridge beams:

> As a cultural artifact, the ridge beam is the center of the roof that covers human habitation. It is this center that preserves the human mind and spirit, as well as the needs of the human body, and thus this unique building element has gained a special place in the collective human memory of place or, perhaps more importantly, of being in places. The ridge of a house not only centers its roof structure but in so doing becomes a symbol for a

centered existence within that form. It is a unique place in a dwelling that has come to secure the human psyche as it gathers the live and dead loads of the roof rafters that it helps to support.[13]

While still on the subject of roof structure, and considering the meaning embodied in a vaulted roof, La Vine continues:

> A flat surface may extend indefinitely without ever protecting an inhabitant at its edges. To be covered is to have something that wraps around human beings . . . The vault of the house covers inhabitants as blankets cover their bed, as the sky covers the earth.[14]

Angus Macdonald also acknowledges the symbolic role of structure in architecture. In his categorization of possible relationships between structure and architecture he includes a category her terms 'structure symbolized'. Here 'structure is emphasized visually and constitutes an essential element of the architectural vocabulary . . . the "structure symbolized" approach has been employed almost exclusively as a means of expressing the idea of technical progress'.[15] He explains that symbolic intent can encompass issues other than celebrating technology, and explores the implications of structure symbolizing an ideal like sustainability.

An implicit assumption that structure plays symbolic roles in architecture underlies this book. For example, Chapter 2 discusses the multiple readings of the Beijing Olympic Stadium, and how the sombre and giant columns of the Baumschulenweg Crematorium are likely to be a source of strength for those who mourn. At the Arts Centre, Rotterdam, exposed structural detailing that questions conventional attitudes to aesthetics expresses the ethos of a museum of modern art (Figure 7.13), while the elegance of detailing at Bracken House, London, conveys a sense of quality and prestige (Figure 4.45).

Clearly, structure plays a wide range of symbolic roles. While some symbolic readings are unintended by architects, in other cases architecture is enriched quite explicitly by exploiting the symbolic potential of structure, as exemplified in three buildings designed by Daniel Libeskind.

In the Jewish Museum, Berlin, structural members play important symbolic roles. They reinforce the symbolism inherent in the whole project, particularly in the plans and

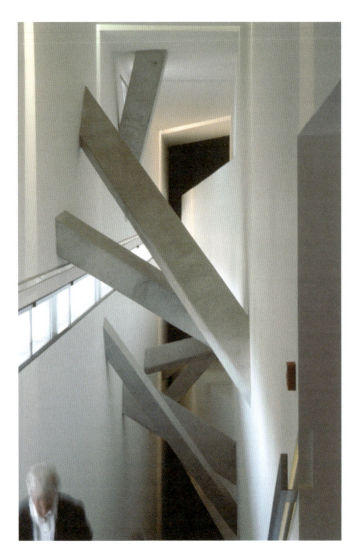

Figure 9.25
Jewish Museum, Berlin, Germany, Daniel Libeskind, 1998. Structural members pass chaotically above the main stairs.

elevations of the fractured building. Concrete struts-cum-beams pass chaotically across the main stairwell leading to the exhibition galleries (Figure 9.25). Orientated at different angles with varied cross-sectional shapes and dimensions, these members symbolize the historical dislocations and horrors experienced by Germany's Jews. The convincing materiality and scale of the struts suggest structurally important roles, even though their chaotic configuration contradicts such a possibility. Although the struts prop the external wall to some degree, their primary role is symbolic. They enhance the architectural concept. This ominous and unexpected structure is laden with meaning.

Figure 9.26
Felix Nussbaum Museum, Osnabrück, Germany, Daniel Libeskind, 1998.
Dysfunctional concrete beams in the Nussbaum Corridor.

Figure 9.27
Beams passing across the light-slot read as the bars of prison cells.

Structure also contributes to the narrative architecture of the Felix Nussbaum Museum, Osnabrück. It helps recount the tragic story of the Jewish painter after whom the museum is named.[16] Structure, together with the building plan, building exterior and architectural details, speaks of violence, isolation and disorientation. For example, structural walls and a ceiling slab enclose the high and dimly lit Nussbaum Corridor that leads visitors to the main galleries. The harshness of the grey concrete, the lack of any detailing to relieve the plainness of the elongated space, and the dysfunctional concrete beams passing over it intensify the sense of loneliness and horror faced by Nussbaum as he entered a period of exile (Figure 9.26). Elsewhere, structure evokes equally poignant emotions. Some structural walls possess sharp and angled edges, and structural members passing through windows and across overhead light-slots read unmistakably as bars of prison cells (Figure 9.27). Together with other architectural elements, as well as the museum collection itself, structure recounts Nussbaum's life in a chilling and jarring manner.

Fragmentation as a design concept is incorporated into the Imperial War Museum-North, Manchester. Its architectural form reflects a view of the world shattered into three fragments, depicting the devastating effect of war. These fragments, or 'shards', brought together to form the main

Figure 9.28
Imperial War Museum-North, Manchester, UK, Studio Daniel Libeskind, 2002. Structural members dominate the Air Shard volume.

museum volumes, represent conflict on land, water and in the air. The main museum space is accommodated in the Earth Shard, while the Water Shard contains a restaurant and café. The Air Shard takes the form of an irregularly shaped and slightly canted tower which houses a viewing platform at roof level.

Open to the elements, the Air Shard is essentially a soaring 30 m-high void – except for its interior structure (Figure 9.28). All museum visitors enter the tower at ground level and pass through it. While rain and wind find their way through the generous gaps between its aluminium cladding battens and accentuate the bleakness of the space, the greater assault upon the senses arises from the structure that fills the volume. Steel tubes fly through the space, seemingly at all angles. They form a multi-member spatial framework that appears chaotic. To me, the structural members map the three-dimensional trajectories of war planes through the sky.

Libeskind's works may have influenced the design of Federation Square, Melbourne. The fragmentation of its façade surfaces and their supporting structures is recognized as symbolizing a number of aspects of Australia's culture – the

Figure 9.29
Federation Square, Melbourne, Australia, Lab Architectural Studio and Bate Smart Partners, 2002. The tangled structure of the atrium roof.

individuality of the country's states, its ethnic diversity, and its relationship with the indigenous people. Behind the fractural patterned glazing mullions and cladding panels, structural form intensifies the idea of fracture through its 'random' three-dimensional frameworks that support some roofs and exterior walls.

From within and outside two of the main public spaces, the atrium and the interior BMW Edge amphitheatre, structural forms appear totally chaotic (Figures 9.29 and 9.30). Load-paths are impossible to trace. There are no recognizable structural systems such as frames, arches or trusses, and no geometrical predictability. Most structural rules and traditions are broken as horizontal and vertical members are avoided, and eccentric connections between members become commonplace. This is an example of structural anarchy. When lit at night the structure appears as a tangled thicket of bare tree branches.

As well as symbolizing some of the realities of Australia's national life, most of which are in fact universally applicable, other fundamental issues are raised by the welded and rigidly connected steel frameworks. Given our inability to categorize them and understand their workings, we are forced to accept that their structural performance is beyond understanding, so we must trust in the expertise of those few structural engineers responsible for their digital structural analyses and designs. This structure forces its viewers to

Figure 9.31
Industrial Park Office Building, Völkermarkt, Carinthia, Austria, Günther Domenig, 1996. The framed block supporting the cantilever with the lift and stair tower behind.

Figure 9.30
A perimeter walkway through the wall structure of the BMW Edge amphitheatre.

accept the unknown and live beyond their prior experiences. It also acknowledges the reality of the irrational and the unpredictable – the environment in which many of our lives are lived.

By comparison with the explicit structural symbolism in the previous four projects, any intended meaning in the exposed structure of the Industrial Park Office Building, Völkermarkt, is far less obvious. Even though the nature of its exposed structure is far more flamboyant than those of previous examples, it solicits different interpretations and creates a refreshing degree of mystery, in the same manner as the Church of the Autostrada.

Providing office accommodation, the building is a gateway for a light industrial park dedicated to start-up or emerging business enterprises. It consists of a narrow concrete-walled structure housing stairs and a lift that connects to the main concrete frame, rising five storeys above a ground-level podium. The frame supports an interesting curved cantilevered steel structure (Figures 9.31 and 9.32). After commenting on a previous design by the same architect that was interpreted as a criticism of the capitalist system, Peter Davey writes:

Figure 9.32
Steel cantilever structure.

It is difficult to see how this building is a criticism of the system . . . perhaps it is a claw against the sky, or possibly a tattered crow's feather with its filaments flying. But the main impression is of welcome and thrust, the swirling curve of a powerful living, glossy bird's wing: a signal of strength, virility, generosity and hope.[17]

Another interpretation might focus on the different characteristics of the frame and the cantilever. Perhaps the heavy, orthogonal and certainly conventional frame epitomizes the capitalistic system, while the light and flexible cantilevered area represents the new enterprises that are twisting, turning and climbing in an effort to break free from it and its constraining rigidity? Then again, perhaps the curvature of the cantilever in plan is merely responding to the geometry of the road which bends around the base of the building?

Summary

After acknowledging how representation and symbolism range from the literal to the ambiguous, this chapter illustrated the individualistic and personal nature of how meaning in structure is discerned. It then continued with examples of representation that draw upon the natural world for their inspiration. Trees and forests are the most common sources, but anthropomorphic and zoomorphic forms are also included. Representation based upon human artefacts is less common, but ship, boat, space-craft and book forms are also represented by structure. The 'Representation' section concluded with the representational and symbolic ambiguity of Michelucci's remarkable Church of the Autostrada.

Structural symbolism, inherent in the concept of reading structure, is implicit throughout this book. Before recalling numerous examples from previous chapters, several other authors were quoted to demonstrate just how widespread is the practice of imbuing structure with meaning. Three buildings by Daniel Libeskind illustrated structure playing explicit symbolic roles, and the chapter concluded by considering a final building where any definitive meaning remains delightfully elusive.

Notes

1. S. Fehn, *The thought of construction*, New York: Rizzoli International, 1983, p. 46.

2. P. Pearce, *Structure in nature is a strategy for design*, Cambridge, MA: MIT Press, 1978, ch. 2.

3. A. C. Antoniades, *Epic space: towards the roots of Western architecture*, New York: Van Nostrand Reinhold, 1992, p. 256.

4. See, for example, J. Cook, *Seeking structure from nature*, Basel: Birkhäuser, 1996.

5. C. Kugel, 'Green academy', *Architectural Review* 206(1232), 1999, 51–5, at 52.

6. The architect comments: 'the Glass Hall structure was always a truss-like element, transparent . . . to minimise its shadow over the garden . . . the tectonics of the building result from the conscious manipulation of the route of main forces to the foundation, and the controlled expression of these routes'. Quoted by I. Richards, 'Space odyssey', *The Architectural Review* 200(1197), 1996, 38–44.

7. A. Bussel, *SOM evolutions: recent work of Skidmore, Owings & Merrill*, Basel: Birkhäuser, 2000, pp. 60–5, at 61.

8. W. Blaser (ed.), *Santiago Calatrava: engineering architecture*, Basel: Birkhäuser, 1989, p. 35.

9. F. Dal Co, 'Giovanni Michelucci: a life one century long', *Perspecta* 27, 1992, 99–115, at 113.

10. R. H. de Alba and A. W. Organschi, 'A conversation with Giovanni Michelucci', *Perspecta* 27, 1992, 116–39.

11. Quoted in K. Frampton, *Studies in tectonic culture: the poetics of construction in nineteenth and twentieth century architecture*, Cambridge, MA: Massachusetts Institute of Technology, 1995, p. 14.

12. P. Tumatatoa, 'Churches illustrate impact of new faith', *New Zealand Historic Places* 29, 1990, 40–4, at 43. Unfortunately, the original church was destroyed by fire in 1995. A replica was opened in 2003.

13. L. LaVine, *Mechanics and meaning in architecture*, Minneapolis: University of Minnesota Press, 2001, p. 125.

14. Ibid., p. 151.

15. A. J. Macdonald, *Structural design for architecture*, Oxford: Architectural Press, 1997, p. 30.

16. After going into exile and evading capture for many years, the young Nussbaum and his partner were killed in a Nazi concentration camp in 1944.

17. P. Davey, 'Spirit of ecstasy', *Architectural Review* 199, 1996, 54–9, at 58.

ten

Hidden structure

Introduction

This chapter completes the analytical section of the book. The previous eight chapters have analysed how structure contributes to architecture other than by fulfilling its primary structural function of resisting and transferring load. Examples have illustrated structure playing many different roles of architectural enrichment in a variety of settings, such as on a building exterior or within. However, in Chapters 11 and 12, the focus changes. Rather than exploring the roles of structure beyond load-bearing, the emphasis is upon expressing design ideas and realizing specific architectural qualities through exposed structure. My aim is to show how some of the most prevalent and compelling contemporary architectural ideas are expressed, reinforced or clarified by structure. By implication, I suggest that structure has the potential to contribute to the successful expression of *any* architectural idea or quality.

The book to this point has not only focused upon the qualitative analysis of structure but has been preoccupied with *exposed* structure. Almost every case-study has highlighted structure that is visible and distinguishable from other surrounding architectural elements. Clearly, the material presented so far is highly selective, for in the real world of architecture most structure is hidden. Approach and enter most buildings and the chances are that the majority of its structural elements will be hidden.

The purpose of this chapter, therefore, is to pause before emphasizing how structure integrates with architectural concepts and qualities. This is where we acknowledge and reflect upon *hidden* structure. A greater awareness and appreciation of structure that is hidden can lead to a far broader range of approaches to incorporating structure in

architecture. Consideration of questions such as the how and why of structural hiddenness leads to an exploration of how structure, even though hidden, contributes architecturally.

It should come as no surprise that something hidden might nonetheless be significant. The nuances of hiddenness are subtle, broad and inviting, as evidenced from a list compiled from a thesaurus. Synonyms include: invisible, absence, vagueness, disguised, mystery, secrecy, camouflage, unnoticeable, unseen, out-of-sight, unknown, concealed, latent, distorted, screened, confined, veiled, masked, shrouded, obscured, disguised, ambiguous, incoherent, unrecognizable, expressionless, secluded, buried, tucked away, and out of the way. It is easy to imagine how some of these aspects of hiddenness could both attract the imagination of designers and be applied in expressive architectural design.

The previous statement – that most building structure is hidden – is explored in detail in the following sections, but it is worth reflecting upon the fact that hidden structure is not only confined to architecture. Most of the structure of inanimate objects, plants and even our own bodies is either hidden or not perceived as structure. Certainly most of us are totally unaware of the drama of the inner structural life and actions that sustain both objects and living organisms, including ourselves.

Consider the simple table upon which I am writing. It consists of a square tabletop supported by four legs, and yet it can also be considered as pure structure. The tabletop can be understood structurally as a two-way slab or plate, transferring the weight of computer and books to the legs. They function as short posts. The sideways or lateral stability of the table arises from the combination of the depth of the tabletop, the diameter of the legs and, finally, the rigidity with which they are connected. In this case, the rigid joints between legs and tabletop transform these elements into two small moment frames that resist lateral loads in each orthogonal direction. The structure of the table is visible, even though we may not recognize it as such.

In an unpainted wooden table we would also see evidence of a smaller scale of structure – in the grain or wood fibres that resist the stresses within the table members. But beyond that, the molecular and atomic scales of structure lie far beyond the capacity of human sight. Similar structural considerations will apply to the chair on which you might well be sitting. Without you realizing it, certain members are experiencing bending, and others compression. Within them, at smaller and smaller scales, structure hidden even to an electron microscope is present and working so that the chair can support your weight.

In plants and trees we can see the primary structure: raised ribs on leaves; or leaves folded in such a way that they cantilever from their stalks; trunks; branches; and twigs. However, bark or other surface coverings may prevent any deeper appreciation of their structures.

Our bodies are somewhat similar. We can readily identify primary structural members like legs, arms and so on, yet they are far more revealing of their internal structural make-up than the members of the plant kingdom. We are able to distinguish individual structural components comprising compression- and tension-capable elements, such as bones, ligaments, tendons and muscles. We can discern their forms and feel them with our fingers, but cannot see them directly, as they are protected by layers of skin and soft tissue, not to mention clothing. Thus, safe from moisture, dirt and mild chemical attack, our bodily structural components can perform optimally.

Even though hidden from view, bodily structure can be more easily discerned than building structure. Where they are reasonably close to the surface, bones are easily recognized, and muscles not only can be felt through our thin and flexible skin but become more pronounced when tensed. In contrast, building structural elements are usually hidden behind or within rigid linings, and rarely reveal their state of stress. For example, in light timber-frame construction, a lightweight alternative to load-bearing masonry, a wall consists of many different structural components. They are hidden behind gibraltar board or other types of drywall sheet linings, which when papered or painted are not usually recognized as structure. Within a wall, including the interior and exterior wall linings, we find vertical studs, nogs or blocking, top and bottom plates, perhaps some form of diagonal braces, and many nailed and screwed connections. The sheet linings, together with the wooden framing within, provide most of the horizontal bracing strength of the wall in the direction of its length. So, even the basic construction components of a house can contain a significant amount and variety of hidden structure.

Note also that not only structure but other technical systems without which buildings would be uninhabitable – such as heating, ventilating, plumbing and electrical systems – are often hidden.

Hidden structural systems and members

Any structural system or element can be hidden if desired. Floor systems are the most commonly hidden. Their upper surfaces are usually covered by floor coverings, and their structure, perhaps comprising primary and secondary beams supporting steel decking and topping concrete, or cast-in-place reinforced-concrete flat slabs, are concealed by suspended ceilings. It is also common for vertical structural systems, primarily designed to resist horizontal loads, to be placed out of view, especially where they form internal structural cores. Braced steel frames, for aesthetic and fire protection reasons, are placed within dry-framed walls, and reinforced-concrete structural walls may be covered by surface finishes. Moment frames, comprising beams and columns connected rigidly at their ends, can also be entirely hidden behind or within partition walls, but usually beams are hidden and columns exposed. In this and similar situations, where some members are exposed and others hidden, the structural system is partially hidden and thereby likely to be incomprehensible.

Partial concealment of structural systems, yet revealing selected members, is commonplace on building exteriors. Opaque curtain walling or enveloping skin can entirely or partially conceal structural members in order to achieve a desired façade pattern (Figure 10.1). An example of this

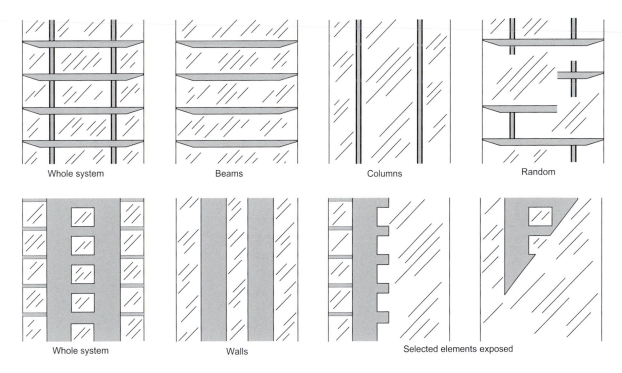

Whole system   Beams   Columns   Random

Whole system   Walls   Selected elements exposed

Figure 10.1

An elevational study of two exterior structural systems, a moment frame (above) and a coupled shear wall (below). Selected structural members are concealed behind the building skin to achieve varied façade patterns emphasizing horizontality, verticality and randomness.

Figure 10.2

China Central Television (CCTV) Headquarters, Beijing, OMA, 2009. Diagonal members of the perimeter braced frames only are selected and expressed. The columns and beams that are equally essential from a structural perspective are hidden.

strategy can be seen on the façade of the CCTV Building (Figure 10.2).

Foundation systems and their individual components, like pile caps, piles or spread footings, are almost always hidden. Exposing these members reduces their effectiveness. Exposed piles lack the confining support from the surrounding ground, increasing their likelihood of buckling, and reducing their ability to resist horizontal forces. Some degree of foundation exposure, perhaps important for the expression of a particular design idea, may be achievable with collaboration between architect and structural engineer. But one exception to the concealment of foundation systems occurs where base isolation is implemented. Placed under building superstructures in seismically active regions to isolate them from the damaging effects of earthquake shaking, base-isolation hardware, such as bearings and damping devices, needs to be accessible for inspection and maintenance. In some buildings this technology can be viewed and is even celebrated (Figure 10.3).

Degrees of hiddenness

One of the fascinations of hidden structure is the *extent* to which it is concealed. At the most extreme, structure is

Figure 10.3
Okumura Memorial Museum, Nara, Japan, 2007. A base-isolation rubber bearing between red-painted base-plates is proudly displayed in the basement. (Raja Hidzir)

completely invisible, both from inside and out – totally hidden. But sometimes perimeter and interior structure is hidden from the exterior, such as by an opaque façade skin, but then revealed inside.

There are numerous possibilities for selectively hiding and revealing structure. Not only individual members but entire structural systems can be selected for concealment or exposure. For example, Figure 10.4 shows an exposed lateral-load-resisting system while the gravity system is hidden.

Then there are different *degrees* of hiddenness. While raw concrete and wood structure might be exposed, often steel structural members are clad or coated for aesthetic or fire-protection reasons. Yet, although concealed, structural form is obvious, as illustrated by the CCTV Building. Here, structure is hidden behind skin but expressed through the cladding treatment. Rafael Moneo takes a similar approach at Columbia University, designing façades clad with panels textured with aluminium ribs (Figure 10.5).

On the HL23 Building (Figure 10.6) the concealment yet expression of structure is literally skin deep. An internal tubular steel-braced frame is visually enhanced by white film applied to the surface of the glass curtain wall, rather like the application of facial make-up. The curved transitions

Figure 10.4
Office building, Wellington, New Zealand. Lateral-load-resisting single-bay moment frames are exposed while the gravity system of beams and columns is concealed.

at structural intersections as portrayed on the exterior are far more elegant than the standard structural steel connections within.

Although in most cases hiding structure involves concealment of structural systems or members, it is also possible to expose structure but to detail it in such a way as to hide or obscure its structural role (Figure 10.7). Such structure, which expresses structural actions other than those actually occurring, recalls the work of the sixteenth-

Figure 10.5

N.W. Corner Building, Columbia University, New York, USA, Rafael Moneo, 2011. Panels with aluminium fins express the structure behind. (Chad Carpenter)

Figure 10.6

HL23, New York, USA, Neil M. Denari Architects, 2009. White film expresses and visually enhances the structure behind. (William McLaughlin)

century Mannerists. They delighted in decorative motifs such as broken-bed pediments, 'slipping' keystones and other structural improbabilities. In contrast, contemporary cases of structural obscuration are not achieved through plasterwork, but by actual manipulation of real structure. The roof structure of the Tokyo International Forum, discussed in the previous chapter, is an example of structural behaviour obscured by detailing (see Figure 9.12).

Techniques for hiding structure

Most structure is hidden by screening, like suspended ceilings, which hide most of the horizontal structure of suspended floors. Columns and diagonal braces are also often screened from view by opaque cladding or non-load-bearing walls, which may be mistaken for actual structure. This is the situation in the San Francisco Museum of Modern Art. The primary structure consists of a braced steel framework, hidden behind non-structural masonry façade panels, structurally separated from the main structure. Nevertheless, they give the impression of a building supported by load-bearing masonry walls (Figures 10.8 and 10.9).

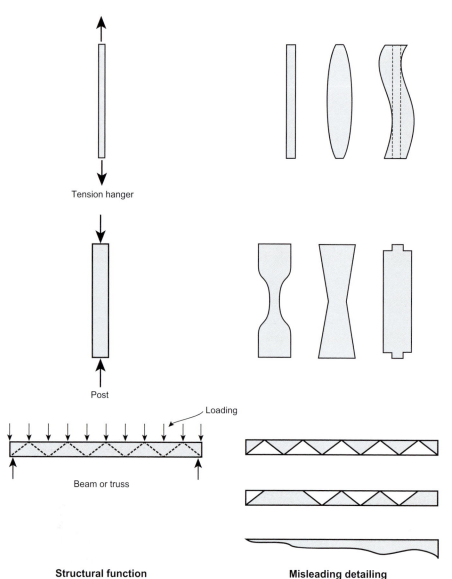

Figure 10.7
Examples of structural function being hidden (misrepresented) by structural detailing. Structural actions are shown on the left and misleading detailing to the right.

Structural function   **Misleading detailing**

We can also find many other methods of concealing structure. Masking, confining, veiling or obscuring, or disguising it to render it unrecognizable as structure are all discussed below.

The wooden cladding over the structural framework of the Serpentine Gallery Pavilion (Figure 10.10) can be considered *masking*. In this case, where the design intent was for wooden structure, steel was required to resist the highly eccentric gravity loads applied to the beams. The thickness of the wood cladding significantly increases the apparent structural dimensions. This example is rather unusual. The more common scenario is for designers to specify steel beams in order to achieve minimum structural depth, and then hide them behind the softer and more natural materiality of wood, without greatly deepening the beam.

The practice of hiding structure by *confinement* is widespread and driven by the desire for planar wall surfaces, undisturbed by pilasters. This means columns especially, but in some cases beams as well, being narrow enough to fit within the width of partition walls. Once a wall with its confined column is plastered over there is no evidence of the structure. Structure is also hidden within 'confined masonry' construction, which is growing in popularity, as a result of its good performance during damaging earthquakes. In this construction method, masonry panels are first constructed with vertical slots, and only then are reinforced columns and

Figure 10.8
San Francisco Museum of Modern Art, San Francisco, USA, Mario Botta, 1995. The structural steel framework during construction.

Figure 10.9
A view of the building with its non-structural masonry cladding panels indicative of load-bearing masonry construction.

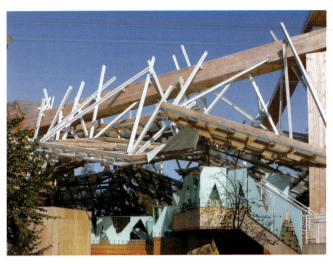

Figure 10.10
Serpentine Gallery Pavilion, London, UK, Frank O. Gehry, 2008. The primary structure that appears to be wooden from a distance is in fact a steel structure clad with wood.

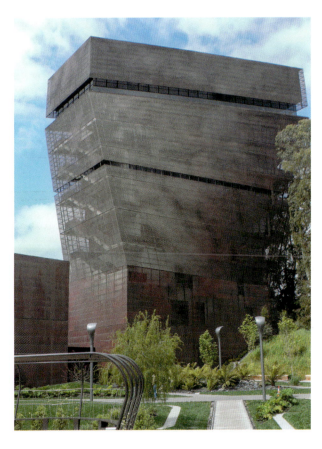

Figure 10.11
De Young Museum, San Francisco, USA, Herzog & De Meuron, 2005. Perforated copper cladding of varying degrees of translucency veils the structure.

beams cast. They are thoroughly bonded to, and confine, the masonry. Even though the composite confined panel is fully structural, a coat of plaster hides that fact from view.

Compared to confinement, *veiling and obscuring* is less commonly encountered. Examples include veiling of structure behind perforated copper cladding at the De Young Museum, San Francisco (Figure 10.11), and even more literally at the Lowry Centre in Manchester (Figure 10.12). Perimeter structural elements of the Kursaal Congress Centre and Auditorium, San Sebastian, are obscured from both inside and out by placing them between curved and thick translucent

Figure 10.12
The Lowry Centre, Salford, UK, Michael Wilford, 2000. Perforated steel sheet veils the tower structure.

Figure 10.13
Kursaal Congress Centre and Auditorium, San Sebastian, Spain, Rafael Moneo, 1999. Structure is obscured from inside and out by glass cladding panels.

glass panels (Figure 10.13), and at the Beijing Olympic Stadium the conceptually simple primary gravity framework is totally obscured by the many other members of identical external dimensions that curve and weave in seemingly random patterns (see Figures 2.1 and 2.2). Some years ago, the few free-standing columns within a large basement space of the Institut du Monde Arabe, Paris, were supplemented by tens of visually identical plastic 'columns' to recreate a modern equivalent of an Egyptian hypostyle hall. So effectively was the presence of the structural columns obscured that the only way to distinguish real from fake was by tapping.

Occasionally, architects detail structure so it is not clearly read as such, thereby diminishing our ability to determine the extent of its structural function. At Colegio Teresiano, Antoni Gaudí designed two types of columns, both of which could almost be mistaken as decorative elements (Figures 10.14 and 10.15). In the far more contemporary MUMUTH music

building, Graz, a remarkable spiralling concrete element not only supports the staircase immediately above it but provides essential support to two suspended floors (Figures 10.16 and 12.59). At the Minnaert Building, Utrecht University, the front of the building is propped on posts that form letters of the alphabet (Figure 10.17).

While the forms and detailing of some of the structures discussed above *disguise* structural functioning, much structure, particularly walls, can be considered hidden not only because of a coat of plaster and paint but due to a lack of perception that they might be structure. This situation arises from the fact that, because walls play so many different roles architecturally, their structural roles may be forgotten or at least downplayed. Consider the following quote from Tadao Ando, in which he fails to mention the load-bearing properties of a wall:

> A good wall, as you call it, is a matter of its physical relationship to people and the way it can create space around us, a system of spatial relationships. It is very basic, but something that people, including architects, often forget . . . If you look at one wall in front of you, you can perceive it as an object. If you see it from the side, you understand that it divides space. If it connects with another wall, you begin to see it as a container of space.

Figure 10.14

Colegio Teresiano, Barcelona, Spain, Antoni Gaudí, 1889. A spiral brick masonry column that is not immediately recognized as structure.

Figure 10.16

MUMUTH Music School and Theatre, Graz, Austria, UN Studio, 2008. A spiralling concrete element that defies structural categorization supports stair and floor plates above. (Brayton Orchard)

Figure 10.15

Slender single brick columns that appear too fragile to function as structure.

Figure 10.17

Minnaert Building, University of Utrecht, The Netherlands, Neutelings Riedijk Architecten, 1997. Steel lettering provides structural support.

At that point, the wall functions as a shelter, protection, a sense of security from the elements . . . The wall is the most basic tool of architecture.[1]

Motivations for hiding structure

In the Introduction to this book I explained how design ideas current within certain periods of architectural history, such as the Renaissance and the Baroque, meant that structural exposure was never a consideration. However, in these early years of the twenty-first century, no single dominant architectural style or movement demands allegiance. A cursory review of internationally acclaimed architects' works indicates that anything and everything goes with respect to hiding or exposing structure.

Given a lack of ideological pressure on architects to take a particular stance towards structural exposure or concealment, practical or pragmatic concerns exert their influence. If we consider a building façade, there are numerous advantages in placing structure behind the skin. First, skin detailing, weatherproofing and maintenance are simplified. Also, separation of skin and structure can improve thermal performance by avoiding thermal bridging and creating opportunities for air circulation inside the skin.

Within a building, a combination of practical and aesthetic choices driven by interior design requirements leads to the ubiquitous use of suspended ceilings. They fulfil many roles, including avoiding the need for high-quality forms and finishes of otherwise exposed structure, and hiding a plethora of pipes, ducts, cables and mechanical equipment. Meanwhile, the practical advantages of providing planar wall surfaces, which are the most accommodating for the hanging of paintings and the positioning of furniture, explain the popularity of hiding columns by confinement to avoid pilasters, as discussed earlier. And the pragmatics of the building programme itself might lead to structure being hidden. For example, if a programme requires an opaque building skin (as for most of the San Francisco Museum of Modern Art), then interior structure becomes invisible from outside.

It is rare for structure to be hidden behind services, but we observe one elegant example at Delft Technical University's library, where structure and services are also highly integrated. Structural steel I-columns are concealed

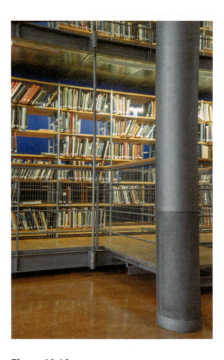

Figure 10.18
Library, Delft Technical University, The Netherlands, Mecanoo Architekten, 1997. A structural steel column is concealed by a tube, perforated at its base for ventilation.

within steel tubes that read as columns. The tubes channel air to their perforated bases as part of the ventilation strategy (Figure 10.18).

A particularly architecturally defensible reason for concealing structure is to realize or reinforce the design concept. Awareness and interrogation of the design concept should always be the basis for decisions regarding hiding or exposing structure. Any architecture where exposed structure detracts from the design concept is flawed.

In the remainder of this section several examples illustrate how hidden structure enhances architectural concepts. A concept requiring sleek and fluid forms to be experienced both within and from outside a building, like the London Aquatic Centre, would all but be ruined with the exposure of deep and geometrically complex roof structure (Figures 10.19 and 10.20). Also, how could a cloud-like undulating roof form have its massive structure exposed from inside and out at the BMW Welt centre? Over 15 m deep in places, trusses form an enormous and complex space frame requiring a minimum of interior supports. All this structure is hidden behind exterior cladding and roofing, and ceiling panels (Figures 10.21 and 10.22).

Figure 10.19
London Aquatic Centre, London, UK, Zaha Hadid, 2011. This photograph, taken during construction, shows the extensive and complex roof structure necessitated by only three points of support. (John Dee)

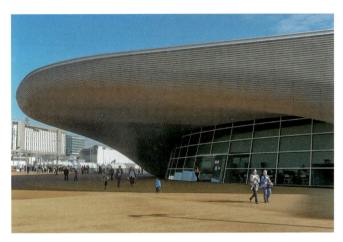

Figure 10.20
The sleek form is uncompromised by exposed structure. (John Dee)

Figure 10.22
Large open spaces are achieved by deep and complex roof structure hidden by the ceiling panels. (Trent Roche)

Figure 10.21
BMW Welt, Munich, Germany, Coop Himmelb(l)au, 2007. Exterior form with the 'cloud' roof emanating from the vortex of the 'double cone' on the right. (Martin Luechinger)

Figure 10.23
Forum Building, Barcelona, Spain, Herzog & De Meuron, 2004. Extensive cantilevering and bridging is achieved in the absence of any visible structure. (Detlef Schobert)

Figure 10.24
Guthrie Theater, Minneapolis, USA, Jean Nouvel, 2006. The means of support of this cantilevering form are revealed only upon close inspection. (Margaret E. Poggio)

Curiosity is aroused by irregular or daring architectural forms when structure is hidden. We might ask: how is the form held up? Due to its perceived absence, a sense of intrigue or mystery is raised regarding the means of structural support. Particularly attracting this sort of response are buildings where structure so often dominates, like those with long-span roofs, buildings that bridge or cantilever, or very tall buildings. Returning to the CCTV Building (see Figure 10.2), how does that building work structurally, given only diagonal members are expressed? How does the Forum Building, Barcelona, manage to cantilever so far (Figure 10.23)?

What about the 'Endless Bridge' of the Guthrie Theater, Minneapolis? A sloping fissure along its length appears to reduce its strength, and there are no deep cantilever beams, or inclined tension-ties to support its free end (Figure 10.24). In the Forum Building, cantilevering and bridging are achieved by 4.0 m-deep steel trusses from which the lower and main floors are hung. As for the 'Endless Bridge', close inspection reveals vertical and diagonal steel members crossing the fissure, and the mystery is solved – deep steel trusses embedded between exterior skin and internal lining cantilever from the main building.

Curiosity is also certainly aroused by the Leutschenbach School (Figure 10.25). What supports the floor of the uppermost storey, a gymnastic hall and, even more significantly, *all* of the floors above ground? No ground-floor structure is visible. The riddle is solved by studying a scaled-down model of the structural steel framework.[2] Internal storey-height trusses under the gymnastic hall provide adequate force-paths, and at ground-floor level a series of squat steel tripods, set deep within the plan, provide necessary vertical support and lateral bracing. For some observers, initial curiosity might lead to feelings of concern, or even anxiety, given the apparent structural weaknesses. Could the designers have made a mistake, unnoticed during the checking and building permission process?

Figure 10.25
Leutschenbach School, Zürich, Switzerland, Christian Kerez, 2008. A lack of exposed structure on two floors of the building raises curiosity. (Matthew Lacey)

Figure 10.26
Office building, Wellington, New Zealand. The eccentric bracing on one floor of this building appears to be missing, but on closer inspection it is hidden behind louvred cladding.

Figure 10.27
Office building, San Francisco, USA. Slender structural steel columns are 'increased' in size by masking them with façade panels, giving them the appearance of greater strength and a scale in keeping with other architectural elements.

Occasionally, a localized area of structure is hidden, causing anxiety until a more careful examination is undertaken. In a Wellington office building it *appears* that the eccentric bracing, absolutely necessary for adequate seismic resistance, has been omitted from one floor, perhaps left out during construction and introducing a fatal structural flaw (Figure 10.26). Fortunately, it is merely hidden behind cladding.

Another motivation for hiding structure is to make it appear larger. This is reasonably common in multi-storey steel-frame buildings. Due to the strength of internal structural cores, exterior columns can appear too skinny and unsubstantial. The solution is to mask them so they *appear* stronger than they are, to avoid possible perceptions of fragility or lack of safety (Figures 10.27 and 10.28).

On other occasions, however, an architect increases the apparent size of structure to strengthen its architectural presence. This was Mario Botta's decision when designing the Bechtler Museum of Modern Art (Figure 10.29). The vertical loads from the cantilevering floor and roof above required a concrete-filled steel tube. Its structural diameter, which is maintained up its height, is delicately revealed top

Figure 10.28
Removal of some cladding to a column reveals its true size.

Figure 10.29
Bechtler Museum of Modern Art, Charlotte, USA, Mario Botta, 2010.
A plain column near the main entry is masked by a steel frame and tile
cladding. (Peter M. Eimon)

and bottom, and the enlargement is achieved by a light steel
framework bolted to the column and clad with terracotta tiles.
While the structure of this column is masked by cladding, all
the other columns of the building are hidden: 'For all of its
uniqueness, the swollen column does, in fact, belong to the
building's regular 29-foot-by-29-foot column grid – it's just
that all of the other columns are concealed within walls, and
six of the 20 grid points are left empty.'[3] This building, then,
exemplifies two different motivations for hiding structure: first,
to increase its architectural presence; and, second, to achieve
an interior architectural quality that exalts 'surface'.

No doubt there are other reasons why designers hide
structure. Perhaps some of these are illustrated by buildings
known to you?

Summary

This exploration of *hidden* structure restores the balance of
the book, which otherwise focuses upon *exposed* structure.
In most buildings, a significant proportion of the structure is
hidden, and there are many possibilities of achieving different
degrees of hiddenness. A whole structural system, like that
to resist horizontal forces, or just individual members, such
as floor slabs, may be hidden. Structure can be hidden from
the exterior yet revealed internally. It can be hidden, perhaps
behind façade panels, yet simultaneously expressed. It can
be exposed, but not perceived as structure, either due to
obscuration by other elements or by how its detailing prevents
us comprehending its true structural function.

Architects employ a wide range of techniques for
concealing structure. Screening by opaque elements, like
suspended ceilings or partition walls, is common, as is the
cladding of structural members. Particularly in countries
that use masonry walls, structure is often incorporated and
confined within the walls.

Even more numerous than the strategies of concealment
are reasons for hiding structure. Pragmatic considerations
of thermal performance, weather tightness, maintenance
and the desire to hide services are the primary reasons. But
the most interesting motivations, and those most likely to
result in engaging architecture, are linked to design ideas and
concepts. For example, by skilfully hiding structure, we are
able to create a sense of intrigue or mystery, arouse curiosity
and convey opposing qualities of strength or instability, and
even generate emotions as divergent as safety and anxiety.

Even though the hiddenness of structure prevents it
from adding richness visually or spatially, or participating
representationally or symbolically, it can fulfil other
architectural roles. Its unique contribution is to communicate
design ideas with a clarity exposed structure would otherwise
cloud. In so far as pragmatic issues allow, decisions about
exposing, hiding but expressing, or complete hiding of
structure must always reinforce the design concept. There
is no question that structure must be hidden when certain
metaphoric or conceptual ideas demand it – hidden structure
enables these architectural visions to be realized, as has been
illustrated in the many buildings studied in this chapter.

Notes

1. M. Auping, *Seven interviews with Tadao Ando*, Fort Worth, TX:
    Modern Art Museum of Fort Worth, 2002, and R. Peltason and G.
    Ong-Yan (eds), *Architect: the Pritzker Prize laureates in their own
    words*, London: Thames & Hudson, 2010, p. 186.

2. 'Christian Kerez, Leutschenbach School, Zurich, Switzerland', *A+U*
    479, 2008, 12.

3. G. F. Shaprio, 'Structural column', *Architect* 99(7), 2010, 21–2.

eleven

Expressing architectural concepts

Introduction

As we move into this chapter the emphasis changes from *analysis* of how structure contributes architecturally to *design*. Whereas the preceding chapters have examined how structure, mainly exposed but also hidden, plays many architectural roles other than load-bearing, here and in Chapter 12 we consider structure from the perspective of a designer. So, rather than beginning with structure, the starting points are now architectural concepts and qualities.

The intent of this section is to demonstrate how structure can express or reinforce a wide range of architectural concepts and qualities, and, by extension, to suggest that there will be few situations where exposed structure cannot enrich an architectural design. However, before commencing to make this case, there is a need to clarify the term *architectural concept*. Pressman offers a definition and then explains its importance:

> [Concept] refers to the essential formative scheme, idea, or basic organizing principle of a building design . . . A strong initial idea is valuable because design decisions can be imprinted by it and then relate to it (or even express it), thereby ensuring coherence among all elements of a project . . . When design decisions are less arbitrary, i.e., they are informed by the concept, the architecture becomes greater, more powerful, and meaningful.[1]

White takes the idea of concept for granted, and then a step further, by emphasizing the need for designers to *reinforce* their concepts:

> Reinforcement involves the statement of the principal messages of the form in as many ways as possible. There are several ways that the building conveys messages to those using it . . . The more ways that the designer can mobilize his [or her] vocabulary of forms to convey the message he intends, the more clearly and strongly his building will communicate the desired information. A design message said in five ways with form has a better chance to be perceived and understood than if only said one way.[2]

While acknowledging the importance of concepts and the need to reinforce them, White also notes that an architectural project may benefit from several concepts. These may exert their influence on a design in a hierarchical manner. In other words, rather than inspiration being confined to one central idea, there may be several ideas of greater and lesser importance influencing different areas and aspects of a project.

As has been noted by others, architects do not readily articulate their design concepts or central ideas.[3] So, it is rather revealing when they are explicitly asked to describe the concepts for buildings they have designed. At least for the past four years, most of the six shortlisted candidates for the annual, prestigious architectural RIBA Stirling Prize have been interviewed.[4] While some have acknowledged an overriding concept or central idea, most have described how their design ideas emerged after consideration of the building programme or context. Yet even in the absence of articulated central ideas, some of the works of these architects incorporate design moves that clearly communicate some of the concepts explored in this chapter. For example, concepts related to floating, being grounded, dynamism and order can be distinctly perceived in their work.

Given the intent of this chapter to demonstrate how structure can express and reinforce architectural concepts, it is necessary to pose and answer the question: what are the recurring, predominant or popular concepts in contemporary architecture? Due to the previously noted reticence of architects to describe their concepts, finding a definitive answer to this question proved rather difficult. I describe the process briefly, not only to explain a certain rigour in the way selections have been made, but also so readers can appreciate the limitations of the approaches taken.

A literature search that included a review of all relevant texts and articles from reading lists provided in my school of architecture course outlines led to a preliminary list of approximately seventy individual concepts and architectural qualities, including contrasting pairs, such as protection–exposure. Building-programme- and site-specific-led concepts were not included due to their specific factors. This list, far shorter than expected, was then supplemented using another approach that involved making architectural readings of existing buildings. The group of approximately three hundred mainly twentieth-century buildings researched for the first edition of this book were reanalysed or 'read' to discern possible concepts underlying their architectural forms, as well as their notable architectural qualities. After categorizing and sorting, the following most common groupings of concepts emerged, listed in order of frequency of occurrence:

- order–chaos;
- stability–instability.
- static–dynamic; and
- grounded–floating;

The list of prevalent architectural qualities comprises:

- open–closed;
- heavy–lightweight;
- light–darkness;
- elegant–rough;
- simple–complex; and
- soft–hard.

For the sake of ordering and presenting this material, a somewhat artificial working distinction has been made between concepts and qualities. Some concepts can be considered qualities and vice versa, but in general the concepts are more applicable to an entire project and the qualities are more likely to be descriptive of a space or spaces within such a project. None of these groups can be precisely defined. There is certainly some overlap between them. Some structures discussed below express concepts from more than one group, or could even be considered part of another group altogether.

These groups of concepts and qualities are the focus of attention in the remainder of this chapter, and in the next. Each group of contrasting concepts is considered separately, beginning with a theoretical study exploring the potential for structure to express or reinforce the range of concepts within that pairing. Then the range of concepts is illustrated by brief case-studies of existing works of architecture.

Order–chaos

This section explores how structure has, is currently and potentially might express concepts or ideas anywhere on the spectrum between order and chaos. Throughout architectural history, beginning with monumental Egyptian construction and continued by the Greeks and Romans, geometrical order has dominated plans and sections. The early temples, for example, were notable for their symmetry, at least about one major axis, and columns were always vertical and usually regularly spaced on an orthogonal grid. In circular or semi-circular forms, regular structure reflected the ordering geometry. The desire for order was just as apparent three thousand years later during the Renaissance. Façades of significant buildings are notable for the order of their structural elements, be they repetitively or rhythmically disposed.

A strong preference for order in architecture is still apparent now, at the beginning of the twenty-first century. Today, most buildings have regularly spaced columns or walls adhering to rectilinear grids. Very rarely is structure positioned off a grid-line, or a column or wall anything other than straight and vertical. Order suits the pragmatics of architecture, such as the practicality and economy of construction, the ease of both architectural and structural design, and even the shape and layout of furniture. However, over the last twenty years or so, architects have generated concepts and design ideas that challenge the notion of order and, increasingly, they are attracted to less orderly architectural form. Perhaps in keeping with the 'spirit of the age', many contemporary architectural concepts and built works offer far more diverse visual and spatial experiences. This is possible where architectural elements, including structure, are freed from the limitations of verticality and orthogonality.

Before case-studies illustrate structure expressing concepts ranging from order to chaos, theoretical design studies explore the ability of structure to express or reinforce these concepts.

Design studies

These studies, initially undertaken in a graduate architecture class, investigate how structure might express differing degrees of order and chaos. The primary precedent was the Kanagawa Institute of Technology (KAIT) workshop (see Figure 6.20). This is a single-storey building, approximately 46 m square with a light roof supported by 305 interior steel posts. They are seemingly randomly distributed throughout the plan, on average 2.6 m apart, but distances between any two vary from 0.4 m to 8 m. The design brief for the studies envisage a smaller space, 15 m square, to accommodate a café or restaurant, also containing relatively closely spaced and slender posts.

Three shapes of posts were studied: straight, curved and faceted. Figure 11.1 presents a summary of the outcomes for straight posts. The degree of disorder increases from (a) to (d) in both plan and section. Each structural layout represents one point on the order–chaos continuum, and expressing a different concept offers a unique spatial experience. Only four designs are presented from an infinite number of possibilities.

Case-studies

We begin with two examples of structural order before illustrating a progression towards chaotic structural assemblages. The sequencing of case-studies illustrating the progression from order towards chaos is irregular rather than linear. Disorder has many different architectural manifestations. For example, a building can have a highly ordered perimeter structure, but its interior structure may be randomly configured, as in the Baumschulenweg Crematorium (Figure 2.10). Or the converse may apply, as in the National Stadium, Beijing (Figure 2.1). Perhaps one area of a building plan is ordered while the structure in another area breaks loose from geometrical constraints, or a gradual progression from order to chaos might be evident as we move through a building. Also, we need to remember that our perception of order is affected by our viewpoint. At a distance, the iconic form of the Eiffel Tower exudes a sense of order, but close up or within, its assemblage of members appears chaotic (Figure 11.2). Such an observation is common for complex three-dimensional structural frameworks.

Any number of buildings within an urban precinct, and many in your own city centre, will be admirable models of structural order. However, Figures 11.3 and 11.4 illustrate how structure expresses geometric order in different architectural periods, and through vastly different materials, structural systems, scales and densities of structural footprint.

The first example of moving away from geometric order can be described as expressing a sense of informality. The random inclination of columns at the Melbourne Museum, as well as their colours, can also be interpreted as playful (Figure 11.5). In this project the architect 'breaks away from conventions for making an architecture that expresses statics, programme and human scale. Instead they play with an architecture that avoids or confuses scale, celebrates destabilization and courts chance . . . and allows the possibility of randomness without chaos.'[5]

A greater degree of randomness is conveyed by the corner portion of a long office and residential development in Vienna by Coop Himmelb(l)au (Figure 11.6). Occupied space is held within an irregular exoskeletal mega-frame. The top double-storey frame appears to have been designed independently of the lower frame, also two storeys high, but then forced to sit on top. Several columns are misaligned, and coupled with the different inclination of columns on the two frames the structure appears decidedly awkward.

This structure and many others in this chapter are considered highly irregular from a seismic design perspective. Fortunately, Vienna is located in a zone of relatively low seismicity. However, structures with this degree of irregularity, in this case a misaligned primary column, should be designed for gravitational forces only, and not resist seismic loads.

Structural wall

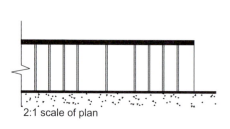

(a)

2:1 scale of plan

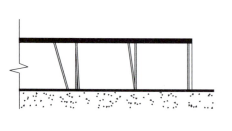

(b)

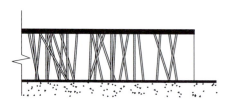

(c)

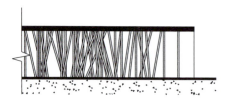

(d)

Plan

Section
(Note: 2:1 scale of plan)

Figure 11.1

Theoretical studies of how structural configuration can express order (a) through to chaos (d). Plans and sections (not to scale).

Figure 11.2
Eiffel Tower, Paris, France, G. Eiffel, 1889. From within one of the legs of the tower the structure appears chaotic.

Figure 11.3
Piazza of St Peter's, Rome, Italy, Bernini, 1667. The epitome of structural order in an oval form.

Figure 11.4
New Gallery, Berlin, Germany, Mies van der Rohe, 1968. Highly ordered, vertical and horizontal structure.

Figure 11.5
Melbourne Museum, Melbourne, Australia, Denton Corker Marshall, 2000. Randomly placed and orientated columns support an exhibition gallery.

Figure 11.6
Apartment and office building Schlachthausgasse, Vienna, Austria, Coop Himmelb(l)au, 2005. Irregular and awkward exterior structure.
(© Pablo Sanchez Lopez)

Although structural engineers permit irregular structure to resist gravitational forces, regular seismic-resisting structure is required elsewhere in plan. Sophisticated structural detailing of the irregular structure, such as creating pin joints between members, might also be required. By combining separate irregular gravity structure together with regular seismic-resisting structure, architects can introduce a degree of structural irregularity while achieving safety against earthquake attack.[6]

A location in a benign seismic zone has permitted structural irregularities to be incorporated into 1111 Lincoln Road, Miami Beach (Figure 11.7). Its structure *appears* to break every rule in a seismic design textbook. Even though reinforced-concrete structural walls are present within the plan, and mindful of the need for every structure in a seismic zone to resist twisting in plan, this configuration would definitely not be recommended in an active seismic region. Assembled from precast-concrete elements and post-tensioned concrete floor slabs, structure is the architecture of this building. The irregularity of inter-storey heights is surpassed by the lack of continuity of the vertical structural elements. While they might display some sense of order on one floor, when all floors are considered together it once again appears that each floor, to some extent, was designed without reference to adjacent floors. This structure very successfully reinforces an architectural idea closely linked to randomness and the chaotic.

Figure 11.7
1111 Lincoln Rd, Miami Beach, Florida, USA, Herzog & De Meuron, 2010. A vertical assemblage of walls and piers verging on the chaotic.
(Audrey Rosario)

Figure 11.8
Serpentine Summer Pavilion, London, Frank O. Gehry, 2008. A random quality in the structural framing speaks of constructional naivety.

Figure 11.9
Michael Lee-Chin Crystal, Royal Ontario Museum, Toronto, Canada, Daniel Libeskind, 2007. Two contrasting architectures and structures.

The same can be said of the very different structure that visually dominated the temporary Serpentine Summer Pavilion (Figure 11.8). The primary structure consisted of four large wood-clad steel posts and beams. What is of particular interest is the seemingly careless or casual layout of these structural members. Posts were not on a grid, were of different heights, and none of the beams was parallel to another. Even more surprising was the naivety of the post–beam connections. They looked as if they had been just flung together, or were reproducing a model constructed by a child. Many different readings of this structure are possible, but they all lie well away from the ordered end of the order–chaos continuum.

Since the completion of the Michael Lee-Chin Crystal, occupying the forecourt between two wings of the historic Royal Ontario Museum, Toronto, and integrating new and old, structural order and chaos exist within the one complex (Figures 11.9 and 11.10). The existing building is notable for its structural symmetry, gridded layout, verticality and regularity. In contrast, the random structuring of the Crystal dispenses with upright columns in favour of inclined members that slash through interior spaces. A greater disparity in structural language is hard to imagine. Yet the internal structure of the Crystal complements its jagged exterior prismatic surfaces, always reminding occupants of the dramatic form they inhabit.

Figure 11.10
The chaotic quality of interior structure near the main façade.

Stability–instability

Large structural members possess and communicate strength. If they are vertical, triangulated, arched or rigidly interconnected, as in the case of moment frames, they also provide stability against horizontal forces. Cross-braced frames, structural walls including buttresses, are examples.

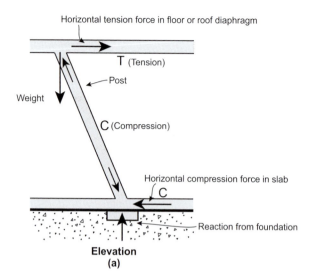

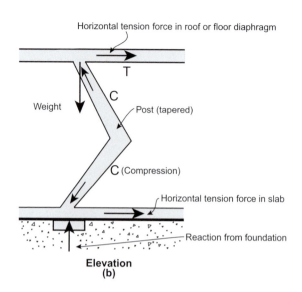

Figure 11.11

The additional structural actions or cross-sectional dimensions to achieve stable leaning and bent posts. They require horizontal forces top and bottom to stabilize them. A bent post also requires greater bending strength near the bend.

Size is important. Slender members, particularly posts or columns, can appear unstable due to their perceived vulnerability against buckling or sideways collapse. Frequently, as noted in Chapter 10, when architects consider that columns appear too slender or lack the required gravitas, they bulk them out with non-structural material. The progression towards both perceived and actual instability is hastened where columns lean or are bent. Leaning posts require horizontal forces acting at their tops and bottoms to assure stability, and bent posts require increased cross-sectional area to resist the greater bending moments to which they are subject (Figure 11.11).

The following case-studies illustrate a range of design approaches that express different degrees of instability. Recall that every structure, if it is code-compliant, will be stable under gravity as well as able to withstand horizontal forces.

Design studies

Figure 11.12 summarizes studies where the degree of instability expressed by structure varies. The background to the studies is as described in the Order–Chaos section. Apart from Figure 11.12 (a), where each cluster of four posts

is vertical, in the other three designs the posts sloping in the same direction not only appear unstable but *are* unstable. In these cases the roof must function as a structural diaphragm, strongly connected to the four perimeter structural walls that will ultimately prevent the building collapsing. In (c), instability potentially occurs in one direction – the direction of the slope of the post – but in (d), since the directions of slope vary, the posts exert a twisting action on the roof. Again, without the strength of a roof diaphragm and perimeter walls, the building would collapse in a twisting or corkscrew action. Figure 11.13 illustrates the horizontal components of post forces acting on the roof diaphragm, and the forces within the walls to maintain the roof in equilibrium. Note that when a wall cantilevers from the foundations, as in this case, it resists forces acting only in the direction of its length. It needs support from the roof diaphragm when it is subject to forces perpendicular to its length.

Case-studies

To begin, we visit two buildings that exemplify stability. Then we consider instances of increasing degrees of instability. There is no difficulty finding buildings that are stable, but most do not actively *express* stability. How a building is stabilized is not usually expressed overtly, and is certainly rarely celebrated.

In the Vancouver Law Courts, as the higher floors step back in the atrium, free-standing concrete moment frames rise up

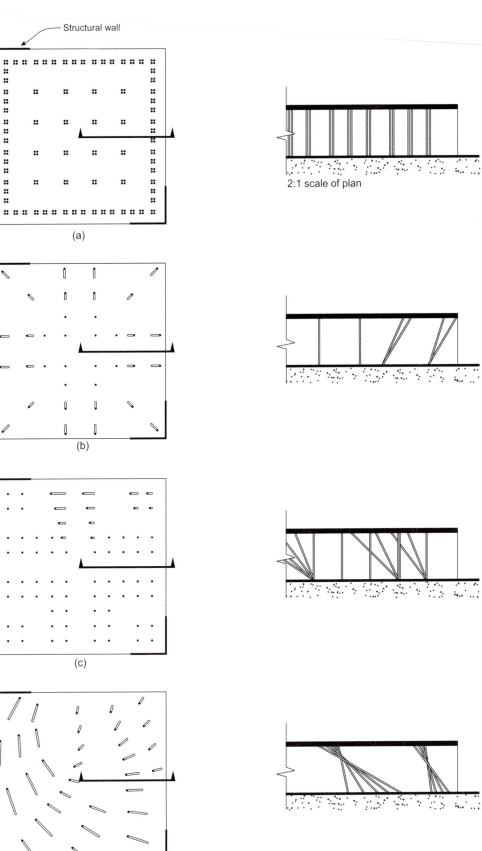

Figure 11.12

Structural configurations expressing stability (a) through to instability (d). Plans and sections (not to scale).

Structural wall

(a)

(b)

(c)

(d)

2:1 scale of plan

Plan

Section
(Note: 2:1 scale of plan)

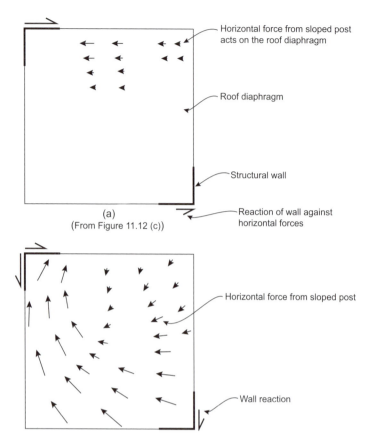

Horizontal force from sloped post acts on the roof diaphragm

Roof diaphragm

Structural wall

(a)
(From Figure 11.12 (c))

Reaction of wall against horizontal forces

Horizontal force from sloped post

Wall reaction

Figure 11.13

Horizontal forces acting on the roof diaphragm from the sloping columns, and the necessary stabilizing forces from the perimeter walls for the layout in Figure 11.12 (c) and (d).

an additional storey (Figure 11.14). Their structural role is to support the sloping space-frame roof. They also modulate their side of the atrium, and due to their dimensions and materiality convey a sense of strength and stability.

In many buildings, though, walls provide and express stability. This is the case above the ground floor in the Cathedral of Christ the Light, Oakland (Figure 11.15). Exposed both outside and within, thick concrete walls surround the body of the cathedral, providing security and support for curved wooden ribs and louvres within the striking fully glazed envelope. This cathedral, which replaces one irreparably damaged during the 1989 Loma Prieta earthquake, not only has been provided with a strong base perimeter but, to lessen future earthquake damage, the entire building weight is supported by lead-rubber bearings for the purpose of seismic isolation.

Whereas the previous two buildings are characterized by strength and stability, the slender columns at Jussieu University, Paris, might well induce worry in some observers – particularly when they realize the columns support five suspended floors (Figure 11.16). The concern might not arise so much from gravity as from wind forces (Paris is located in a seismically inactive zone). During wind storms one can visualize the columns flexing and the floors vibrating sideways in an alarming fashion – if there were no strong floor diaphragms and vertical structure present. Therefore,

Figure 11.14

Vancouver Law Courts, Vancouver, Canada, Arthur Erickson, 1980. Concrete frames support the space-frame roof and convey a sense of stability.

Figure 11.15

The Cathedral of Christ the Light, Oakland, CA, USA, C. Hartman, 2008. Enclosing concrete walls express security.

Figure 11.16
Jussieu University, Paris, France, Edouart Albert, 1965. A multi-story building supported by very slender columns.

the floor slabs of these lightly supported blocks need to function as diaphragms that are connected to strong vertical concrete cores providing the necessary stability at each end of a block. If we study the floor plans of the entire building we can see how the structural cores that provide the horizontal strength are placed adjacent to the areas supported by the slender columns.

Feelings of unease with respect to stability keep intensifying as we move to more overt expressions of instability. Consider the audacious raising of the Sharp Centre, Toronto, 26 m above street level (Figure 11.17). The perceived instability is induced by the height of the elevated two-storey volume and the relatively slender posts. Fortunately, the splaying of the posts and their triangulation some distance in plan away from the structural core tend to reduce anxiety. Yet again, the presence of floor diaphragms and their connections into a core that is strong against horizontal loads is the secret of this building's real stability.

The Mediathéque, Marseille, located within an atrium between two much larger buildings, also has splayed legs. But this time the configuration of the supports represents the

Figure 11.17
Sharp Centre, Ontario College of Art & Design, Toronto, Canada, Alsop Architects, 2004. The two-storey volume is supported by splayed steel tubes and a concrete core. The sloping red-coloured element houses an escape stair.

antithesis of stability due to the way they converge towards a point at floor level (Figure 11.18). It seems that unequal floor loading within the Mediathéque could cause it to topple. Only the relatively large diameters of the props and their considerable bending strength avert such a catastrophe.

Even more explicit expressions of instability are found in the Beehive, Culver City, whose architect explores ideas of 'balanced unbalance'.[7] Several interior posts are kinked like a bent knee-joint and the detailing is suggestive of bending failure (Figure 11.19). The rotation at each post joint

Figure 11.18
Mediathéque, Marseille, France, Alsop & Störmer, 1994. The inward-sloping legs express instability.

Figure 11.19
The Beehive, Culver City, USA, Eric Owen Moss Architects, 2001. A 'broken' post at first-floor level.

Figure 11.20
Spittelau Viaducts Housing, Vienna, Austria, Zaha Hadid, 2005. Sloping columns suggest instability. (Addison Godel)

is expressed graphically by a triangular 'crack' between the upper and lower sections of the posts. Notions of instability, fragility and damage are conjured up in one's mind. Only upon closer inspection do we see how steel plates welded within the hollow sections provide enough structural strength.

Sloping columns can certainly communicate instability, especially where there is no triangulation or where the column slopes do not oppose one another to cancel out any out-of-balance horizontal forces. This situation occurs at Spittelau Viaducts Housing, Vienna (Figure 11.20). Although some vertical columns are present, most are sloped in one direction, causing instability. The elevated two apartments need to be connected through their floor diaphragms to other blocks that provide the strength to resist horizontal forces, from both the sloping columns and wind.

In the final example of instability, all four supporting piers are straight but none has the same geometry as another, is vertical, or appears to be connected strongly to the roof.

The whole structural layout exudes a state of precariousness which is slightly reduced by the outward splay of some piers (Figure 11.21).

Static–dynamic

This continuum of architectural concepts has some overlap with the previous concept pairs of order–chaos and stability–instability. While the architectural expression of order, stability and static is similar and hard to distinguish between, at the other end of the spectra differences become more apparent. For example, chaotic structure may not be perceived as unstable. Depending upon the nature of its randomness, it could be read as dynamic, however. Dynamic structure also need not be considered unstable. It must convey a sense of movement, which might include relating to our movement or causing our eyes to move as they follow the structural form.

Figure 11.21
Photovoltaic pergola, Barcelona, Spain, Architectos Architects, 2004. A lack of verticality and horizontality contribute a sense of structural instability. (Roger Ibánez)

Design studies

Using the same procedure as outlined previously, four designs are presented that trace expressions of static through to dynamic (Figure 11.22). Typically, a sense of the dynamic in a post-and-beam structure is achieved by some combination of post inclination and non-orthogonal placement.

Case-studies

As noted above, a regular structure consisting of vertical and horizontal members, or even arches, can be considered to express all or any of order, stability and static. This could mean, as it often does, that the structure is essentially dumb or non-expressive. Most building structures fall into this category unless designers introduce some expressive and therefore architecturally transformative qualities. Consider the post-and-beam structure of the Museum of Anthropology, Vancouver (Figure 11.23). Here, the most basic of all structural systems is manipulated in height and width to move a potentially bland, ordered, stable and static form to one with a sense of the dynamic.

In many buildings, however, dynamism is achieved simply by sloping columns or posts, as in the Vancouver Convention Centre (Figure 11.24). Columns placed along the sea wall acknowledge the inlet beyond. They slope outwards towards it and create exciting viewing areas from within (Figure 11.25). Secondary structural elements have the same capacity to introduce a dynamic quality when sloped, even when primary structure is orthogonal. Jean Nouvel introduces this technique to enliven a façade of One New Change, London (Figure 11.26).

A fine example of structure expressing movement (of people) is the entry canopies to the Bilbao Metro (Figure 11.27). A transparent skin sheathes eleven tubular steel arched-frames. As well as articulating circulation, other aspects of their design provide a great deal of architectural enrichment. The front frame leans slightly outwards over the threshold in a subtle but effective welcoming gesture. While the second frame is orientated vertically, those behind it lean over incrementally in the other direction. Eventually they align perpendicular to the slope of the escalator or stairs inside. Due to their changing orientation from the vertical, the frames invite entry and then graphically indicate in elevation the transition from horizontal to downwards movement and vice versa. They therefore both express and respond to movement within, and even their roundedness echoes the

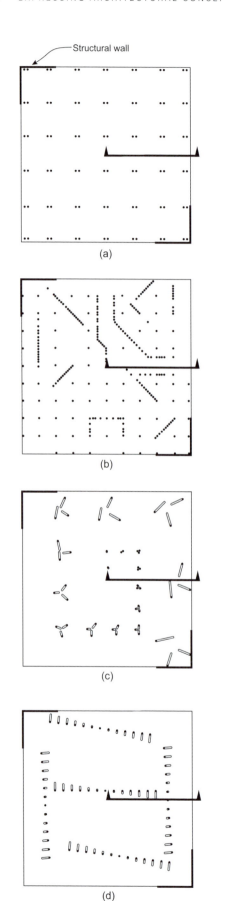

(a)

(b)

(c)

(d)

Plan

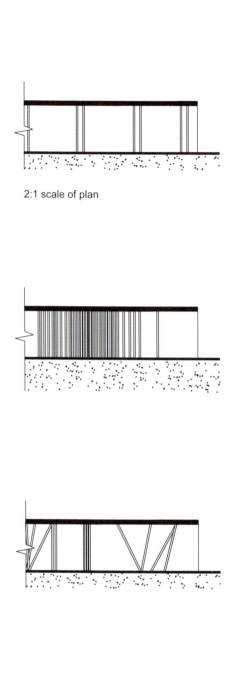

2:1 scale of plan

Section
(Note: 2:1 scale of plan)

Figure 11.22

Structural configuration varies from static (a) to dynamic (d).

Figure 11.23

Museum of Anthropology, Vancouver, Canada, Arthur Erickson, 1976. Creative post-and-beam construction.

Figure 11.25

Sloping columns intensify the experience of viewing from inside.

Figure 11.24

The West Building, Vancouver Convention Centre, Vancouver, Canada, LMN Architects, MCM Architects and DA Architects + Planners, 2009. External columns slope towards the inlet.

Figure 11.26

One New Change, London, UK, Jean Nouvel, 2010. Steel mullions slope and intersect against a backdrop of orthogonal primary structure.

Figure 11.27

Bilbao Metro, Bilbao, Spain, Foster and Partners, 1996. Progressively changing frame inclinations express movement into and from an underground station.

Figure 11.28
Mexican Embassy, Berlin, González de León and Serrano, 2000. Dynamic column-walls.

Figure 11.29
Barajas Airport, Madrid, Spain, Richard Rogers Partnership, 2006. A combination of a playful and dynamic structure dominates the main spaces.

forms of the underground tunnels and platform areas to which they lead.

The main façade of the Mexican Embassy, Berlin, is another example of exterior dynamic structure (Figure 11.28). Forty closely spaced and over-structured concrete mullions-cum-columns satisfy security and aesthetic requirements. Several subtle geometric manipulations of the 17 m-high columns transform a potentially repetitive façade into one comprising two columned planes, both angled inwards, and one warped to achieve a dynamic visual effect. Beginning at the left-hand side of the embassy as seen from the street, vertical columns step back progressively from the pavement towards the entrance. To the right of the entrance, column bases lie on a straight line between it and the corner of the building. However, the set-out lines for the tops and bottoms of the columns are not parallel. This simple geometric variation between top and bottom set-out lines creates a warped surface, profoundly affecting the visual impact of the columns. As the eye moves relative to the columns, they also appear to move.

Pairs of inclined bifurcated tapered struts lead the eyes upwards towards a wave-like roof in Barajas Airport, Madrid (Figure 11.29). All struts lean towards the outside of the building, irrespective of the viewing point. Their dynamic radiating gesture helps create the quality of fun desired by the architect, while at the same time their supporting piers define

the principal linear circulation route. The struts are painted in bright colours that continually change along the 1.2 km-long terminal. The colours accentuate the structure, reinforcing its dynamic qualities.

Now we move on to examples where structure plays even more dynamic and dramatic roles. First, we visit the Berlin Philharmonie. The fragmentation of its surfaces, used so effectively to break up undesirable sound reflections in the main auditorium, continues into the main foyer. Two pairs of raking columns support the underside of the sloping auditorium floor (Figure 11.30). The foyer space is visually

Figure 11.30
Philharmonie, Berlin, Germany, Hans Scharoun, 1963. Some of the diverse structural elements in the foyer.

Figure 11.31
The Cooper Union, New York, USA, Morphosis, 2009. Inclined columns at street level introduce a dynamic quality. (William Kimber)

Figure 11.32
Choreography Centre, Aix-en-Provence, France, Rudy Ricciotti Architecte, 2004. Exposed perimeter structure expresses the building's function. (Jacqueline Poggi)

dynamic with many different structural elements – columns, piers, walls, bridges and other circulation elements, like staircases and walkways. The structure appears irregular, even spontaneous, and certainly not constrained to an orthogonal grid.

At the Choreography Centre, Aix-en-Provence, every perimeter structural element is exposed (Figure 11.32). The design brief prohibited internal structure that might disrupt building function so, apart from each end of the building, floor structure spans the entire width of the building. The dynamism of the façade is achieved by the irregular inclined columns. Unlike the exposed members at the National Stadium, Beijing, these members vary in dimensions and the larger members taper, reducing in size towards the roof. Also, in comparison to the stadium's structural members, they are quite upright but sufficiently angled to create a triangulated pattern able to resist horizontal forces. The dynamic appearance of the structure raises numerous questions: might

structure be symbolizing the straight limbs and pointed feet of dancers, and do the different-sized structural members represent the different ages of dancers participating in choreographed productions? However we read this structure, we are likely to agree that it expresses a certain graceful and dynamic, dance-like quality.

Animal movement, specifically that of horses, was the inspiration for the final case-study that illustrates the extreme end of the static–dynamic architectural concept continuum (Figure 11.33). This extension for the Library for Architecture, Art and Design, Münster, sits in front of a building that was

Raking columns also enliven the ground floor of the Cooper Union, New York (Figure 11.31). They splay to collect forces from vertical columns above that are concealed behind the sculpted façade. Although it would have made a lot more structural sense to keep columns vertical at ground level, the architects design and expose this dynamic structure to reinforce their design ideas.

Figure 11.33
Library addition, Leonardo Campus, Münster, Germany, Zauberschoën and Buehler and Buehler Architects, 2010. The shape of the columns was inspired by the movement of horses' legs. (Arch. Facchetti Davide)

formerly the campus stables. As part of an architectural class design exercise, students studied photographs of legs of galloping horses from which they derived the forms and details of the three double-columns.

Grounded–floating

Structure can also be an effective means of expressing concepts positioned anywhere between grounded and floating. The two natural objects to which 'groundedness' most applies are rocks and trees. Both rise from below the ground yet are firmly embedded within it, in a completely continuous manner. What is seen above ground continues underground. While exposed rock is merely an extrusion of what is below, a tree's root system ensures its stability. As well as their continuity through the ground plane, rocks and trees usually reduce in size as they rise. Tree trunks taper towards the highest branches and sometimes, just before plunging into the ground, their diameters increase to facilitate connectivity to their widely spread root systems.

Where structure explicitly expresses groundedness, it will display some of the characteristics of rocks and trees noted above. It will anchor, both literally and figuratively, a building to its site. It will be apparent that the stability of the building, especially against wind and earthquake, will be due to the strength and rigidity of connection between superstructure, foundation and ground. This aspect is explored in the design studies below.

Floating, on the other hand, is denoted by a visual or possibly even a physical interruption of vertical structure, like columns, walls or arches at the base of a building. Alternatively, particular elements of a building can be designed to *appear* to float. Roofs, cantilevering sections or even entire buildings can be raised above the surrounding ground plane in such a way they are read as floating.

There are no hard and fast definitions of when an element or a building may be perceived to float. The eye of the beholder obviously plays a large role. Imagine someone who has spent years surrounded by thick earthen-walled construction seeing for the first time modern concrete and steel buildings with their slender columns. The structural footprint would appear so small as to suggest the building was floating. Usually a perception of floating is most intense where structural supports are small compared to the bulk of the supported form, or where supports are hidden or located away from what appears to be floating.

Of course, some lightweight roofs do almost float, at least when subjected to high winds. They act like aerofoils and require holding down. Tension membranes or fabric structures, and inflatable structures, must be held down even in the absence of wind.

Design studies

The first design study explores grounded and floating structures (Figure 11.34). Three structural systems, often used for resisting vertical and horizontal forces, are illustrated. First, (a) and (b) show structural walls functioning as vertical cantilevers in the direction parallel to their lengths. They project above their foundations that are firmly embedded in the ground. Wall (a), which is tapered in elevation, and in section if required, expresses groundedness. Wall (b) is typical. It lacks any overt expressive qualities. The cantilever columns (c) cantilever from their footings. Like trees, they taper to accentuate the reduced strength required towards the top. Larger footings than those required for gravity forces alone prevent the columns overturning in the event of horizontal forces. Alternatives to footings are either to extend the columns deep into the ground, like fence posts, or to use smaller footings joined by a ground beam rigidly connected to the base of each column. Frame (d) requires strong and rigid joints between columns and beam to resist horizontal forces. Due to the pin joints at the base of the columns, it is structurally rational to taper the columns and connect them to the foundations with compact but strong joints. These columns touch the ground as lightly as structurally possible, and depending on the detailing at this junction might be perceived as floating.

It is possible to reduce a wall's footprint and its sense of being grounded as illustrated in Figure 11.35. If a horizontal slot is created in the middle of a wall, the wall can resist nominal horizontal forces even if it is connected to the footing only by two strong pin joints (a). If a wall is grounded by a centrally placed pin joint (b), it is unable to resist horizontal forces by cantilever action and needs to rely upon other structure to support it. Finally, it is possible to separate a

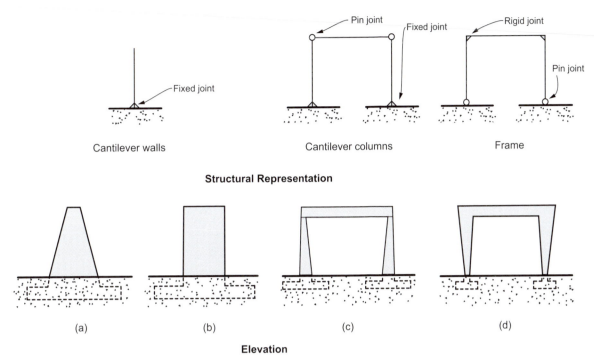

Structural Representation

(a) (b) (c) (d)

Elevation

Figure 11.34

Different degrees of grounding: structural (cantilever) walls, cantilever columns and columns of pin-jointed frames.

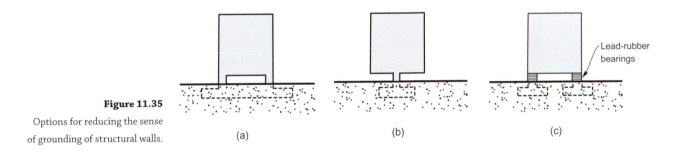

Figure 11.35

Options for reducing the sense of grounding of structural walls.

(a) (b) (c)

wall fully from the foundation and literally float it on rubber (or lead-rubber) bearings, as when seismically isolating a building. There are many buildings in seismically active countries floating on such bearings, but architects have rarely articulated the physical reality of this floatation. For example, the Cathedral of Christ the Light (see Figure 11.15) is base-isolated, but almost everyone is completely oblivious of it.

Case-studies

The case-studies begin with buildings that read as grounded and then progress towards those that are perceived to have elements or major volumes that appear to float.

At the Ordrupgaard Museum, Copenhagen, cast-in-place reinforced-concrete walls either rise up directly from the ground or begin as a horizontally cantilevered slab that then wraps around to become an inclined wall (Figure 11.36). In both instances the concrete is embedded into the ground, clearly anchoring the building to its site.

Both the Rolex Learning Centre, Lausanne, and the Mellat Gallery, Tehran (Figures 11.37 to 11.39) are supported by concrete structures that emerge from under the ground and then, in the form of gentle vertical curves, span to where the concrete again becomes one with the site. Since these buildings are not continuously grounded, but connected to their sites at discrete areas, they are not nearly as firmly grounded as possible. At the Mellat Gallery the raised

portion of the concrete base provides a source of entry from under and within the underbelly structure. The main entry and exit doors are flanked by deep beams supporting the superstructure.

At the Porta Church, Brissago, ground-floor beams that would normally be embedded are elevated above the ground

Figure 11.36
Ordrupgaard Museum extension, Copenhagen, Denmark, Zaha Hadid, 2005. (Hans Nerstru)

Figure 11.37
Rolex Learning Centre, Lausanne, Switzerland, SANAA, 2009. The undulating slab is grounded at discrete areas. (Asli Aydin)

Figure 11.39
Mellat Gallery, Tehran. The main entry is at ground level between two deep beams supporting the superstructure.

Figure 11.38
Mellat Park Cineplex, Tehran, Iran, Fluid Motion Architects, 2008. Grounded at each end of the building, beams gently curved in plan and elevation raise the building and create an entry foyer.

cladding overhangs and partially conceals a conventional concrete foundation.

All the previous differing degrees of groundedness are apparent from the exteriors of buildings, so now we visit Beijing Airport's Terminal 3, where grounding is expressed *within* the terminal (Figure 11.42). Tapered columns support the roof over the immense volume of the arrivals hall. Their scale is reassuring, and their increased base diameter indicates they are capable of resisting horizontal forces acting at roof level. These columns are rigidly connected to substructure that provides the strength from which to cantilever.

Figure 11.40
Church at Porta, Brissago, Switzerland, Raffaele Cavadini, 1997. Front elevation with a visible gap under the ground beam.

by 100 mm (Figure 11.40). By visually separating the tiny, cube-like church from its foundations the architect conveys a sense of the building not being *of* the site but rather built *over* it. This approach respects the site's previous medieval chapel, the demolition of which caused considerable controversy.

The lack of any visible structure at the base of the Splash Leisure Centre, Sheringham, conveys an impression that the building is transportable (Figure 11.41). This perception arises from the lightweight materiality and a simple construction detail. The double-layered plywood

Figure 11.42
Terminal 3, Beijing Airport, Beijing, China, Foster and Partners, 2008. Tapering columns support the roof structure.

Figure 11.41
Splash Leisure Centre, Sheringham, UK, Alsop & Lyall, 1988. Wall-to-foundation detailing conveys a lack of grounding.

By way of contrast, the wide columns of the Taisei Sapporo Building begin to taper three storeys above ground. At ground level their depths are halved (Figure 11.43). This column treatment means the building appears to be far less strongly anchored to its foundations than it could have been. During an earthquake, structural strength is mainly provided by rigidly connected concrete columns and steel beams at each floor, rather than the column-to-foundation strength. However, the strength of some column bases is enhanced by diagonal damping devices.

The columns at Paddington Station, London, sit on pinned bases. Lacking bending strength at the pins, the columns rely upon support at roof level for their stability (Figure 11.44).

Having considered various degrees of grounding buildings through structural expression, we now visit buildings, or

Figure 11.44
Paddington Station addition, London, UK, 2011. Canopy columns are pin-jointed at their bases.

Figure 11.43
Taisei Sapporo Building, Sapporo, Japan, Taisei Design Planners Architects and Engineers, 2006. Reduced column widths near ground level lessens the physical and visual connection of superstructure to the foundations. (Taisei Corporation)

significant portions of them, that are considered to float. The first reading of flotation, at the Unilever Building, Rotterdam, is due to the slenderness of the exposed elevating structure, as compared to the massiveness of the supported volume (Figure 11.45). The new building, which oversails an existing historic building, is supported at three points along its 133 m length. Two four-storey-deep trusses span between them. If the two end vertical cross-braced frames were of similar dimensions to the central braced core, their masses would tend to ground the building far more strongly and dilute any reading of floating.

The University of Alicante Museum displays a similar contrast of scale between the supports and the supported (Figure 11.46). Pairs of V-shaped steel props along each side

Figure 11.45
Unilever Building, Rotterdam, The Netherlands, JHK Architekten, 2005. The slender vertical structure contrasts with the large supported volume. (James Milles)

of the box-like form seem structurally inadequate due to their fineness, and reinforce a perception of floating.

The metaphor of floating is emphasized in a review of the Vanke Centre, Shenzhen (Figure 11.47). A reviewer comments:

> Nothing determines the character or architecture more than its desire to defy gravity and the manner and style with which this desire is fulfilled. The Horizontal Skyscraper-Vanke Center in Shenzhen on the South Sea of China is as long as the Empire State Building in New York is high. Suspended on eight core structures on which it floats above the ground, it gives the observer a lift as if he were a surfer riding a very large wave . . . Indeed, the choice to float an immense structure right

Figure 11.46
University of Alicante Museum, Alfredo Payá Benedito, 1999. Delicate structure contrasts with the massing of the 'box'. (Christopher Tweed)

Figure 11.47
Vanke Centre, Shenzhen, China, Steven Holl Architects, 2009. A project strongly expressing floating. (Trevor Patt)

under the 35-meter height limit, instead of several smaller structures each with its own specific program, generates the largest possible green and water grounds open to the public.[8]

In this complex, the cantilevering structure utilizes cable-stay bridge technology. Some internal spaces are disrupted by huge diagonal cables.

The 30 m cantilevering gallery of the Hoki Museum, Chiba, conveys a similar perception of floating (Figure 11.48). In a welcome note to visitors on a wall near Reception, the director writes: 'The Hoki Museum building was specifically designed and constructed for this collection. Made up of three stories, one above ground, two below, the galleries are layered, long corridors filled with images. A section of the structure floats in the air.' This gallery, which curves gently in plan, is approximately 100 m long and is supported at only two points. The welds joining the sheets of steel plates on the three visable surfaces clearly express the materiality of the steel tube construction. Careful detailing which suggests the steel floor and walls are only the thickness of one sheet of steel increases the sense of lightness. Note that the structural tube action has been severely compromised by the continuous glazed slot above floor level (Figure 11.49). Although this feature introduces natural light and connects visitors with the outside, it 'breaks' the structural tube action, adding significantly to design complexity and construction cost.

Figure 11.49

Hoki Museum. From within the gallery the curve in plan is apparent. The glazed slot allows views outside and the absence of supporting structure reinforces the sense of floatation.

To end this chapter, we consider four examples where portions of buildings seem to float, beginning with Marina Bay Sands, Singapore (Figure 11.50). The SkyPark, which comprises outdoor gardens and a 150 m-long pool, bridges the three hotel towers, each well grounded by curved and splayed walls. The SkyPark's canoe-like form cantilevers a massive 66.5 m with its complex structure hidden behind the cladding of its belly. V-shaped supporting struts are exposed but barely visible due to their height above ground as well

Figure 11.48

Hoki Museum, Chiba, Japan, Yamanashi, Nakamoto, Suzuki and Yano, 2010. The steel tube, housing a gallery, cantilevers well beyond the last support, creating an impression of floating.

Figure 11.50

Marina Bay Sands, Singapore, Safdie Architects, 2010. Three towers support the bridging and cantilevering SkyPark.

as their slenderness. The structural design and construction of the SkyPark, given the differential wind movement of the towers necessitated separation gaps along its length, is a remarkable feat of structural engineering.[9]

Long cantilevered roof canopies can also be perceived as floating, particularly if their span-to-depth ratios are high, as in the following two cases (Figures 11.51 and 11.52). At the De Young Museum, San Francisco, steel trusses cantilever from the main structure, which itself is floating on (hidden) rubber bearings that together with fluid viscous dampers comprise the seismic-isolation system.

Figure 11.51

De Young Museum, San Francisco, USA, Herzog & De Meuron, 2005. A roof canopy cantilevers over an outdoor café.

At the Trumpf factory, Stuttgart, the 22 m cantilevered roof is supported by just four columns. A translucent screen suppresses their presence and attention is drawn to the dominant horizontal element. The sense of lightness of the canopy is even more pronounced due to the lack of vertical support structure directly under the side trusses. Internal canopy structure collects and channels forces from all the trusses into the four columns. Especially under snow loads, very high compression forces occur in the front two columns, while foundations weighing 20 tonnes counteract the tension in those at the rear.

Architects frequently seek to accentuate the lightness of roofs. Saint Benedict Chapel has already been mentioned (see Figure 6.3). Its opaque roof is supported by regularly spaced slender perimeter posts. Especially in sunlight, which has a dematerializing effect on the posts, the roof appears to hover. Another fine example of a floating roof is found at Maggie's Centre, London (Figures 11.53 and 11.54). From the outside, the roof of this two-storey building hovers above, and in places over, the ground-floor enclosing walls. As usual, the sense of roof lightness is enhanced by the fully glazed first-floor perimeter walls, which are set back. This leads to impressive roof cantilever beams which taper to points. A second level of roof flotation is observed from within the building. The core of the building is defined by two one-bay

Figure 11.52
Gatehouse canopy, Trumpf Factory, Stuttgart, Germany, Barkow Leibinger, 2010. Shallow structure cantilevers from columns obscured by a translucent screen. (Frank Stahl)

Figure 11.53
Maggie's Centre, London, UK, Rogers Stirk Harbour & Partners, 2008. The roof cantilevers from set-back posts along the glazed first-floor walls.

Figure 11.54
The roof is supported by fine steel tubes that raise it above the beams defining the core of the building.

and two two-bay precast-concrete frames. Rather than the roof bearing on top of the frame beams, it is raised above them on slender tubular posts located above the columns.

Before completing this discussion on how structure contributes to a perception of floating, a final example demonstrates almost invisible vertical structure. The interior structure of Notre Dame de la Duchère, Lyon, fades into the background (Figures 11.55 and 11.56). Four slender cantilevered steel posts support the whole roof and resist lateral loads above eaves level. Lateral loads on the perimeter walls are resisted by regularly spaced piers that form the walls. Compared to the scale of the deep glue-laminated wooden roof beams, the visual solidity of the ceiling, and the

width of perimeter piers, the posts are barely discernible. Strip glazing that separates the perimeter walls from the roof reinforces the impression of the roof floating.

Summary

This chapter has addressed the question: how can structure reinforce architectural design concepts in order to enrich architecture? After acknowledging the relevance of design concepts in architecture, recurring concepts in

Figure 11.55
Notre Dame de la Duchère, Lyon, France, F. Cottin, 1972. Posts supporting the roof are barely discernible.

Figure 11.56
The exterior wall is structurally separated from the roof by glazing.

contemporary architecture were identified. The most prevalent concepts found, excluding those that were programme- or site-specific, can be summarized as pairs of opposing concepts: order–chaos, stability–instability, static–dynamic, and grounded–floating.

Having identified the concepts, two research approaches attempted to answer the question posed above. First, theoretical design studies demonstrated structure expressing concepts positioned anywhere along the continuum defined by each pair of concepts. Although the studies are at a conceptual level of design, they are informed, and to some extent calibrated, by a contemporary precedent. This gives confidence that the schemes are realizable. The second approach, involving a large number of case-studies, consisted of showcasing works of architecture where structure communicates and reinforces design concepts within the selected pairs of concepts.

These two approaches have demonstrated the ability of structure to reinforce readings of many different concepts. It is hard to imagine any concept not inspired by programme or site that structure cannot reinforce by virtue of its form, configuration or detailing. Where concepts are reinforced by expressive structure, architecture is enriched.

Notes

1. A. Pressman, *Designing architecture: the elements of process*, London: Routledge, 2012, p. 23.
2. E. T. White, *Concept sourcebook: a vocabulary of architectural forms*, Arizona: Architectural Media, 1975, p. 25.
3. P. Johnson, *The theory of architecture: concepts, themes and practices*, New York: Van Nostrand Reinhold, 1994, p. 338.
4. For example, refer to *The Architects' Journal* 234(9), 2011.
5. H. Beck and J. Cooper, 'Reinventing the institution', *Domus* 830, 2000, 49.
6. See A. W. Charleson, *Seismic design for architects: outwitting the quake*, Oxford: Elsevier, 2008, ch. 9, 'Vertical configuration'.
7. D. Hutt, 'In Culver City, California, Eric Owen Moss builds the Beehive – a playfully sculptural structure and a creative workplace abuzz with activity', *Architectural Record* 8(2), 2002, 130–5.
8. Y. E. Safran, 'Gravity and grace', *Abitare* 506, 2010, 71–8, at 71.
9. M. Safdie, 'Case study: Marina Bay Sands, Singapore', *CTBUH Journal* 1, 2011, 12–17.

twelve

Facilitating architectural qualities

Introduction

Whereas the previous chapter explored how structure can emphasize architectural concepts, we now focus on achieving a wide spectrum of architectural qualities. The process of identification and classification of the qualities discussed below is described in the introduction to Chapter 11. The following pairs of contrasting qualities that are reinforced by structure are discussed and illustrated:

- simplicity–complexity;
- open–closed;
- lightweight–heavy;
- soft–hard; and
- elegant–rough.

As acknowledged previously, the process of categorization is imprecise. Some qualities can be discussed in the context of more than just one pair of qualities, and could even be considered architectural concepts, and vice versa. However, the purpose here is not to pigeon-hole a quality, but rather to illustrate the amazing variety of ways structure can help realize these qualities in built work. We can assume that all the qualities studied in the following sections were desired by the architect and responded to a client's brief.

Many case-studies illustrate how structure contributes different architectural qualities, both on façades and within buildings. Structure works in this way at different scales, ranging from structural form to the detailing of structural members. And, depending upon the force of expression of the architectural qualities, structure can communicate them at different levels of intensity. For example, a concrete member

can convey either a hint of roughness or extreme roughness by the treatment of its surface finish.

Simplicity–complexity

In many periods of architectural history, structural form and the detailing of structural elements have contributed to both architectural simplicity and complexity. The simple repetitive structural forms of Egyptian, Roman and Greek architecture gave rise to the complexity of the Gothic period, which was then moderated during the Renaissance. Then, the primary structural materials consisted of stone and brick. With the advent of iron, steel and reinforced concrete, structural forms other than arched, vaulted and post-and-beam were introduced. Just like the materials that preceded them, these 'new' materials were able to express different degrees of complexity.

We begin the following brief case-studies with examples where exposed structure bestows a sense of simplicity upon the architecture, and commence with one of the best-known buildings of the Modern movement. LaVine describes the exterior ground-floor columns of the iconic Villa Savoye, Paris (Figures 12.1 and 12.2), as 'classically placed but unadorned, slender cylinders, reflecting a technological stance of the twentieth century'.[1] Consistent with the plainness of the columns, the floor beams are rectangular in both cross-section and elevation. Their widths, which equal the diameters of the columns and result in tidy beam–column junctions, are evidence of detailing being pared back to the most basic and simple. It is certainly not attention-seeking.

Figure 12.1
Villa Savoye, Paris, France, Le Corbusier, 1929. The front and side elevation.

Figure 12.2
Plain exterior column and beam detailing.

At the Millennium Seed Bank, Sussex, also constructed from reinforced concrete, details have similarly been reduced to the bare minimum (Figures 12.3 and 12.4). A 'less is more' approach complements the simple geometries of barrel-vaulted and frame forms. This simple and restful architecture achieves the architect's design concept to 'evoke a sense of spirituality and create a space for private reflection where both adult and child should leave feeling enriched'.[2]

Figure 12.3
Millennium Seed Bank, Wakehurst Place, UK, Stanton Williams, 2000. Barrel-vaulted roof forms.

Figure 12.4
Detailing matches the simple structural forms.

Similar qualities of simplicity are also evident in two buildings which utilize the sleekness of steel hollow sections. At the Vancouver Convention Centre West, horizontal steel vierendeel trusses support vertical glazing mullions (Figure 12.5). In a three-storey-high foyer area, three levels of trusses provide face-load resistance for wind forces acting on the mullions. Had there been fewer trusses, or none at all, significantly larger mullion depths would have been required, reducing façade transparency. The trusses, spanning horizontally between primary columns, are simply detailed.

Figure 12.5
Vancouver Convention Centre West, Vancouver, Canada, DA Architects + Planners, 2009. Exterior glazed walls are supported by geometrically simple vierendeel trusses.

Figure 12.6
Entrance canopy, Terminal 3, Heathrow Airport, London, UK, Foster and Partners, 2009. A simple structural framework.

The decision to use trusses rather than solid beams maintains a lightness of construction that respects the primacy of the vertical columns.

It would be difficult to conceive of a more simple entrance canopy than that of Terminal 3, Heathrow Airport, London (Figure 12.6). All roof members are in the same plane and fully welded to achieve maximum plainness of connection. There is no distinction between primary and secondary members. All depths are equal, and their widths are similar to the diameter of the posts. The only detailing refinements are the tapering of the cantilevered primary beam and the reduction in post cross-section where it connects to the roof structure. The final notable aspect of this structure's simplicity is the absence of roof purlins, and therefore of any hint of structural hierarchy. The fixing details of the ETFE inflated cushion roof are confined to and hidden along the top edges of roof beams so nothing detracts from the simplicity and purity of the structural framework.

However, structural detailing possesses the potential to introduce complexity and decorative qualities that enhance architecture. The ribbed concrete floor soffits of the Schlumberger extension building, Cambridge, are reminiscent of Pier Luigi Nervi's isostatic ribs (Figure 12.7). Floor construction was achieved with permanent ferro-cement formwork, subsequently infilled with reinforced concrete.

Figure 12.7
Schlumberger extension building, Cambridge, UK, Michael Hopkins and Partners, 1992. Exposed ribbed soffits around the perimeter.

We observe simple primary structure with an overlay of more complex secondary structure at the *Financial Times* printing works, London (Figure 12.8). The functional benefits of the regularly spaced perimeter columns have already been discussed in Chapter 5, but now we note the complexity of the horizontal brackets, connecting glazing to columns. The brackets are significantly more complex compared to more conventional (horizontal) girts often used to support cladding or glazing. This architecture would be all the poorer without this simultaneous display of simplicity and complexity.

The final case-studies in this section exemplify structural complexity in the form of two roof structures. The multiple pitched-roof form of the Verbier Sports Centre suits its surroundings (Figures 12.9 and 12.10). Roof planes step down the mountainside slope and relate comfortably to the pitched roofs of adjacent chalets. Roof trusses over the main swimming pool follow the slope and are articulated on the exterior, where they bear on exposed concrete buttresses.

Figure 12.8
Financial Times printing works, London, UK, Grimshaw & Partners, 1988. Elegant repetitive exterior columns support complex cantilevered brackets.

Figure 12.9
Verbier Sports Centre, Switzerland, André Zufferey, 1984. Complex stepping roof form.

Figure 12.10
Visually complex roof structure.

Figure 12.11
Louvre Pyramid, Paris, France, I. M. Pei, 1989. Visually complex structure within a simple form.

However, the stepping roof profile increases the truss complexity and a lack of structural hierarchy among the many structural members obscures the primary structural form to the extent that the structure appears chaotic.

The Louvre Pyramid, on the other hand, is very simple in form and structural layout – four inclined triangular planes – but the structural detailing introduces a high degree of visual complexity (Figure 12.11). Rather than frame the pyramid conventionally with solid sloping rafters spanning between the base and four ridge beams, the architect opted for a diagonally orientated system – a two-way grillage of stressed cable-beams. While small-diameter stainless-steel members offer a high degree of transparency, from many viewing angles the profusion of rods, cables and connections results in extreme visual complexity. The effect is compounded by the curved bottom-chords of the cable-beams whose geometry reflects the internal forces of the beams but is at odds with the prismatic form they support.

Open–closed

Structure can facilitate a quality of openness in buildings in several ways. If openness refers to the relationship between the interior and exterior, then we try to minimize the perimeter structure that would otherwise negate such an intention. In this case 'open' is synonymous with light, and 'closed' with darkness. A suitable structural strategy might be

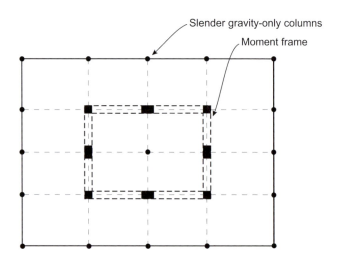

Figure 12.12
A strong internal core is required where perimeter structure is minimized to create openness between the interior and exterior. In this case the structural core consists of four two-bay moment frames.

to place gravity-only columns or posts around the perimeter. Alternatively, the outer bays of floors can be cantilevered so that nothing larger than a glazing mullion is required on the façade. Where a minimum perimeter structure solution is adopted we need to increase the structural footprint density in plan within the building to provide adequate resistance to horizontal loads. Moment frames, cross-braced frames or structural walls will be required (Figure 12.12). Because they are not situated on the perimeter where they are most effective at resisting any twisting of the building during an earthquake or wind storm, they need to be stronger than normal to provide that torsional resistance.

If, however, openness is a quality required in the interior of a building, then *that* is where structure must be minimized. Gravity-only structure may be used there, or long-span horizontal structure, or a combination of the two. Openness is highly prized in airport terminals, exhibition halls and sports venues which demand large structure-free areas. In these situations, larger structural members required for horizontal forces, like structural walls, are placed around the perimeter.

Throughout this book many examples of architectural openness have already been illustrated, so just two more are given here. Behind the western façade of the extension to the Natural History Museum, London, rises an impressive eight-storey atrium (Figures 12.13 and 12.14). Vertical 30 m-long mullions support a glazed wall and roof beams above.

Figure 12.13

Extension to the Natural History Museum, London, UK, C. F. Moller Architects, 2009. The west-facing façade with the 'cocoon' behind.

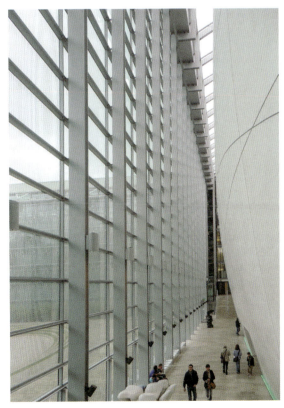

Figure 12.14

The 'cocoon' can be appreciated in the absence of internal structure or other elements.

Figure 12.15

Evelina Children's Hospital, London, UK, Hopkins Architects, 2005. The 100-metre-long atrium is effectively a light-filled conservatory.

The atrium, by virtue of its fully glazed perimeter, opens out towards the exterior while providing enclosure for the one significant intrusion – a giant 'cocoon' that protects and accommodates displays and offices. The lack of structure and other elements within the atrium enable the 'cocoon' to be fully appreciated. By comparison to the Natural History

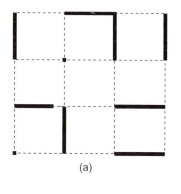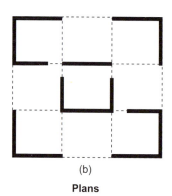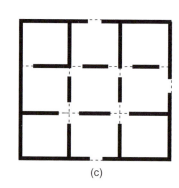

(a)   (b)   (c)

Plans

Figure 12.16
Floor plans become more and more closed as the number of walls increases from (a) to (c).

Museum, the atrium at Evelina Children's Hospital, London, is only five storeys high, wider, and visually more dynamic with its curved tubular diagrid roof (Figure 12.15). It is also far more open, punctuated only by two sets of elevator towers and bridges. It is read and experienced as one single volume.

Where structure facilitates openness, it does it best by being absent from that area. A greater structural footprint density is required elsewhere in plan, be it in the interior or on the perimeter. Totally structure-free buildings are no more possible than perpetual motion. However, where a more closed architectural quality is intended, structure can play more active roles – shielding, protecting, blocking or subdividing. For such introverted settings, we turn to structural walls because they can achieve all these qualities. Regarding wall materiality, reinforced-concrete walls are probably the most versatile due to their ability to resist horizontal loads, but masonry is more common, especially in non-seismic areas. Many lightweight buildings rely on plywood or other lining materials for their stability. But irrespective of their materiality, structural walls, which for structural purposes are continuous from foundation to roof, are ideal agents of a closed architecture. The degree of physical security or amount of natural light or views required will inform the number, size, shape and locations of wall penetrations. Figure 12.16 shows the effect of increasing the number of walls to create fully closed architecture.

Mention has already been made of how exterior walls can express protection and enclosure by virtue of materiality and shape, such as at Fitzwilliam College Chapel (Figure 4.40), but three further examples follow. From the exterior, the Museum of Roman Art, Merida, appears like a large brick-walled warehouse (Figure 12.17). Its solid walls, apart from near roof level, which are essential to protect the collection, lack

Figure 12.17
Museum of Roman Art, Merida, Spain, Rafael Moneo, 1985. Unpenetrated perimeter walls.

Figure 12.18
Lyon School of Architecture, Lyon, France, Jourda et Perraudin, 1988. A wall encloses offices and an atrium within.

Figure 12.19

The atrium surrounded by offices and the perimeter wall beyond.

Figure 12.20

FDA Laboratory, Irvine, CA, USA, Zimmer Gunsul Frasca Partnership + HDR, 2003. A segment of the curved wall enclosing a library.

penetrations. Natural light is introduced through large areas of translucent roofing. Within the building, as shown in Figure 5.14, interior walls subdivide interior space. Some connection between inside and outside is provided by slotted windows at the Lyon School of Architecture and the FDA Laboratory, Irvine (Figures 12.18 to 12.20). At Lyon, the walls shield offices around the perimeter of the semi-circular form from excessive light and heat and create a spacious internal atrium. On a far smaller scale, the curved wall of the FDA Laboratory encloses a library while providing similar protective functions.

Lightweight–heavy

This section explores how the size and details of structural members affect the architectural qualities of space. Designing and detailing exposed structural members offers an opportunity for structure to exhibit qualities of fineness or, conversely, heaviness. For example, in many situations solid beams can be replaced by trusses that use less material and are visually lighter and more transparent as a consequence of their far finer and widely spaced members. Of course, it must be remembered that the disadvantages of this type of construction include greater fabrication costs, vulnerability to corrosion and fire damage, and increased maintenance for cleaning and painting.

If designers seek to maximize ingress of natural light and to achieve a high degree of transparency in external walls and roofs, as discussed in Chapter 8, they may adopt a strategy entailing many slender, rather than fewer larger, members. As observed at the Louvre Pyramid, while structure might exhibit acceptable qualities of lightness and transparency, from some viewpoints its appearance may be less successful due to visual disorder. We need to remember that people mostly view and experience structure from positions other than those used to generate plans, sections and elevations.

An exemplar of structural lightness has already been noted in the lace-like roof structure at the TGV station, Lille (Figure 3.45). Another example of structural detailing for lightness is found in Terminal 2F, Charles de Gaulle Airport, Paris. Whereas in our first visit to the building we noted how massive exterior structure signalled entry (Figure 4.35), now we experience structural lightness inside the terminal. A 200 m-long 'peninsula' that houses departure lounges and aircraft walkways juts out from the airside of the main terminal building. A series of transverse portal frames whose detailing is so 'light' that the whole structure almost reads as a space-frame supports its roof (Figures 12.21 and 12.22). Structural detailing is not locked into an orthogonal grid but responds to the curved roof form. The truss nodes map the gently curving roof contours, and the trusses wrap around the floor slab via innovative 'tension-spokes'. The structure delivers a light-filled space while displaying a remarkable degree of lightness. Compared to the heaviness of the terminal's landside concrete wall and ceiling surfaces, this airside structure looks as if it could take off itself!

Figure 12.21
Terminal 2F, Charles de Gaulle Airport, Paris, France, Aéroports de Paris, 1999. Lightweight 'peninsula' roof.

Figure 12.22
Tension-spokes allow roof frames to wrap around the cantilevered floor slab.

Lightness for flight can also be read in the sunshade structure at the National Library, Singapore (Figure 12.23). Like the wings of biplanes, six 6 m-wide sunshades span 20 m. They are supported by a truss-like structure including diagonal rods and compression struts. Both struts end in sharp points, accentuating the attention being paid to lightness. Each structural member is very fine given the overall span of the system.

The Arab World Institute, Paris, also illustrates a successful detailing strategy utilizing multiple fine members, rather than fewer solid members. Open vierendeel box-trusses span the width of the main façade (Figure 12.24). Positioned in front of the cladding, they support it at each floor level. With their outer chords curved in plan, they contribute a diaphanous softness to the façade. Other internal box-trusses support the skin in double-height or higher spaces. But these are

Figure 12.23
National Library, Singapore, T.R. Hamzah and K. Yeang, 2004. A lightweight structure supports sunshade blades.

Figure 12.24
Arab World Institute, Paris, France, Jean Nouvel, 1987. Light vierendeel trusses support the front façade.

Figure 12.25
Ornate internal horizontal trusses by virtue of their detailing.

detailed completely differently. Diagonal web members, together with four tubular chords, achieve new qualities of intricacy and ornateness (Figure 12.25). Their transparency and visual complexity complement similar qualities present in the glazed and mechanically shuttered curtain-walls. It is worth reflecting on how much the aesthetic qualities of the space would change if the existing trusses were replaced by solid box beams.

Use of multiple elements in a structural member is also an effective strategy to prevent people from feeling overwhelmed by otherwise large structural elements. The visual mass of the chords of the trusses in the Centre Pompidou, Paris, are reduced to a minimum by the use of double tubes (Figure 12.26), and the clustered columns of the United Airlines Terminal, Chicago, have a similar effect (Figure 12.27).

Figure 12.26
Centre Pompidou, Paris, France, Piano and Rogers, 1977. Double-chords reduce the visual mass of the truss.

In the progression towards examples of visually heavier detailing we visit two buildings that incorporate instances of both light and heavy detailing. The Learning Resource Centre, Thames Valley University, London, consists of three forms. A main rectangular block housing bookcases, seminar rooms and offices is structured by typically dimensioned solid beam and column members; then a lightweight curved roof encloses a three-storey volume; and finally, within it, a single-storey concrete structure supports computing and study areas (Figures 12.28 and 12.29). Lightness of structure is most

Figure 12.27
United Airlines Terminal, Chicago, USA, Murphy/Jahn, 1987. Two smaller-diameter tubes substitute for one large solid column.

Figure 12.28
Learning Resource Centre, Thames Valley University, UK, Richard Rogers Partnership, 1996. Both heavy and lightweight forms are visible from the exterior.

Figure 12.29
Lightened by the use of tension-ties, shallow curved beams arch over a computing area.

evident in the curved roof. Its beam depths are minimized by ties that connect to intermediate points along the beams, effectively deepening them structurally, but without increasing their visual mass. Beam legibility, highlighted by yellow paint, is further enhanced by concealing roof purlins behind perforated ceiling cladding.

This method of reducing structural depth by forming composite members is particularly popular when utilizing wood construction. It is illustrated in Figure 7.1 and we have already seen it in several buildings, such as the Lyon School of Architecture (see Figure 6.19), the Mont-Cenis Academy

Figure 12.30
Portland Building, University of Portsmouth, UK, Hampshire County Council Architects Department, 1996. Composite wooden-steel construction lightens bridge and roof beams.

(see Figure 4.32). It is also found in the bridge and roof at the Portland Building, Portsmouth (Figure 12.30). Here the wooden members are just chords of the composite truss, so their depths are a fraction of that usually required.

Trees exhibit a progression from heaviness to lightness within their structures. Trunks reduce in size with increasing height eventually to become fine and fragile twigs. This transformation in scale is exaggerated since member cross-sections reduce simultaneously as viewing distances increase, as observed at Brookfield Place, Toronto (Figure 12.31). Here, a non-literal attitude towards representation sees the girth of the galleria columns display their greatest bulk at the first floor where they are stabilized by adjacent multi-storey buildings. The columns then branch twice before supporting a canopy of parabolic arches and light-filtering battens.

Figure 12.31
Brookfield Place, Toronto, Canada, Santiago Calatrava, 1993. A general progression of structural members towards lightness at roof level.

So far in this discussion of structural lightness and its move towards heavier construction, the only mention of concrete has been where it contrasts with more delicate steel or wooden elements. Concrete, as used traditionally in elements like beams, trusses, arches, walls and columns, cannot be described as lightweight due to both member size and density. This situation of concrete being synonymous with heaviness is likely to change, though. Architects and engineers are beginning to exploit the opportunities presented through the recent introduction of self-compacting and ultra-high-strength concretes. Low-viscosity and high-strength concretes, which reach compressive strengths comparable to mild steel, enable smaller and more complex shapes to be cast than those achievable in the past. White cements also eliminate the greyness with which concrete is associated, and which also increases that sense of heaviness.

Visually heavy concrete elements are usually not popular with designers, except where accentuating a sense of protection or the monumental. They are often a consequence of heavy loads and long spans. For an example of protection, we revisit the Wöhlen High School library, where the centrepiece is a concrete roof canopy resting upon a single steel post (Figure 12.32). The slenderness of the post, even though spindle-shaped, and the mass of concrete above it induce a sense of unease. This is heighted due to the apparent instability of the construction – all this concrete supported by a single pin-jointed post! However, anxiety subsides when perimeter stainless-steel ties connected to stabilizing structural walls are observed. As I sat at a desk on the mezzanine floor beneath the roof, the overwhelming sense was one of protection – from the weight and strength of the concrete, and also from its gentle curved surfaces in the form of an open book, the source of inspiration for its form. I identified with the sense of security that chicks experience when gathered under the sheltering wings of a hen. Here, heaviness plays a positive role, introducing tangible architectural qualities.

Invariably, underground structures are deep and heavy, even though designers may reduce the visual impacts by sensitive detailing. The Stadelhofen Station underground mall, Zürich, exemplifies detailing that visually lightens large concrete members (Figures 12.33 and 12.34). Pier detailing incorporates two set-backs in plan that reduce visual mass and scale, rendering the space more amenable to human habitation. The thinnest portion of a pier cross-section when traced from its base up to the beam and down to the base of the opposite pier reads as a portal frame. The next-thicker area appears to be supporting and connected to the keel-like ceiling shape. Such structural details reduce our perception of structural size towards the human scale, to create friendlier and more humane environments. A similar example is seen in the subterranean Museum of Gallo-Roman Civilization, Lyon (see Figure 6.35). Chamfering the lower third of the beams and their smooth curved transitions with columns soften their visual impact and render the structure less formidable.

Figure 12.32
Wöhlen High School, Switzerland, Santiago Calatrava, 1988. Concrete roof structure over the library.

Figure 12.33
Stadelhofen Railway Station, Zürich, Switzerland, Santiago Calatrava, 1990. Cambering the beams and the 'sloping columns' visually lighten the structure.

Figure 12.34
Pier detailing reduces visual mass.

After describing his wonderment at the setting and form of another concrete structure – that of Robert Maillart's Salginatoblel Bridge, Schieirs, Switzerland – Alain de Botton states:

> the bridge testifies to how closely a certain kind of beauty is bound up with our admiration for strength, for man-made objects which can withstand the life-destroying forces of heat, cold, gravity and wind . . . It follows from this that the impression of beauty we derive from an architectural work may be proportionally related to the intensity of the forces against which is it pitted.[3]

Crucially, later he notes that elegance is also a prerequisite for this type of beauty. We can all identify with that, given the large numbers of deep, heavy and featureless bridges spanning across our motorways.

While this line of reasoning may hold true for works of civil engineering, the situation is more complex in the context of buildings where elements displaying strength are exposed within different-sized spaces or volumes. The massive concrete arches that support the roof and public space above the underground Moscone Exhibition Center, San Francisco, are on the cusp of creating either awe or intimidation (Figure 12.35), whereas the columns of the Hong Kong and Shanghai

Figure 12.35
Moscone Center, San Francisco, USA, Hellmuth, Obata and Kassabaum, 1981. Deep arch members support the roof of the underground exhibition hall.

Figure 12.36

Hong Kong and Shanghai Bank, Hong Kong, China, Foster Associates, 1986. The columns seem large even in a double-height space.

Bank appear oppressively large within a single-storey space (Figure 12.36). While the same column appears well scaled on the building façade (see Figure 4.1), when encountered within the building its visual heaviness exerts an overbearing presence on the area around it.

Examples of exposed structure detailed to accentuate a sense of heaviness rather than lightness are rare in contemporary buildings given the general preoccupation with transparency and its offer of light and views, and a generally greater aesthetic appreciation of slender rather than chunky objects. The visually heavy structural detailing at the Centre for Understanding the Environment (CUE), London, is a consequence of its ecologically sustainable design, rather than any other reason. Primary structural members are hollow, exemplifying the highest possible level of structure and services integration (Figures 12.37 and 12.38).[4] Structural members function as air conduits in this naturally ventilated building. Column and beam cross-sections are therefore larger than normal, even accounting for the weight of its turf roof. Warm air is extracted through circular penetrations in the triangular plywood web-beams, and channelled horizontally to columns. Columns that terminate above roof height function as ventilators. For such a relatively small building, the structural members appear heavy.

While previous case-studies have provided examples of

Figure 12.37

Centre for Understanding the Environment (CUE), Horniman Museum, London, UK, Architype, 1997. Front façade with chimney-like columns.

Figure 12.38
Interior column and beam.

structure exhibiting qualities of lightness and heaviness, sometimes coexisting in the same building, the final two examples of stair structures illustrate how these contrasting qualities are achieved by architects in response to their individual design aims. Although the Suntory Museum, Tokyo, is housed within a massive commercial development, its architect sought to introduce a domestic scale to spaces and other elements. Therefore, the beam supporting internal stairs had to be as shallow as possible. Spanning 7 m, the depth of the wide slab-like beam is only 100 mm, less than half the normal depth (Figure 12.39). Needless to say, the structural engineer had to resort to sophisticated design details, including the use of damping devices, to avoid an overly lively structure. Compare these stairs with those at 21_21 Design Sight, Tokyo (Figure 12.40). Here, cantilevering only approximately 1.2 m from a supporting wall, they are over twice as deep as we might expect. However, the architect has employed here the same heavy detailing used elsewhere.

Figure 12.39
Suntory Museum, Tokyo, Japan, Kengo Kuma & Associates, 2007. An exceedingly shallow stair stringer avoids introducing an element greater than domestic scale into the space.

Figure 12.40
21_21 Design Sight, Tokyo, Japan, Tadeo Ando & Associates, 2007. Cantilevering concrete stairs are over twice as deep as necessary.

The structures of these two stairs remind us how we can vary the cross-sections of structural members for the sake of our design ideas. Beams, and other members for that matter, can be designed to be shallow (and wide), deep and wide, or even deep and thin.

Soft–hard

Qualities ranging from softness to hardness are experienced in works of architecture. Softness is not about physical softness or elasticity, or even the strength of materials, but about *visual* softness. It takes the forms of roundedness, perhaps exhibiting some of the sensual qualities associated with the human body or other natural forms. It is also about materiality. Exposed wood conveys a sense of softness due to its natural properties, and this quality can be enhanced by the ways wooden members are detailed. Without going so far as to turn a circular cross-section on a lathe, just chamfering the corners of a wooden member increases its sense of softness. Softness, then, is communicated through curved structural forms, through the detailing of structural members, and through the choice of material (mainly wood). Hardness, however, prefers straight or linear members. It is conveyed through orthogonality of structural form and member cross-section. As far as detailing is concerned, it thrives on sharpness of corners, edges and ends. Concrete, even with the edges of members lightly chamfered to facilitate formwork removal, masonry and, to a lesser degree, steel are the closest allies of hardness. Most steel plates and hot-rolled sections are characterized by sharp edges.

Let us then visit some works of architecture that are notable for their expression of differing degrees of softness and hardness. We begin at the soft end of the continuum with the parabolic arches at Colegio Teresiano (see Figure 5.30). Softness is bestowed by the arches that spring from their vertical piers at shoulder height. The material of construction, brick masonry, is concealed beneath the plastered and white-painted surfaces. Other architectural readings – such as peacefulness or tranquillity – are also invited by this structure.

These same architectural qualities, and more, are evident in the interior of the Tama Art University Library, Hachioji City (Figures 12.41 and 12.42). Although the arch also forms the basis of the architecture, linear repetitive structure is replaced by three-dimensional irregularity. Here, the visual softness inherent in arches is accentuated by their three-dimensional layout, defined by gently curved lines in plan and by changing span lengths of the arches along each line. Thus the rounded and subtle irregular flow of arches dominates both storeys of the building. Apart from thin steel mullions, structural members are curved and few straight lines or right

Figure 12.41
Tama Art University Library, Hachioji City, Japan, Toyo Ito & Associates, 2007. Two curved exterior walls express the surface of structure that takes on three-dimensional form inside.

Figure 12.42
Structure, curved in elevation and in plan. Imbued with subtle geometric irregularity, it imparts a flowing softness to interior spaces.

angles, even in bookcases and tables, disrupt the quality of softness imparted by structure. The overwhelming sense of structural softness and flow is even more remarkable given its realization in concrete, even though centrally located steel plates within the 200 mm-thick members provide most of the structural strength.[5] The plate thickness increases greatly within the bases of the intersecting arches whose delicacy is, in part, due to the seismic isolation system at foundation level.

Figure 12.43
Law Faculty extension, Limoges, France, Massimiliano Fuksas, 1997.
Curved wooden ribs wrap around a lecture theatre.

The Law Faculty extension, Limoges, contains two
rounded lecture theatres. Curved glue-laminated wooden
ribs define the interior volume of the smaller theatre (Figure
12.43). Smaller, also curved, horizontal ribs accentuate its
three-dimensional curvature and visually emphasize the form
of the womb-like interior. Primary and secondary ribs express
enclosure as they wrap over and around the volume. The
organic form, its small scale, the sympathetic configuration
of the structural elements, and the materiality of timber all
combine to realize a warm, intimate and embracing space
imbued with softness.

To a lesser extent, these same qualities are present at
the Säntispark Health and Leisure Centre, St Gallen, with its
curved forms (Figure 12.44). In the recreational and pools
areas, structure follows an organic geometric layout. It is as
if the designers considered a rectilinear grid antithetical to a
recreational environment. In plan each roof truss is straight,
but an obvious sag acknowledges its informal architectural
intention (Figure 12.45).

Curved forms also dominate the Licorne football stadium,
Amiens (Figure 12.46). Elegantly curved and tapered ribs
shelter the spectators and reinforce a sense of enclosure. The
combination of widely spaced ribs and glazing provides an
unusually high degree of transparency. A prop at the base of
each rib provides its base-fixity and stability in the transverse

Figure 12.45
Säntispark Health and Leisure Centre. Roof structure with its deliberate
sagging profile.

Figure 12.44
Säntispark Health and Leisure
Centre, St Gallen, Switzerland,
Raush, Ladner, Clerici, 1986.
The roof curves down from
the ridge.

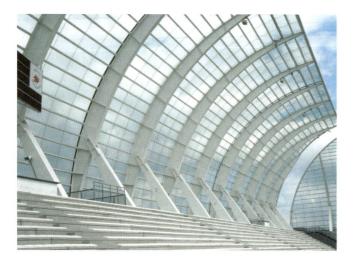

Figure 12.46
Licorne football stadium, Amiens, France, Chaix & Morel et Associés, 1999. Curved ribs enclose the pitch and spectators.

direction. Unusually configured moment frames within the ribbed surface resist longitudinal loads. In these frames the curved ribs function as columns, and the horizontal tubes or girts, rigidly connected at 1 m spacing up the ribs, are the moment-resisting beams. The integration of girts with ribs to form these multi-bay moment frames avoids the need for a more common and economical form of resistance, such as diagonal bracing, whose geometry would clash with the softness conveyed by the curving ribs.

Figure 12.47
Barcelona Fair GranVia Venue, Barcelona, Spain, Toyo Ito, 2007. Organically shaped walls are consistent with the plan. (Pablo Axpe)

Figure 12.48
Faculty of Law Building, Cambridge, UK, Foster and Partners, 1996. Raking concrete columns 'softened' by a rounded cross-section and a sand-blasted finish.

Softness is also conveyed in concrete construction through both form and detailing. Responding to the irregular curved plan shape of the Barcelona Fair GranVia Venue, Toyo Ito has designed several sets of organically shaped perimeter structural walls to resist horizontal forces (Figure 12.47). As well as being read as fun elements, the curved shapes of the walls are totally consistent with the building form. If desired, concrete structure like this could be further softened by rounding the edges, or by curving the walls in plan to follow the shape of the roof slab above. Where left unpainted, concrete surfaces can also be softened in a tactile and visual sense by sandblasting, as in the Law Faculty Building, Cambridge (Figure 12.48), or by light bush-hammering.

Leaving curved and rounded cross-sections behind, we next visit examples of a visually harder genre and return to the Museum of Anthropology, Vancouver (Figure 12.49), whose post-and-beam structure was shown in Figure 11.23. The structural elements in the main hall are linear, sharp-

Figure 12.49
Museum of Anthropology, Vancouver, Canada, Arthur Erickson, 1976. Part side elevation of main exhibition hall.

edged and assembled in a pure orthogonal layout. This uncompromising adherence to the right angle is typical of most buildings, but usually not so starkly expressed. No other architectural elements, like infill walls, soften its visual impact.

Structure is also inseparable from the form of a Barcelona swimming pool that is sited on a beach and subject to a harsh marine environment (Figure 12.50). Its concrete walls express a hardness and permanence necessary to withstand the destructive elements of nature. The material and structural form are reminiscent of coastal defence structures, cast in anticipation of enemy attack. For these situations a hard-edged, strong architecture is entirely appropriate, but should it be used in buildings designed for a more gentle type of habitation? This is the question that the church at Porta raises (Figure 12.51.) We observed its rather tenuous attachment to its site in the previous chapter (see Figure 11.40). Apart from two small wooden elements, every surface is either concrete or stone masonry. No details ameliorate the sense of coldness and harshness that pervades the tiny space.

For the final example of the architectural quality of hardness we return to the Felix Nussbaum Museum, whose narrative architecture tells a story of loneliness, horror and, eventually, death (see Figure 9.26). All the exposed concrete walls and beams express hardness. They are all straight and edges are sharp. In fact, the end of one wall that juts out into a gallery is angled, and the leading edge is so sharp as to cause injury (Figure 12.52). In these structural elements the architect has refused to place triangular 25 mm wooden fillets into the corners of the formwork to prevent voids in the concrete causing rough edges, and has done everything possible to support the narrative of harshness and terror.

Figure 12.50
Swimming pool, Barcelona, Spain, J. Antonio, 1996. A hard concrete building to withstand the marine environment.

Figure 12.51
Church at Porta, Brissago, Switzerland, Raffaele Cavadini, 1997. The hardness of masonry and concrete permeates the church.

Figure 12.52
Felix Nussbaum Museum, Osnabrück, Germany, Daniel Libeskind, 1998. A sharp-edged wall is part of the narrative.

Elegant–rough

Although we might expect elegant structural detailing in most, if not all, recognized works of architecture, this certainly is not the case. Qualities of elegance – or, for that matter, roughness – should be consistent with the architectural design intent. In successful architecture we delight in how the design ideas are expressed through the placement of structural elements and their detailing, even down to the layout and orientation of nuts and bolts. Any judgement passed upon the appropriateness of an expressed quality, like elegance, must be guided by the need for that quality to be integrated with the concept.

Elegant structural details are those that are pure and refined. Any extraneous material and componentry has been edited away. We are left with the impression that the detail could not be improved. It has undergone an extensive process of reworking, leaving the designer satisfied with the outcome – technical and aesthetic requirements have been resolved in a synthesis of structural necessity and artistic sensibility. Alain de Botton defines elegance in similar terms:

> a quality present whenever a work of architecture succeeds in carrying out an act of resistance – holding, spanning, sheltering – with grace and economy as well as strength; when it has the modesty not to draw attention to the difficulties it has surmounted.[6]

Rawness, crudeness and coarseness are included in the quality of roughness. Although we regularly observe these qualities in buildings around us, often as indicators of poor construction quality or budget cuts, in acknowledged works of architecture they are not accidental but integral with a deliberate design strategy.

The following case-studies illustrate how structure, through its configuration and detailing, expresses qualities ranging between the extremes of elegance and roughness.

The expression of architectural quality on the exterior of Bracken House has already been discussed and some of its exposed details noted (see Figure 4.45). The building exterior provides other examples of elegant detailing, such as the entrance truss that supports a translucent canopy (Figure 12.53). Metal bosses articulate the joints between the bottom-chord members and the others that are inclined. The spoke-like diagonals, ribbed and tapered, possess the same visual qualities as elegant mechanical or aeronautical engineering

Figure 12.54
Generously chamfered interior columns reflect the curved plan shape of the new insertion. Partition walls are yet to be constructed.

components. Within the building, concrete columns provide the primary gravity support to the suspended floors. Their rounded cross-sections, which relate to the plan shape of the new insertion between the existing blocks, inject a degree of elegance into the building interior with which most of the columns we meet in day-to-day life are totally unacquainted (Figure 12.54).

A similar high degree of structural detailing elegance is evident at Queen's Building, Cambridge (Figure 12.55). In describing it, one reviewer observes: 'One would say that the

Figure 12.53
Bracken House, London, UK, Michael Hopkins and Partners, 1991. Elegant truss members meet at a joint.

Figure 12.55
Queen's Building, Cambridge, UK, Michael Hopkins and Partners, 1995. Main façade.

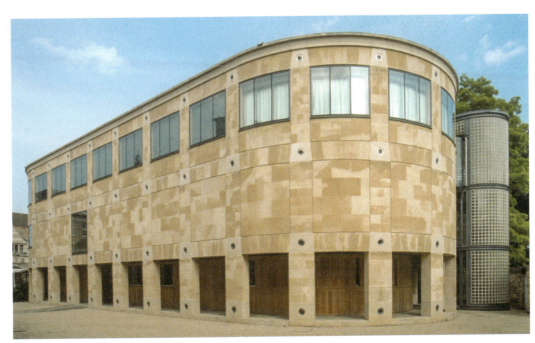

Figure 12.56
Refined roof truss detailing.

Figure 12.57
A post-tensioning node detail.

Figure 12.58
Sainte-Geneviève Library, Paris, France, Henri Labrouste, 1850. Decorative curved iron beams over the reading room.

the anchorages of an innovative post-tensioning system that reinforces the solid limestone masonry piers (Figure 12.57). Specially selected aggregates for the concrete blocks housing the nodes match the colour of the surrounding stone blocks.

The exquisitely detailed wrought-iron beams of the Sainte-Geneviève Library provide a fine example of both elegant and decorative structural detailing (Figure 12.58). A flowing pattern resembling stars and sickles replaces standard diagonal web members. Structural detailing and artistry merge in these members.

An elegant concrete structural element dominates the first-floor foyer space at MUMUTH Music School and Theatre, Graz (Figures 10.16 and 12.59). Defying structural categorization, 'the Twist' functions as an inclined structural prop. This is one of several concrete members with highly sculptural qualities that are located in the foyer of the building. The construction of such a complex form with a high-quality surface finish required the highest standard of workmanship plus self-compacting concrete pumped into the base of its formwork.

As with the other pairs of architectural qualities considered in this chapter, there is little point in providing examples of the mid-point of the continuum – in this case half-way between the extremes of elegance and roughness. We can assume they would lack expression and therefore fall into the category of the bland architecture we mostly inhabit.

So we move on to examples where structure conveys a sense of roughness, beginning with Coop Himmelb(l)au's attic conversion, Vienna (Figures 12.60 and 12.61). Raw

building was a montage of Hopkins' motifs, were it not such a unified, monolithic form – more like a beautifully crafted piece of furniture than a building.'[7] The composite wooden and stainless-steel roof trusses incorporate elegant structural details (Figure 12.56). Precisely located bolts pass through stainless-steel plates inserted between wooden members. Rods elegantly connect to and fan out from a plate at the truss apex. The building exterior also features notable exposed structural detailing. Small stainless-steel ring-nodes denote

Figure 12.59
MUMUTH Music School and Theatre, Graz, Austria, UN Studio, 2008. A concrete structural element with sculptural qualities. (Brayton Orchard)

and irregular detailing abounds. Such a deliberate lack of refinement is entirely appropriate within this chaotic structural assemblage, described variously as 'an eagle', 'a crazy composition',[8] 'a snapshot of a disastrous collision' and 'a constructional thunderstorm'![9] Details therefore mirror the general absence of structural rationality. Their random and fractured qualities verge on the crude and recall similar

Figure 12.61
Irregularity of the form is reflected in the roughness of the detailing.

Figure 12.60
Attic conversion, Vienna, Austria, Coop Himmelb(l)au, 1988. The attic roof oversails the existing building.

qualities at the temporary Serpentine Gallery, with its flung-together appearance (see Figure 11.8).

A less random expression of roughness characterizes LASALLE College of the Arts, Singapore (Figure 12.62). Severe perimeter walls that enclose the rectilinear site are interrupted by jagged openings. Experienced as canyons weathered from rock, irregular in plan and section, they divide the complex into six free-standing blocks, connected by bridges.

For the final examples of structure contributing to the quality of roughness, we return to the Güell Colony Crypt. Figure 6.8 focused upon the wonderfuly rich ceiling surface texture provided by the shallow brick arches. While their gentle curved profiles and their fineness introduce a degree of elegance, without a plaster coating they display basic masonry construction – bricks and mortar. The full richness of roughness is introduced by the rough-hewn stone posts (Figure 12.63). It would be difficult to find architectural elements rougher than these and their capitals, on which the brick masonry sits. While we absorb the fact that this is structure at its most raw, it is easy to forget that the inclination of the posts was determined precisely by Gaudí using his catenary model. That ensured that the orienation of the posts aligned perfectly with the lines of thrust from the ceiling arches and the superstructure piers above (unfortunately, never built).

Figure 12.63
Güell Colony Crypt, Barcelona, Spain, Antonio Gaudí, 1917. Roughly hewn stone posts exemplify structure expressing roughness.

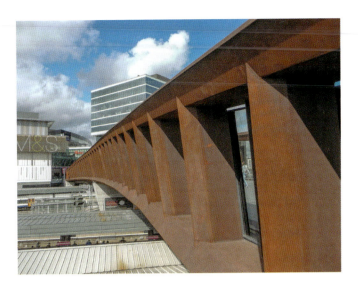

Figure 12.64

Pedestrian footbridge, Stratford, London, UK, Buro Happold Services and Knight Architects, 2009. A vierendeel truss fabricated from weathering steel.

The crypt reminds us that we can introduce a quality of roughess into any material. It is very easy to achieve a rough and irregular concrete finish. If formwork is not tightly abutted, grout will leak from that area to leave a honeycomb finish (usually swiftly plastered over). If fresh concrete is over-vibrated the aggregate separates from the grout and settles to the bottom of the formwork, again leading to irregular and defect-ridden surfaces. If formwork is removed too early and roughly, surfaces and edges will suffer damage. Even steel can be treated to create a rusticated or raw finish. Weathering steel, formulated so that its initial rust prevents severe corrosion in the future, is already quite common (Figure 12.64). Steel plates and sections can also be cut roughly by gas torches, or connected crudely by coarse runs of weld left unground, or by bolts misaligned or of diffent lengths. We just have to be mindful of the risk of injury from brushing against jagged steelwork. This ease of constructing roughly extends to all other materials. Expression of roughness is limited only by our own creativity.

Summary

Provision of particular architectural qualities is a fundamental characteristic of any successful work of architecture, unless its intent is to portray blandness! Using five pairs of common contrasting pairs of qualities – simplicity–complexity, open–closed, lightweight–heavy, soft–hard and elegant–rough – this chapter has shown, primarily through case-studies, how structure assists their reinforcement. Although the focus has been on the extremes of each pair of qualities, it is easy to convey more moderate qualities by reducing the intensity of expression. For example, we can imagine how an exposed steel post including its connections to other members could be detailed to express many different degrees of roughness.

The intent of this explanation of how structure increases perception of architectural qualities is to enrich our own designs. Once a preliminary structural design is resolved, the following question should be addressed: how should the structural forms and members continue to be transformed to exhibit qualities that reinforce the architectural concept(s)?

Notes

1. L. LaVine, *Mechanics and meaning in architecture*, Minneapolis: University of Minnesota Press, 2001, p. 163.

2. R. Bevan, 'Seed capital', *Building Design*, 27 October 2000, 15–19, at 17.

3. A. de Botton, *The architecture of happiness*, London: Hamish Hamilton, 2006, pp. 204–5.

4. For a ranking of levels of structure and services integration, refer to R. D. Rush, *The building systems integration handbook*, New York: John Wiley, 1986, p. 12.

5. For several construction photographs and a fascinating account of the twists and turns of the design process which began by envisaging a cave-like interior, see 'Toyo Ito & Associates, Architects, Tama Art University Library', *Japan Architect* 67, 120–9.

6. A. de Botton, *The architecture of happiness*, p. 206.

7. C. Davies, 'Cambridge credo', *Architectural Review* 199(1188), 1996, 47–51, at 49.

8. P. Cook, 'Spreadeagled', *Architectural Review* 186(1112), 1989, 76–80, at 76.

9. W. Bachmann, 'Coop Himmelb(l)au attic conversion', in S. Tiel-Siling (ed.), *Icons of architecture: the 20th century*, Munich: Prestel, 1998, p. 152.

thirteen

Conclusions

Introduction

The fact that most of the previous chapters in this book focus on specific areas or aspects of architecture suggests a need to summarize the main themes emerging from this study. This final chapter, then, draws together the three principal strands that weave through each of the proceeding chapters.

Before tying off these threads, it is necessary to recall briefly the main purpose of the book – to understand and appreciate structure architecturally rather than structurally; that is, to observe and read structure through the eyes of an architect and a building user, rather than adopting the narrower and more technically focused eye of a structural engineer. I therefore view structure as a mainstream architectural element rather than as a secondary element originating from the often self-contained 'Structures' discipline of schools of architecture.

Drawing upon many case-studies, this book has presented a comprehensive analysis and categorization of the roles that structure plays in contemporary architecture, including reinforcing the most common architectural concepts and qualities. As such, it functions as a source book for designers. Although careful not to advocate the *necessity* of incorporating exposed structure into a building, it presents a vision of structure as a potentially exciting architectural element, and one that should always be integral with the design concept. Precedents in the book will trigger designers' imaginations and suggest ways for them to develop their design ideas further. The book can also be used as a mirror against which designs may be assessed. It may, for example, help designers to reflect on the architectural qualities of their own interior surfaces and spaces, and to ponder

whether they have fully exploited structure. Does structure contribute explicitly to their architecture and help realize and communicate their design concepts?

In most cases, structure contributes to architecture aesthetically – stimulating our senses and engaging emotions and minds. Given its dominant visual presence, it impacts most significantly upon our sense of sight. However, in some situations the surface smoothness of a structural member, or the manner in which it has been hand-crafted, might encourage us to connect with it physically, through touch. We rarely experience structure through smell, although the fragrance of freshly milled and erected wooden members might well be savoured. And, apart from an awareness of the acoustic screening or the reverberation properties of concrete and masonry structural walls, structure rarely impinges upon our sense of hearing.

Transformative power of structure

Throughout this book many examples have illustrated how structure transforms otherwise bland surfaces and spaces, both exterior and interior. By virtue of its composition-making and space-making qualities, structure introduces visual interest and character. Surfaces take on a degree of interest and 'spaces become places'. Additional architectural enrichment flows from the interaction of structure with light, or by offering meaning to viewers through its representational and symbolic qualities.

Structure is not a neutral architectural element. It influences the space around it, and its very presence invites architectural analysis or readings. This book encourages architects and engineers to develop a strong proactive stance towards structure, rather than resign themselves to treat structure as purely utilitarian. Architects should allow their design ideas to drive the structural design. They should make the most of structure as an architectural element, beginning with its form and layout, and further enliven their designs through structural detailing. The architectural success of any structure should be assessed by the extent to which it helps to realize a design concept, or, in other words, enriches a design. In numerous situations that will mean concealing structure.

This perception of structure creates opportunities rather than constraints. Such a positive attitude releases structure from the shackles of conventional practice and its two masters of constructability and economy, and frees it to play more substantial functional and aesthetic roles in architecture. Just as a structural overlay upon an architectural plan or section bestows an additional sense of constructional reality to an otherwise diagrammatic representation, exposed structure transforms surfaces, spaces and our experiences of built architecture.

Structural diversity

There are a surprisingly large number of modes by which structure enriches architecture – the most important being to assist in the realization of the design concept. In order to achieve this goal, exposed structure will be prominent in one or more of the areas of architecture discussed in the previous chapters, such as in intensifying or contrasting with architectural form, or modifying the visual appearance of the exterior or interior of a building. Structure, in all likelihood, will also be carefully integrated with building function, for example by articulating spaces for circulation. It will often play a role in introducing daylight into a space and modifying qualities of light. Success with the big picture is achieved where structure relates to all aspects of the design, down to the smallest structural detail.

Within each area of architecture the contribution of structure can take one of many possible forms. Consider the large number of examples illustrating the different ways in which structure interacts with daylight. Diversity also

abounds given the number of structural systems available. For example, designers can choose between three-dimensional surface structures, spatial frameworks, and essentially two-dimensional systems like structural walls and moment and cross-braced frames. As well as a choice of structural materiality, designers have a huge diversity of structural scale at their disposal – from cables 10 mm in diameter to trusses that are over 5 m deep.

Given the huge number of structural possibilities, designers have considerable freedom of choice. This sets the scene for innovative and creative structural designs. But because of the goal that structure should actively reinforce the design concept, each structural decision must be thought through strategically. Future technological advances in structural materials and in analysis and design techniques will inevitably continue to increase both the diversity of structural options and their architectural implications.

The impacts of structure upon those who experience it are also diverse. One structure, conveying a sense of tranquillity, soothes emotions. Another sets nerves on edge. A raw and inhospitable structure contrasts with one that welcomes and expresses a sense of protection. Structures are also capable of conveying an enormous range of meanings to those who read them.

Implications for the architectural and structural engineering professions

With its emphasis on structure as an architectural element, this book encourages a broad, creative and critical stance towards structure. It presents an alternative approach to some current practice where the most expedient structural engineering solution is adopted unless its impact upon the architectural concept is considered disastrous. For structure to enliven architecture, collaboration between the architect and the structural engineer needs to be extensive and intensive.

Architects need to take an active role in all stages of structural design, working with the structural engineer in order to achieve mutually acceptable outcomes. Beginning with preliminary structural layouts and proceeding through to detailed design at the working drawing stage, both groups of professionals need to wrestle in collaboration with the various options. Structure is owned by both professions and it must satisfy the requirements of both simultaneously – load-bearing as well as architectural expression.

My hope is that this book will help bridge the gap between the two professions. Through it, architects will become more aware of how structure can enrich their designs. This will lead them to ask structural engineers to explore how less conventional structural responses might integrate better with their design concepts. Through such a process, structural engineers will develop their awareness that the systems and members they design and detail for strength and stiffness possess considerable architectural value and represent far more to architects and the general public than merely a means of load-bearing.

Architecturally enriching structure is likely to require greater analytical and design skills. It challenges designers' reliance upon a formulaic approach to structural design where the most construction-friendly and economic design is adopted. Finally, an increased appreciation of how exposed structure plays important architectural roles will increase a sense of pride among structural engineers and strengthen the sense of partnership between them and architects.

Given that structure is of vital importance to both professions, the teaching of 'Structures' in schools of architecture should be subject to ongoing reflection. At present, in most schools, engineers tend to teach this subject within the 'Architectural Technologies' section of the programme. Little mention is made of structure's architectural roles. By increasing the integration of 'Structures' with architectural design, students' interest in structure and their awareness of its relevance to their designs will increase, as will the quality of their architecture.

Index